FOR THE LOVE OF LITERATURE

FOR THE LOVE OF LITERATURE

*A Celebration of Language
and Imagination*

Christy MacKaye Barnes

Francis Edmunds, A.C. Harwood, Adam Bittleston,
Isabel Wyatt, and Others

Douglas Gerwin, Editor

🖉 Anthroposophic Press

in collaboration with the
Association of Waldorf Schools of North America

Several contributions to this volume have been drawn from previously unpublished lectures and essays, which are copyrighted by their respective authors. We gratefully acknowledge permission to reprint various other essays in this book and the courtesy extended by their original publishers: "Can Imagination Be Trained? A Crucial Question for Schools Today" from *Educating As An Art*, edited by Ekkehard Piening and Nathan Lyons, © 1979 by the Rudolf Steiner Press. "Poetry, Music and Imagination" from *Journal for Anthroposophy*, Number 53, © 1991 by The Anthroposophical Society in America."The Crisis of the Word Today" from the *Journal for Anthroposophy*, Number 47, © 1988 by The Anthroposophical Society in America."The Role of the Poet and the Importance of Imagination" from *Journal for Anthroposophy*, Number 36, © 1983 by The Anthroposophical Society in America."Why Write? A Few Suggestions and Exercises" from *Journal for Anthroposophy*, Numbers 35 and 36, © 1982/1983 by The Anthroposophical Society in America."Literature and the Drama of Polarities" from *Journal for Anthroposophy*, Number 29, © 1979 by The Anthroposophical Society in America."Schooling Capacities through the Study of Literature" from *Journal for Anthroposophy*, Number 36, © 1983 by The Anthroposophical Society in America."Backgrounds for Russian Literature: With Special Emphasis on Soloviev and Dostoyevsky" from *Journal for Anthroposophy*, Numbers 18 and 19, © 1974 by The Anthroposophical Society in America. "A Conversation with Christy MacKaye Barnes" from *The Hawthorne Valley Newsletter*, Spring 1991. "The Future of the English Language" from *The Golden Blade*, 1957, © by *The Golden Blade*. "Literature in the Upper School" from *Child and Man Abstracts*. "Chaucer and the Modern Consciousness" from *Anthroposophical Quarterly*, Vol.14, Nos. 1-4, 1969. "Fair Mountain and Fine City: A Study of the Images in *The Merchant of Venice*" from *The Golden Blade*, 1950, © by *The Golden Blade*. "Shakespeare's Troubled Kings" from *The Golden Blade*, 1967, © by *The Golden Blade*. "In Quest of the Holy Grail" from *The Golden Blade*, 1981, © by *The Golden Blade*."The Trials of Parsifal" from *The Golden Blade*, 1981, © by *The Golden Blade*. "Grail Mountain and Garden of Marvels" from *The Golden Blade*, 1981, © by *The Golden Blade*. "Wolfram and Wagner" from *The Golden Blade*, 1981, © by *The Golden Blade*. "Christopher Fry and the Riddle of Evil" from *The Golden Blade*, 1955, © by *The Golden Blade*. "We Love Grammar" from *Journal for Anthroposophy*, Number 35, © 1983 by The Anthroposophical Society in America.

Published by Anthroposophic Press,
RR 4 Box 94-A1 Hudson, N.Y. 12534

Library of Congress Cataloging-in-Publication Data

For the love of literature : a celebration of language and imagination : essays / by Christy Barnes ... [et al.] ; Douglas Gerwin, editor.
  Includes bibliographical references.
  ISBN 0-88010-416-3 (paper)
  1. Literature—Study and teaching. 2. English philology—Study and teaching.
I. Barnes, Christy MacKaye, 1909– . II. Gerwin, Douglas.
PN59.F67 1996
807—dc20   96-30735

10 9 8 7 6 5 4 3 2 1

Printed in the United States of America

Contents

Introduction by Christopher Bamford   vii

Foreword by Christy MacKaye Barnes   xvii

A Conversation with Christy MacKaye Barnes by Andree Ward   xix

I

CHRISTY MACKAYE BARNES

Can Imagination Be Trained?   *3*

Poetry, Music and Imagination   *17*

The Crisis of the Word Today   *31*

Speech As Awakener and Healing Force   *40*

Poetry: Nourishment and Medicine   *55*

Why Write?   *61*

Literature and the Drama of Polarities   *71*

Schooling Capacities through the Study of Great Authors   *83*

Backgrounds for Russian Literature   *92*

II

The Future of the English Language
Adam Bittleston 129

Literature in the Upper School
L. Francis Edmunds 145

In the Footsteps of Dante
Linda Sawers 175

Chaucer and the Modern Consciousness
Isabel Wyatt 186

Fair Mountain and Fine City
A. C. Harwood 220

Shakespeare's Troubled Kings
Adam Bittleston 228

In Quest of the Holy Grail
Ursula Grahl 245

The Trials of Parsifal
L. Francis Edmunds 257

Grail Mountain and Garden of Marvels
Hugh Hetherington 268

Wolfram and Wagner
Eileen Hutchins 274

Christopher Fry and the Riddle of Evil
Adam Bittleston 284

Questing toward a True Understanding of Grammar
Susan Demanett 300

We Love Grammar
Dorit Winter 315

Biographical Information 327

INTRODUCTION

Language plays a significant—some would even claim divine—role in human evolution and development. Although psychologists may argue about whether and in what sense apes in a learning laboratory demonstrate linguistic ability, the fact nevertheless remains that humanity has always recognized that with speech and all that goes along with it the gods gave us a part of themselves. From time immemorial speech and language have been considered something sacred. To speak was to participate in divine creativity; it was the paradigm of action in the world. Thus the ancient Hebrew "spoke with his foot" instead of walked, and throughout the ancient world to speak was to act, to *create*—to participate in creation.

We find this view of language powerfully articulated at the beginning of written tradition in the Vedas of ancient India. Here, the creation of the world by the gods and its re-creation by the Vedic poet-priest are both accomplished by speech: the word, the goddess *Vac*. Accordingly, in a hymn dealing with the birth of the gods, the priest-poet sings:

Let us now speak with wonder of the births of the gods—so that one may see them when the hymns are chanted in a later age.
The speaker, like a smith, fanned them together. . . .

Elsewhere, we find that when the poet-seers first set speech in motion and uttered names, "their most pure and perfectly guarded secret was revealed through love." And, further, that:

When the wise ones fashioned speech with their thought, sifting it as grain is sifted through a sieve, then friends recognized their friendships....

Through sacrifice they traced the path of speech and found it inside the sages. They held it and portioned it out to many; together the seven singer-sages praised it.

In still another hymn the Goddess, who is the sole means of communion between heaven and earth and embraces and unites all things, says of herself:

I move with the Rudras, with the Vasus, with the Adityas, and all the gods. I carry both Mitra and Varuna, both Indra and Agni, and both of the Asvins.

I carry the swelling Soma.... I bestow wealth on the pious sacrificer....

I am the queen, the confluence of riches, the skillful one who is first among those worthy of sacrifice. The gods divided me up into various parts, for I dwell in many places and enter into many forms.

The one who eats food, who truly sees, who breathes, who hears what is said, does so through me. Though they do not realize it, they dwell in me....

Word and thing, word and archetypal cosmic-creative idea, word and thought, inspiration and inner experience were not then yet separate, but formed a dynamic picture-filled continuum mediating between heaven and earth and scripting the dramatic content of human life. Language was experienced as the cosmogenic archetype of the gods' creativity. Panini, the great Sanskrit grammarian, still knew this. Hence his account of the structures and interconnections of words and their roots is really a cosmological treatise: an account of how the world was and is created. Human consciousness was not then so concretely located in the skull or so closely bound to the brain. Nor was it so abstract and literal as we experience it today: it was "the house of being." When reading the documents that have come down to us from those times—the hieratic picture-language of the Egyptian hieroglyphics, for instance—we have the sense that these ancient ancestors still participated in what we might call the Divine Imagination, wherein the forms and processes of earthly things are woven and unwoven.

By Greco-Roman times all this had begun to change. Language and thought separated. Plato's *Cratylus* dialogue could now debate whether words (and sounds) were natural (and hence "true") or merely conventional. Nevertheless, there was still something inherently magical about language. Though to a lesser degree than Hebrew, Greek was still a sacred language: the letters still had names (alpha, beta, omega, and so on) and these names also represented numbers. Thereafter, with the period of Latin dominance, single sounds lost their names and became mere sounds, foreshadowing the nominalism of our own times.

Rudolf Steiner spoke of this (and more) in a lecture called *The Alphabet* (given in Dornach, Switzerland, on December 18, 1921):

In Greek culture, we still have a name for the first letter of the alphabet, but in Latin it is just "A." As we pass from Greek to Latin, something living in speech, something eminently concrete, changes into abstraction. We might say that, as long as human beings experienced the first letter of the alphabet as "Alpha," they experienced a certain amount of inspiration in it, but the moment they called it just "A," the letters became conventional and the prose of life replaced inspiration and inner experience. Here one can see the actual transition from everything Greek to what is Roman and Latin. Cultural life leaves the poetic-spiritual world and enters the "prose of life."

The Romans, as I have often remarked, were a sober, prosaic people who transmitted prose and jurisprudence into later culture, while what lived in Greece unfolded in cultural life more or less like a kind of cultural dream which the people approached through their own revelations when they had inner experiences and wished to give expression to them.

Steiner goes on to show how when the letters of the alphabet were still names, each name or letter symbolized a living reality:

If we seek the nearest modern words to convey the meaning of "Alpha," these would be: "The one who experiences his own breathing." Here we have a direct reference to the Old Testament words, "And God formed man in his own image and breathed into him the breath of life." Thus, the first letter of the alphabet expresses the reality that it is breathing that makes human beings earthly beings, beings who experience the imprint of their humanity through the experience of breath, by receiving into themselves the experience of breathing. And the Beta, considered with an open mind, turning to the Hebrew equivalent, Beth, represents something of the nature of a wrapping, covering, or dwelling. Thus, if we were to put our experience on uttering "Alpha, Beta" into modern language, we would say: "The human being in his house." And we could go through the whole alphabet in this way and, simply by saying the names of the letters of the alphabet one after another, express a concept, a meaning, a truth about human nature. We would be uttering a comprehensive sentence that expressed the whole mystery of human nature. This sentence would begin by showing the human being in its building, its temple. It would then go on to express how humankind conducts itself in its temple and how it is related to the cosmos. In short, what would be expressed by speaking the names of the alphabet consecutively would not be the abstraction we have today when we mindlessly say "A, B, C," but it would be the expression of the Human Mystery and its roots in the universe.

Thus, as Steiner confirms, the alphabet—language, grammar—considered as a single sentence, a whole, was not in its origins simply a conventional way of referring to external things and events but humanity's own expression, through the larynx and speech organs, of a "divine-spiritual Mystery." This "mystery" arose out of the cosmos. It was what the heavens revealed through the fixed stars (the Zodiac) and the planets moving across them. The ancient understanding of linguistics therefore included, at the very least, all of what later came to be known by the Middle Ages as the Seven Liberal Arts: the Trivium of grammar, rhetoric, and logic; and the Quadrivium of arithmetic, geometry, astronomy, and music. All of these "sciences," of course, are now dead and abstract—they play no part in any literature curriculum—but for such as Alain de Lille in his *Anticlaudianus*, they were the living practices, virtues, and faculties that shaped the perfect human being.

This understanding has been largely lost in modern times, although the poets (as Steiner points out)—by avoiding the "prosaic" element and seeking always to return language to its inner dimension and feeling for the good, the true, and the beautiful—have from generation to generation striven to regain "the lost word," each in his or her own way. For this great gift we owe our poets and writers an equivalent debt, one that we can repay adequately only when we integrate their contributions within *our* being while at the same time continuing their work.

This, of course, is where the study—and, above all, the love—of literature enters in. For, paralleling the descent of language and imagination into abstraction and literalism, there has always been an evolving tradition comprised of those who, honoring humanity's changing place and role in the cosmos, have striven to bear existential witness to the highest and deepest experiences available to human beings. Beginning with Homer and continuing on through Hesiod, Pindar, the Pre-Socratic philosophers (Thales, Pherekydes, Empedocles, Heraclitus, and Pythagoras) and the great tragedians (Aeschylus, Sophocles, and Euripides), Western literature grows out of the profound intuition of the unity of religion, science, and art—an imagination of humanity as entwined with the gods in a relationship that is both knowing and loving:

> For from of old the gods appear visibly to us,
> When we honor them with holy festival hecatombs—
> They sit among us in our rows, and eat of our meal.
> Even when one single man, a wanderer meets them,
> They do not hide themselves from him, for we stand near to
> them.

Not for nothing, then, is Orpheus—a poet, musician, religious prophet, guide of souls, and proto-scientist—considered the founder of the Western tradition of imagination. From Orpheus, as Rilke knew, we learn the *task* of literature—namely, to transform, or rather resurrect, the world; while from the philosopher Plotinus, we can glean something of its method or medium, *love*:

> It is sound, I think, to find the primal sources of Love in a tendency of the Soul toward pure beauty, in a recognition, in a kinship, in an unreasoned consciousness of friendly relation.... Pure Love seeks the beauty alone, whether there is Reminiscence or not; but there are those who feel also a desire of such immortality as lies within mortal reach; and these are seeking Beauty in their demand for perpetuity.... Love, thus, is ever intent upon that other loveliness, and exists to be the medium between desire and the object of desire. It is the eye of the desirer; by its power what loves is enabled to see the loved thing. But it is first; before it becomes the vehicle of vision, it is itself filled with the sight....

In the history of Western vernacular literature—from the troubadours, the minnesinger, Dante, Chaucer, and the authors of the epic Grail cycles (Chrétien de Troyes, Wolfram von Eschenbach, and others) to the great authors of the Renaissance (like Petrarch, Montaigne, Rabelais, Spenser, and Shakespeare himself)—we see imagination, an "eye... filled with vision," incarnate deeper and deeper into human experience. Studying and learning to love this tradition we learn to understand what was vision for the ancients becomes, forms, the experience of the open heart for us.

We do not usually think first of the heart—or love—when we think of the study of literature. But that, in fact, is where one must begin. For, without the painful openness to experience that these demand, art can neither be created nor understood. I mean here *love* in the sense that the German romantic poet Novalis meant it when he wrote, "to love is to hold the wound always open." Or, in the words of Christy MacKaye Barnes:

> A wound awoke me,
> Opened the lids that lie closed
> Over the eyes of the longing
> That lives in the sleeping soul
> To be whole;
>
> And a word woke me
> To reach
> Into the wounds of the world—
>
> And the wounds
> Became speech.

Here we have the counterbalance to the chaos, confusion, literalism, and abstraction that surrounds us and threatens our own and our children's humanity. The love and study of literature and language, when pursued in conjunction with work in science from the phenomenological perspective—where the imagination is further trained and enhanced by the practice of the observation of nature in her place—gives young people more than a simple sense of history, more even than membership in a culture or a sense of human solidarity. For what is involved is, in the profoundest sense, "soul-making." Today, we are so overwhelmed by information—and esteem it so highly—that we forget that information without knowledge and wisdom is without meaning or value as far as the primary human task is concerned. For our human task, as John Keats knew well, has nothing to do with information, it has to do with "soul-making"—individuation, human freedom:

Call the world if you Please "the Vale of Soul-making" [Keats writes in his famous letter]. Then you will find out the use of the world. (I am speaking now in the highest terms for human nature admitting it to be immortal which I will here take for granted for the purpose of showing a thought which has struck me concerning it.) I say "*Soul making*" Soul as distinguished from an Intelligence—There may be intelligences or sparks of divinity in millions—but they are not Souls till they acquire identities, till each one is personally itself. Intelligences are atoms of perception—they know and they see and they are pure, in short they are God—How then are Souls to be made? How then are these sparks which are God to have identity given them—so as ever to possess a bliss particular to each ones individual existence? How, but by the medium of a world like this?...

But the world alone is not sufficient; and so, Keats continues:

[Soul-making] is effected by three grand materials acting the one upon the other for a series of years—These three Materials are the *Intelligence*—the *human heart* (as distinguished from intelligence or Mind) and the *World* or *Elemental Space* suited for the proper action of *Mind and Heart* on each other for the purpose of forming the *Soul* or *Intelligence destined to possess the sense of Identity*. I can scarcely express what I but dimly perceive—yet I think I perceive it—that you may judge the more clearly I will put it in the most homely form possible—I will call the *world* a School instituted for the purpose of teaching little children to read—I will call the *human heart* the *horn Book* used in that School—and I will call the *child*

able to read, the Soul made from that *school* and its *horn book.*
Do you not see how necessary a World of Pains and troubles
is to school an Intelligence and make it a soul? A place where
the heart must feel and suffer in a thousand diverse ways! Not
merely is the Heart a Hornbook, It is the Minds Bible, it is
the Minds experience, it is the teat from which the Mind or
intelligence sucks its identity....

To these propositions, and to the greater human good, Christy
MacKaye Barnes—the occasion of this celebration collecting her
writings and those of other Waldorf teachers and anthroposo-
phists—has dedicated her life. The daughter of the poet-dramatist
and American man of letters, Percy MacKaye, and his wife, the
poetic soul, Marion Morse, Christy Barnes grew up amid the
dynamism of the creative life. At her father's knee, she learned to
love the music of the English language in its most characteristic
voices. Chaucer, Shakespeare, Milton, the Romantic poets, and
the American Transcendentalists—these were the familiars of her
childhood. Percy MacKaye himself was one of the last Romantics,
an idealist, a spiritual poet of the imagination, a passionate lover
of nature and humanity. From him, Christy must have imbibed
her fundamental premise—which was Rudolf Steiner's also—that
the creative person was the doer, the experiencer, and that true
learning (like true being) must at all costs avoid sterile intellectu-
alism. Drama, poetry, novels—the words human beings spoke and
wrote—were alive. The works of the past were not corpses to be
analyzed and dissected, but living beings. One could encounter
them as one encounters a friend, a teacher, an angel. Participating
in them, one's soul was given shape and nourished—given the
form and beauty, truth and goodness that one could then, like the
ancient Vedic priest, give back to the world and the gods, stamped
with one's own existence.

On the basis of such intuitions it is not surprising that it was in
Rudolf Steiner's spiritual science or Anthroposophy that Christy

Barnes, like the other authors in this book, found the guidance her heart needed in its quest. Thus, although a published and accomplished poet, she dedicated her life not to establishing a career as a literary figure but to helping to establish Waldorf education in North America and to teaching literature and vocal recitation to teenagers. In this, again, she was like the other contributors to this volume, each of whom has devoted his or her life to the stewardship of youth and to the education of the next generation of teachers.

Waldorf education, in fact, is one of the great open secrets of our time. In its curriculum for the lower and the upper schools, we find an education that unfolds strong, centered, responsible, and compassionate human beings with a historical, holistic, and global view of life. In the early grades, studying the myths of different times and cultures—not only of India, Persia, Egypt, Greece, and Rome, but also the Norse legends and the stories of the Old Testament—the children are confirmed as world citizens, members of a single human family. Thus, by the time they enter high school, they have lived imaginatively in the company of all the great figures who exemplify what is best in human nature. The seeds have been sown.

The high school curriculum then nurtures these seeds and their seed-bearers. And, in this book, readers will find indications of how this is done by the teaching of literature. English teachers, of course, will find here an invaluable resource; but, beyond this, anyone concerned with truly human values, any lover of language and words, anyone with a feeling for the importance of imagination as an organ for the cognition of the truth, will find sustenance in this remarkable collection—remarkable not only for the virtues of the pieces themselves (the writing, the ideas) but also for the human beings who caused them to be. I spoke of Waldorf education as a great open secret of our times: another great secret is the quality of the teachers. This collection salutes a few of them.

— *Christopher Bamford*

FOREWORD

Such articles of mine as are included here have to do with the results of one teacher's work. The most productive aspects of these were inspired by ideas from the work of Rudolf Steiner. The way in which the lessons they tell about evolved—sometimes suddenly, sometimes through long, hard work—and how they were pruned and re-shaped brought about in me something of the joy that accompanies the writing of a poem, especially in the struggle to combine and balance strict form and the fire and chaos of enthusiasm.

A similar joy came from watching and helping the students likewise invigorate, prune, shape and re-shape their work. More than anything else, I wanted to convey to young people how thinking, augmented to imagination, can become a clear, accurate instrument for perceiving an ever greater depth, breadth and height of reality.

My hope is that anything I have done may serve as a spark to kindle or inspire others in their struggles to make their own discoveries and to bring young people to discover *their* own abilities and bring to expression the questions and answers concerning the meaning of life which live half-consciously within them.

—*Christy MacKaye Barnes*

Christy MacKaye Barnes

(photograph by Joan Dufault)

A CONVERSATION WITH
CHRISTY MACKAYE BARNES

Andree Ward

Christy Barnes' lifelong love of literature has led her along many interesting paths, and today in her "retirement" she continues to write and to encourage the efforts of others through her small publishing house, The Adonis Press. But especially dear to Christy's heart is the art of speech formation—the beauty and clarity of the individual sounds of the consonants and vowels as they merge in the spoken word. This art was refined and enlivened by Rudolf Steiner during the early years of this century as he worked with the actors and actresses performing his Mystery Plays, and in a course on drama given at the request of two troupes of professional actors. The Hawthorne Valley Newsletter *visited Christy at her home on a snowy winter's afternoon.*

HVN: Christy, how did the work with speech come to carry this central importance for you?

CB: It all goes back, I think, to my childhood. My mother and father were consummate readers. Hardly a night went by without their reading aloud to us children. Our whole childhood was filled with poetry and the theatre—we breathed that atmosphere.

We children always knew that not we but our father's work came first [Christy's father, Percy MacKaye, was a well-known poet and dramatist in the early years of this century], for he was guided by the ideal that the theatre was the great educative force for humankind. To quote his own words, he believed in:

... The slow education of mankind through the influence of art, particularly cooperative art, the art of the theatre in its full social scope and universal meaning ... [which] stands for the democracy of excellence, not the democracy of mediocrity.

What is art but self-government, the harmonizing of the elements of the mind? There can be no art where there is no discipline, there can be no art where there is no high standard of excellence.

Our house was always filled with artists and actors—Rabindranath Tagore, Robert Frost, Vachel Lindsay and Carl Sandburg came to see us. So I couldn't help but have a sense of the power of the spoken word from childhood on.

When I was in elementary school, we were always moving. At age fourteen I was in my fourteenth school. We spent a lot of time at my Grandma's house in Massachusetts, where there was no electricity or running water, only a pump. We had to chop wood and get ice from the icehouse. This was the home of my uncle Benton MacKaye, the father of the Appalachian Trail. In high school I went to boarding school where I had wonderful teachers.

One summer when I was in my twenties, I went on a walking tour of Ireland with a girl friend and Seamus McManus, a poet-storyteller and friend of my father's. We had a letter to Lady Gregory and were shown around her home by William Butler Yeats. We saw plays performed by the Abbey Players and went out to the Aran Islands, where Synge wrote *The Playboy of the Western World.*

The fields were all gray rock, with a few cabbages growing in the cracks. Ireland was wonderful, and the people were very hospitable and kind.

HVN: What was your experience of the speech training at the Goetheanum in Dornach, Switzerland, and who were your teachers?

CB: I went to Dornach in the 1930s. The Goetheanum stage is one of the largest in Europe. There were plays and eurythmy performances constantly. The scenery, the drama, the beauty and force of the speech chorus—all affected me powerfully. Besides my training in the speech school, where we also learned eurythmy and Greek gymnastics, I worked privately with Erna Grund, one of the chief actresses of the Goetheanum stage. She was a hard taskmaster, with a shining voice and clear technique. Dornach was a stimulating place. There was a great coming and going of people from all over Europe. I received my diploma from Marie Steiner, who directed the eurythmy and most of the dramas. Through my father I came to know Albert Steffen, the Swiss poet-dramatist, who was head of the Anthroposophical Society and editor of the *Goetheanum Weekly*, the newsletter for members of the Anthroposophical Society.

I met Henry Barnes during this time and we were married in 1939, three days after World War II broke out. We left Europe on the last American boat out of the Mediterranean on June 1, 1940.

HVN: You taught for many years at the Rudolf Steiner School in Manhattan. How did you bring this love of language into your teaching?

CB: When I began, Waldorf education was so new in America that I had a free hand. Many of the so-called Waldorf traditions, such as teaching Melville's *Moby Dick* in ninth grade, I began in those early years. It was a privilege to try to give the students an impression of the scope of literature from Homer up through Dante and Petrarch, Chaucer, Shakespeare, the Metaphysical and Romantic poets, and in their senior year to soak them in our great Americans: Emerson, Thoreau, Whitman, Hawthorne and Lincoln. We read the giant Russians as well, from Pushkin, Tolstoi and Dostoyevski to Solzhenitsyn—not to mention Goethe and the African and Norwegian writers.

In their writing I tried to teach my students not self-expression but the subtle and exact expression of the world about them, and that the use of imagination is to see more deeply, truly, and comprehensively into life: to see in a deed its consequence, and in a human being his or her inmost nature.

In looking at the artists of today, I am grateful for those who want to help humanity. Artistic gifts deteriorate if they are not used for an ideal. True art demands tremendous discipline.

I

CHRISTY MACKAYE BARNES

CAN IMAGINATION BE TRAINED?

A Crucial Question for Schools Today

Education has for a long time been oriented toward inform-
ing the mind and training it to respond to facts and problems
as speedily, logically and accurately as possible. Our schools are
based on the indisputable premise that intellectual powers and the
ability to absorb information are necessary and important for life
and progress, and that their efficiency can be improved.

Many of us look upon imagination as a pleasant and admirable
embellishment to cultural life. But there have been and are
people—writers, scientists, statesmen, planners of all kinds—
who say that without imagination we cannot foresee, organize or
originate what is needed for the future.

The relationship of education to intellect and imagination
should be one of the most fundamental concerns of the new generation. Why, for example, are we witnessing such upheaval in
colleges?

There are many answers to this question. Let us consider one of
them. As academic pressures are pushed ever lower down into
high school and elementary school, and as these pressures continue up into the universities, where humanism and human contact are often sacrificed to research and specialization, the young
people experience a kind of soul starvation and revulsion. Theoretical speculation and unrelated facts do not nourish well. The soul
stomach, hungry for the whole kernel of experienced life-wisdom,

undergoes an involuntary reaction. It rejects and vomits whether it will or no. A revolution, a revolt, takes place. Vomit and revolt are neither pleasant nor to be recommended, but they are facts and consequences, spasms not easy to control. The stomach responds urgently and tumultuously; it does not necessarily know what will heal it. Alongside of this revulsion, there appears a craving for imaginative experience which is often so little disciplined and so little understood that it seeks out unhealthy forms. Young people, unable to supply themselves with active, inward experience by their own effort and weakened in their will life, turn to the use of drugs. Why is all this? There are many diagnoses; the search for remedies, however, is the crucial search of our time.

In practical life, one of our greatest difficulties is that we are surrounded by countless instances of "improvements" made by innovators who lack the ability to foresee the consequences of these steps in "progress," or who are unable to estimate the relationship of their acts or discoveries to life and society as a whole. The "practical" scientist discovered DDT, the "expert" advised the "experienced" government official, and whole tracts of wilderness and townships were sprayed with DDT, at cost to the taxpayer. Voices raised against such "progressive" scientific steps were looked upon as the voices of medieval superstition. A lawsuit against such wholesale poisoning and pollution was lost. It took an imaginative and courageous artist-scientist, Rachel Carson, to awaken the world to the "whole" picture in her *Silent Spring*.

Various experiments have been made on tiny children, exposing them, for instance, at the age of a few months to caricatures of human faces for specific periods of time in order to see whether earlier responses can be stimulated and whether in this and other ways the processes of learning can be speeded up. Because these experimenters do not have Wordsworth's eye to see that a child's "whole vocation is endless imitation," or that, like a plant, a child should not be forced to flower too early (but needs time to develop sturdy "root, stem and leaf" in nourishing soil and warm, light-filled surroundings), they do not foresee the tendency to distortion they implant in the child's soul nor the weakened, prematurely exhausted organisms they are encouraging. Still other educators fail to realize that by means of "teaching machines" they encourage a mechanistic mode of thought and tend to stunt healthy imagination. Yet large sums of money are given for such experiments by intelligent and philanthropic persons and institutions. Almost every day there are new instances of similar lack of whole-sight. Can we prevent some of the havoc which attends so many of our "advances"? Must we always experiment unhampered by common sense and have to correct our blunders painfully and pragmatically?

At the beginning of our age, writers such as Emerson, Goethe and Tolstoi were aware that a one-sided trend was developing, especially in the field of science. In his essay, "Modern Science," Tolstoi says:

> Our science, in order to become science and to be really useful instead of harmful to humanity, must first of all renounce its experimental method, which causes it to consider as its business merely the study of what exists, and return to the only wise and fruitful understanding of science, according to which its subject is the investigation of how men should live.

With this statement he adds to the scientist's newly-won competence in objective observation two other human powers: those of imaginative foresight and of moral responsibility.

"The eye of the naturalist," says Emerson in his *English Traits*, "must have a scope like nature itself, a susceptibility to all impressions, alive to the heart as well as to the logic of creation." In a chapter on literature, he makes a complaint similar to Tolstoi's. He observes incipient in England, for which he has deep admiration, a tendency which has taken root in much of specialized science and education throughout the world today.

But English science puts humanity to the door. It wants the connection which is the test of genius. The science is false by not being poetic. It isolates the reptile or mollusk it assumes to explain; whilst reptile or mollusk only exists in system, in relation. The poet only sees it as an inevitable step in the path of the Creator. But, in England, one hermit finds this fact, and another finds that, and lives and dies ignorant of its value. There are great exceptions . . . but for the most part the natural science in England is out of its loyal alliance with morals, and is as void of imagination and free play of thought as conveyancing. It stands in strong contrast with the genius of the Germans, those semi-Greeks [Emerson had been studying Goethe], who love analogy, and, by means of their height of view, preserve their enthusiasm and think for Europe.

The romantic poets—Wordsworth, Shelley, Keats—created their own peaceful revolution and cultivated imagination as "the only means of grasping the unseen": the unseen forces which penetrate into and make sense of the seen and without a knowledge of which we can have no mastery over the visible, practical world; without it we treat symptoms, not causes.

We today have educated our thinking to become accurate, sharp, objective and, we hope, to accord with reality. One of the most effective training grounds in this achievement has been that aspect of nature which can be weighed and measured, that which is dead.

Goethe and Thoreau, however, were not content with this. For Thoreau, a plant torn out of its home and pressed between pages was a half-lie. These men were pioneers with whom we are only just beginning to catch up. They observed the world whole: the qualitative with the quantitative; living, changing forms, each in relationship to the others; and within the multiplicity and diversity of phenomena they also observed invisible laws, such laws as change flower to fruit, grub to butterfly, child to adult. Can we, like them, school the image-forming eye upon the objective, animate analogies and metamorphoses of nature? The following are some of a teacher's attempts in this direction.

Ask students to look at a leaf, the stem branching away from the twig, the veins from the stem, the tinier tributaries angling out from these into the "watershed" of leafy substance. Let them feel their way with eye and heart into the gestures of eager, childlike trust with which a leaf lifts into the sun. Let them observe intently until vagueness and boredom vanish in the face of absorption in these subtleties of living imagery.

Then turn their attention to the great analogy-creating powers of nature. Let them follow in their minds the image of a river, from whose central stem (cut by the currents as they flow downward to the sea) branches extend up into the foothills and multiply into the streams of mountain watersheds. The river system is unlike the leaf in size and substance. Its webbing of field and rock cannot sail on the wind. Its current flows in the contrary direction. Nevertheless, these two images, these two patterns, that of the leaf and of the river basin (reduced now to map size), when overlaid one upon the other, have a certain congruence. This congruence the poet calls metaphor. The leaf is a more individualized and tinier river basin, lifted and given independence by the air; the river basin a giant, continental leaf.

Where the shapes or qualities of two or even several images converge upon or overlap one another, like the intersecting arcs on a surveyor's map, "X" marks the spot where the treasure is buried. And the treasure? An unseen idea or law, in this case a law governing the way in which a flowing substance penetrates a more solid one with the greatest possible economy: a branching which we see made visible in leaf and lung, in blood vessels and the map of continents, in the veins of rocks: an irrigation or circulation. Imagination, the faculty which can grasp the invisible law or idea, unifies and reveals meaning in the seemingly chaotic and the senseless seen. It sees the connections between water, traffic and blood systems, between sleep and death, the organism of human beings and of human society, microcosm and macrocosm. Through analogy we become the surveyors and treasure seekers of a unified and known world.

It was this kind of imagination which informed Thoreau when he wrote in *Walden* in his chapter "Spring":

Few phenomena gave me more delight than to observe the forms which thawing sand and clay assume in flowing down the sides of a deep cut in the railroad.... Innumerable little streams overlap and interlace one with another, exhibiting a sort of hybrid product, which obeys half way the law of currents, and half way that of vegetation. As it flows it takes the form of sappy leaves or vines, making heaps of pulpy sprays ... you are reminded of coral, of leopards' paws or birds' feet, of brains or lungs or bowels, and excrements of all kinds. It is truly... a sort of architectural foliage.... I am affected as if in a peculiar sense I stood in the laboratory of the Artist who made the world and me.... No wonder that the Earth expresses itself outwardly in leaves, it so labors with the idea inwardly. The atoms have already learned this law, and are pregnant by it. The overhanging leaf sees here its prototype. Internally, whether in the globe or animal body, it is a moist, thick lobe, a word especially applicable to the liver and lungs and the leaves of fat ... *externally* a dry and thin leaf.... The feathers and wings of birds are still drier and thinner leaves. Thus, also, you pass from the lumpish grub in the Earth to the airy and fluttering butterfly. The very globe continually transcends and translates itself, and becomes winged in its orbit.

Here Thoreau points not only to analogies in nature, but he traces the forward, upward tendency of creation. He continues:

Even ice begins with delicate crystal leaves.... The whole tree itself is but one leaf, and rivers are still vaster leaves whose pulp is intervening Earth, and towns and cities are the ova in their axils....

The Maker of this Earth but patented a leaf.... *There is nothing inorganic.... The Earth is not a mere fragment of dead history*, stratum upon stratum like the leaves of a book, to be studied by geologists and antiquaries chiefly, but living poetry like the leaves of a tree, which precede flowers and fruit—not a fossil Earth, but a living Earth; compared with whose great central life all animal and vegetable life is merely parasitic [emphasis added].

In such a passage Thoreau touches upon the natural metaphors and metamorphoses composed by "the great Artist in his laboratory." Teachers can do worse than set their pupils' feet upon a path along which they may explore these "ideas" with which "the Earth labors."

Let a student choose some theme, the sun, a leaf, the process of breathing, and trace it through the kingdoms of nature—mineral, plant, animal, human, from stone to star—perhaps through the elements of earth, water, air and fire. Let him see how it works in the human eye and in thought. He cannot help, then, but come upon the embodied metaphor instilled there by that "Artist who made the world and me." What he writes afterward, whether he is gifted or not, will be of the stuff of imagination and the stuff of truth also if he is rightly guided to respect accuracy.

It is up to the teacher to help a student to distinguish between illusion and "real imagination." One means of doing this is to guide him methodically through three steps in the imaginative process: first, the very accurate observation and reproduction of an image; second, the tracing of carefully authenticated analogies to this image, through which he is led to recognize the fundamental law which creates their congruence; third, based upon the study of such actualities, the discovery of that fire which creates and shapes new images out of which may evolve poems, music, works of art, inventions or social reforms. Schooled by reality and respect for truth during the first two steps, he will, one hopes, try to produce and introduce his new creation to the world with a sense of its fitting, constructive relation to nature and society as a whole.

A further exercise of the imagination relates microcosm and macrocosm: "To see," like Blake, "a world in a grain of sand." Take any small object, nature-made, and read from it its greater counterpart, its secret embodiment of large in little. Choose a nut, a shell, a drop of dew, the whorls of a fingerprint, a plank of wood. The following examples, taken from compositions by high school students, were written for such assignments:

SNOWDROP

The snowdrop appears in a pile of damp, rotten, black leaves as soon as the snow recedes. Its form is deceptively delicate; one would never believe that beneath this gently drooping, curved head and graceful leaves sweeping upward, there burns an indomitable spirit which holds it alive through the winter's last fierce frosts and storms. The snowdrop's head is pure white, silky and almost waxen in texture; it curls downward from the smooth green stem, sheltered by strong, upright leaves. It has no smell, as far as I know; it is always found in clusters of modest blooms. As spring finally comes, the three petals and calyx leaves open into a luminous six-pointed star which shines in triumph for a while; then it fades, giving way to the brighter, colorful crocuses and daffodils.

The snowdrop is aptly named; in a way, it brings a drop of winter and re-embodies it in a redeemed form. It is as if, out of the wild whiteness, one drop has been reborn in the form of a flower. When the snowdrop opens, the six-petaled star reminds one of a snowflake, which also, in a way, redeems winter with its beauty. Thus a snowdrop is the last child of snow and frozen earth, but it also is the first to herald the approach of its brethren in a new spring.

—Melissa Merkling

THE GEODE

Splitting open a plain, pock-marked global rock, one usually encounters its constituents, sometimes arranged in delightful patterns, but on the whole uninteresting in their appearance. A geode, however, is a hollow sphere, lined on the inside by the most perfect crystals: droplets of sunshine trapped within the living stone and peering at one another. The many facets reflect a light which is dazzling under their source, the sun. The geode seems truly a symbol of the universe: serene purity enclosed and encrusted in "ordinary" matter, its calyx.

I am always looking for a person who is a geode, someone who may look like any other, but whose soul is so pure and ordered that he blazes with a radiance and thereby activates the minds of those who chance to perceive this inner "crystal array." Such people are rare, and before a geode is found, numerous rocks must be opened; but the discovery of a geode, and of such a person, is an exciting triumph and an occasion which must change the discoverer forever.

—Daniel Szekely

We may also investigate with our students the laws of metamorphosis: how an entity is always in flux, maintaining its essence yet radically changing its form. Let students follow the seed to sprout; the bud, flower and fruit to seed. Let them match this sequence with that of egg to caterpillar; cocoon and butterfly to egg. Let them see how the activities of a child are other than those of an adult: watch how a child's capacities grow: from the wriggling larva of imitation, to the cocoon of dreaming, till from this bursts at last the winged creature—thought.

Perhaps most important of all, such exercises may provide a sense of the meaningfulness and worthwhileness of life which can reach in a healing way to the roots of adolescent disturbance, bitterness and withdrawal, as Olive Schreiner describes in her novel of the conflicts of youth, *The Story of an African Farm*:

In truth nothing matters. This dirty little world, full of confusion, and the blue rag, stretched overhead for sky, is so low we could touch it with our hand.

Existence is a great pot, and the old Fate who stirs it round cares nothing what rises to the top and what goes down, and laughs when the bubbles burst. And we do not care. Let it boil about. Why should we trouble ourselves?...

A gander drowns itself in our dam. We take it out, and open it on the bank, and kneel looking at it. Above are the organs divided by delicate tissues; below are the intestines artistically curved in a spiral form, and each tier covered by a delicate network of blood-vessels standing out red against the faint blue background. Each branch of the blood-vessels is comprised of a trunk, bifurcating and re-bifurcating into the most delicate hair-like threads, symmetrically arranged. We are struck with its singular beauty, and, moreover—and here we drop from our kneeling into a sitting posture—this also we remark: Of that same exact shape and outline is our thorn-tree seen against the sky in mid-winter; of that shape also is delicate metallic tracery between our rocks; in that exact path does our water flow when without a furrow we lead it from the dam; so shaped are the antlers of the horned beetle. How are these things related that such deep union should exist between them all? That would explain it. We nod over the gander's insides.

This thing we call existence—is it not a something that has its roots far down below in the dark, and its branches stretching out into the immensity above, which we among the branches cannot see? Not a chance jumble; a living thing, a One. The thought gives us intense satisfaction, we cannot tell why.

We nod over the gander; then start up suddenly, look into the blue sky, throw the dead gander and the refuse into the dam, and go to work again.

And so it comes to pass in time that the Earth ceases for us to be a weltering chaos. We walk in the great hall of life, looking up and round reverentially. Nothing is despicable—all is meaningful; nothing is small, all is part of a whole, whose beginning and end we know not. The life that throbs in us is a pulsation from it—too mighty for our comprehension, not too small.

And so it comes to pass at last that, whereas the sky was at first a small blue rag stretched over us, and so low that our hands might touch it, pressing down on us, it raises itself into an immeasurable blue arch over our heads, and we begin to live again.

There are a thousand ways, of course, to cultivate the imagination. It goes without saying that teachers create their own ways and means. You can steep a boy or girl in the greatest poems of the great poets, read them aloud, have the children learn them by heart and collect poems as one might collect flowers or autumn leaves, lead the students deep into their childhood memories of nature and into their newest experiences of human beings, minerals and stars; open them to the sounds, rhythms and wisdom of language; show them how with Blake not to "see with but through the eye": how to open eyes within eyes. Let them learn not only to see but to breathe in the color of the sky, the light on a birch, the sunset glow on a snow peak, the grey devastation and tragedy of a city slum. Let this new wind of experience lift them into new flight, to a "new height of view" and wider perspectives from which they may then breathe back not plodding but winged words. This breath stirs more than the mind, it vivifies their whole circulation and strengthens the pulse of the heart. Imagination leads here to inspiration.

The exercises I have suggested earlier are attempts not only to awaken imagination but to help perfect it to as clear and "true" a lens, one as transparent to reality as possible, so that when used creatively it can perhaps become, in Tolstoi's words, a means of dealing "with what man should become." In the foregoing exercises we were following, for the most part, in the footsteps of Thoreau, that Yankee pioneer of modern outlook. He, as well as Emerson and Olive Schreiner, take many hints from Goethe and speak in a like spirit. Rudolf Steiner has called attention to the importance of Goethe as a forerunner of the kind of scientific thinking needed in our day. It is through an exact schooling in imagination that Goethe and, to a far greater extent, Steiner himself arrived at insights which point to new advances in science, education and the arts. And it is this kind of lively but precise and fluid imagination, it would seem, that is going to be necessary in order to do more than bewail the times, and be able to see, sense and maintain stability in the changing complexities and impasses which confront us.

We find a recognition of this Goethean ability in Thoreau in an introduction to *Walden* by Sherman Paul, former Professor of Literature at the University of Iowa, in which he writes with imaginative "whole-sight" of the passage quoted earlier:

The most brilliant passage in "Spring," Thoreau's description of the thaw, was a myth of creation as expression. This elaborate metaphor of the organic process that proceeds from

the inside out, that creates and shapes by means of the Idea—
the process of Nature, art, moral reform and social reform—
was also for Thoreau the metaphor of his purification and
rebirth.... This evolution from the excremental to aerial
forms was a process of purification:... "The very globe
continually transcends and translates itself, and becomes
winged in its orbit...."

As he learned from Goethe, the leaf was the unit-form of
all creation, the simplest form of which the most complex,
even the world, was composed.... "The Maker of this Earth
but patented a leaf." This process, of course, not only applied
to art, but to all re-forming and shaping. It illustrated
Emerson's belief that "Nature is not fixed but fluid. Spirit
alters, moulds, makes it"—that not only poems and
individual lives, but institutions were "plastic like clay in the
hands of the potter...." Thoreau was not the reformer,
however, who broke things, but one whose methods, like the
thaw with its "gentle persuasion," melted things....

Walden is the kind of heroic book that was worthy of
"morning discipline," a book so true "to our condition" that
reading it might date a new era in our lives.

It is just such a "heroic book," one that does not break but
builds, which does in fact appeal to this new generation. Thoreau
has never before been so popular. Consciously or unconsciously,
young people seem to long for this kind of new era, this sort of revolution of vision and action, such a "transcending and translating"
of self and social institutions for which the intellect is a necessary,
sharp cutting tool, but which, alone, it is powerless to produce.

It is not without significance that the emphasis upon analysis, to
which we owe a large portion of the greatness of present civilization,
has had its counterpart in racial splits, the splitting of the atom, and
even in the split personality. To balance this we may do well, now,
to cultivate also analogy which emphasizes the unifying force within

the variety of races and nations, within the individual and in man's relation to nature.

Imagination makes "Cosmos out of Chaos." In educating it we work not with telescope or microscope but upon the exercising and polishing of our own lens of insight.

Such self-evolution is actually the most revolutionary of acts. It is what is needed to help us in the reorganization of colleges and high schools. We might then give the full responsibility to those who have had experience with young people and understand the similes of their nature, their laws of growth and metamorphoses. The so-called "establishment" in many cases consists of the dry, paper-like pupa or shell left behind by the human spirit that longs to build new institutions based upon blueprints of forms more organic to its growing nature. And it is these more living, more evolving forms only that fully justify the casting off of the old ones.

Men and women schooled in imagination might become teachers, scientists, statesmen, businessmen, artists who are better able to conceive new and more practical creations and solutions, a little abler to see their own ambitions in relation to the whole of society, a little less apt to thrust into the present what will become a danger or pollution in the future.

The healthy awakening and training of imagination may well be one of the most crucial challenges that face educators today.

REFERENCES

Rachel Carson, *Silent Spring*
Ralph Waldo Emerson, *English Traits*
Olive Schreiner, *The Story of an African Farm*
Henry David Thoreau, *Walden* (introduction by Sherman Paul)
Lev Nikolayevich Tolstoi, "Modern Science"

POETRY, MUSIC AND IMAGINATION

> I am interested in language as something that fashions destinies and worlds—language as the most important skill—language as a ritual and magic charm—the word as carrier of dramatic movement.... Isn't just the subtle abuse of truth and of language the real beginning of the misery of the world we live in?
>
> —Vaclav Havel, *Disturbing the Peace*

Of what earthly use today is poetry or the study of it in this technological, highly complex and televised world, with its threatened environment, economy and human rifts between races, nations and creeds, the split atom and the split personality? Has poetry any possible power to heal, re-form or transform the times or ourselves?

Why is it that in Russia it is just the poets who have been exiled and incarcerated? Why are they feared? Why is it that we still speak of the ages of Homer, Dante and Shakespeare, Chaucer and Milton? What gave them the ability both to characterize and to form their centuries? What capacities must a poet have to achieve such stature?

What is the very first capacity that marks a poet? Gradually we realize that it is the ability to open oneself to the world. You cannot be nourished by food unless you first open your mouth, nor can you be nourished by experience and grow strong from it unless you first open your eyes and look about you—not with the glazed and passive eye of the TV viewer—but with that gentle opening of the soul which we call wonder.

Yet wonder is still more than this all-embracing openness. An inner stirring begins, a warmth, an inner brooding, a humming, musical mood, a gradual absorbing of the world that can grow to become something like a chewing upon the cud of life, a digesting and transforming of its rich, raw stuff. Now we want to explore the essences and origins of things. Curiosity belongs to the delighted intellect, but wonder to the heart.

In the words of Jacques Maritain:

A kind of musical stir, of unformulated song, with no words, no sounds, absolutely inaudible to the ear, audible only to the heart, here is the first sign through which the presence of poetic experience within the soul is recognized.

"Wonder," the Greeks said, "is the beginning of Wisdom." Rachel Carson in her book, *A Sense of Wonder*, writes:

I could wish as a gift to each child in the world a sense of wonder so indestructible that it would last throughout life as the unfailing antidote against boredom and the disenchantment of later years, the sterile preoccupation with things artificial, the alienation from the sources of our strength.

It is this sense of wonder that led thinkers to ponder the beginnings of the world. What could be created out of nothing, yet hold within itself all the future of creation? What can I as a human being create without any help from outside myself, without the help of clay or wood or paint, and yet can hold in itself and tell about all that is? What but words, which can paint, sculpt forms, describe every detail that exists, but can also pulse with joy, sorrow and life, can command and even have power over life and death! And so the students and I write and recite together the beginning of the St. John's Gospel in English and in Greek:

In the beginning was the Word
And the Word was with God
And the Word was God.

The same was in the beginning with God.
In Him was life
And the life was the light of men.
And the light shineth in the darkness;
And the darkness comprehendeth it not.

En Arche ain ho Logos
Kai ho Logos ain pros ton theon
Kai theos ain ho Logos
Autous ain en arche pros ton theon.
En auto tzoe ain
Kai he tzoe ain to phos ton anthropon.
Kai to phos en te scotia phainei
Kai he soctia auto ou katelaben.

Along the way we learn some basic Greek roots: *Arche*: archaic—the first time, ancient, in the beginning, the first of angels: archangels, archbishop, arch-fiend, archetype. *Theos:* god. *Thea:* goddess—theater, the home of the goddess, en-*thu*-siasm—god within us. And so on, through *Logos, Anthropos, auto, tzoe, phos.*

Words

The poet's problem is to unite freedom with precision. Dante was free imagination—all wings—yet he wrote like Euclid.

—Emerson

And yet, what really is a word? How is it born? Arising as an invisible thought or the impulse of a warm heart, it must build itself a body if it is to be effective in this physical world of ours. And so it does—out of the most ephemeral and intangible of substances: the stuff of sound. With the instruments of lips, teeth, tongue and palate, the delicate yet sturdy consonants are shaped to provide keel, masts, sails and vessel, and in the hull of each syllable is placed a musical, glowing vowel, like a jewel set in the prongs of a ring:

enclosed, protected, cherished, held in place
by many-sided care of consonants.

So the little boats of each word are ushered forth into the world, uttered, born from the human mouth, and then borne outward on the stream of the outflowing, warm, slightly moist breath: wingéd words that fly straight to their goal—another human soul. An impulse arising within us may first appear only as a glint in the human eye, next in a gesture and finally in the transformation of them both, as speech carried on the spearthrow of the breath.

It is characteristic of speech that it is never for itself or its author—always it is for "the other." And it is most itself when it is spoken with the greatest concentration of the *subject's* activity but at the service of scrupulous *objectivity*. In this way a true marriage of subjectivity and objectivity is celebrated. They become one. And when this happens, it gives the speaker a sense of effectiveness in the world, an inner firmness and natural unselfconscious self-confidence.

There are only three arts that need no more than the human body for their performance: the arts of movement, song and speech. Of these, the art of speech can best express thought, the activity most characteristic of human beings. And speech includes within its own nature all the other arts.

Music in Language

A large part of the power of poetry lies in its music. Poems without rhythms and repetitions, onomatopoeia and tone-color, hardly move the heart or awaken us to fresh vision and delight. How and when can we best bring home to young people the full nature and scope of poetry? Waldorf schools provide a History Through Poetry course in the tenth grade. What could be a better time to do this?

Viewed from within, the soul of an adolescent is now a battle-field. A new tide is rushing into the waters of childhood, and the two currents meet in a whirlpool whose vortex can suck them down to depths of loneliness or fascinating hells, and then lift them to breathtaking heights, where the wide view is swept by a light, like dawn on the first day of creation, revealing as has never been revealed before, the beauty of the world. Why is it that older people have been able to disregard or sully it so—an inner world that is deep and secret beyond any telling of it?

These extremes are a tenth grader's realities. Against these, students test their teachers. Do they know anything of these depths and heights? Will they encroach too far on this private world? Can they grasp or answer the riddles of life? This is a time when we can describe how Pythagoras spoke of the great, harmonious motions of the starry worlds as sounding "the music of the spheres," and how out of this the creative ordering of the universe arose. This conception permeated people's imagination up through medieval times, and later it inspired Dryden, in his "Song for St. Cecilia's Day," to write:

> From harmony, from heavenly harmony
> This universal frame began:
> From harmony to harmony
> Through all the compass of the notes it ran,
> The diapason closing full in Man....
> Then hot and cold and moist and dry
> In order to their stations leap,
> And music's power obey....

The astronomer Kepler was convinced that the courses of the planets were musical in their motions and, in his search for the harmonic basis of their orbits, came upon the facts of astronomy which have made him famous. He found a set of mathematical ratios very similar to those that underlie the mathematical ratios of the harmonic series in music. As a result of one of his projects, he wrote the score of the melodies of all the planets, including the Earth. He transposed into musical notes the fractions created by the relation of two speeds: the speed of a planet at its apogee (when it is farthest from the Earth) and its speed when nearest the Earth, its perigee.

That the music of the spheres sounds also in the human soul is a thought that, in *The Merchant of Venice*, Lorenzo ponders as he speaks to Jessica on a star-lit night:

> Look how the floor of heaven
> Is thick inlaid with pattins of bright gold.
> There's not the smallest orb which thou behold'st
> But in his motion like an angel sings
> Still quiring to the young-eyed Cherubims.
> Such harmony is in immortal souls,
> But whilst this muddy vesture of decay
> Doth grossly close it in, we cannot hear it.

We can go further and make a Chladni figure. A violin bow is drawn across the edge of a copper or a crystal plate over which fine powder has been strewn. As the tone grows stronger, the powder forms itself into an harmonious pattern and then into a different form when the pitch changes and a new note sounds. You can show the class a movie of iron filings that stand up on end and perform intricate dances to a passage from a symphony. Now we realize that music can send a similar harmonious pattern not only into iron filings but right into our own physical bodies. No wonder that, on the one hand, music therapy can bring healing into a disordered, disoriented body or soul. On the other hand, noise destroys. Some insurance companies will not insure heart patients if they live on a noisy thoroughfare.

But there is something still more significant to be drawn from this experiment. The plate across which the violin bow is drawn must be either of copper or of crystal. So the diaphragm of the soul, if it is to respond subtly to the world around it, must have the warm, sensitivity and mobility of copper or the purity of crystal. A lead plate or a soul can only respond to a kick. All the world craves drama, especially young people. The copper soul finds it in Shakespeare, the soul allowed to become leaden finds it in drugs and guns.

"What passions cannot music raise and quell," Dryden writes. Music moves the motions of the soul, the e-motions. An iambic rhythm stirs us to activity, the trochaic to thoughtfulness, the anapest to dance, the dactyl to health. Shakespeare again puts it best of all:

> The man that hath no music in himself,
> Nor is not moved with concord of sweet sounds,
> Is fit for treasons, stratagems, and spoils.
> The motions of his spirit are dull as night,
> And his affections dark as Erebus.
> Let no such man be trusted.

The Genius of Language

It is the genius of a language that shapes the architecture of its grammar and the stanzaic forms of its poetry, imbuing it not only with music but with sculpture, color, drama, and the art of black and white, dark and light. We can discover some of the artistry of the English language through the way in which it can build a whole ladder of mysterious shades that span the way from somber darkness to fiery light. Start with the hint of a word such as *glint* and then arrange a mounting sequence such as *gloom, glimmer, glint, glisten, glitter, gleam, glare!* and afterwards assign a composition that starts near a woodland pool and ends with a forest fire. Start out along the trail of *whirl, swirl,* half dance, half sculpture, past *furl* and *curl,* not forgetting, last but not least, *girl!* Make the four elements sound out in a short poem, only one noun, one verb to a line: *Rocks crack,/Winds flow,/Fire flickers,/Rivulets flow.* There are endless such discoveries to be made.

Children have a keen ear for expressive sounds and love such words as *slosh, slush, flop, slop, plop.* When I was little and my sister and I made our beds, we would stand on either side of the white sheets and point out the rimples that had to be smoothed. It was not until college, when I asked my roommate to smooth out the rimples in her sheets, that I was told there was no such word in the dictionary, which only goes to show how *wrong* a dictionary can be! Our sheets had no hummocks or coils in them, so they were not rumpled. Neither were they wet, so not *rippled. Wrinkles* belong in old ladies' faces. No, our sheets were distinctly *rimpled!* Now you might say that we were being creative. But no again. We were being exact. We were going to the source, the origins of things. We were being original but not creative. This was by no stretch of the imagination self-expression. It was world-expression!

Imagination

> Respect for the word is the first commandment in the discipline by which a man can be educated to maturity—intellectual, emotional, and moral. Respect for the word—to employ it with scrupulous care and an incorruptible heartfelt love of truth—is essential if there is to be any growth in a society or in the human race.
>
> —Dag Hammarskjold

This brings me to something which I think is of the greatest importance. It is why I have never taught so-called "creative writing." We all, and young people especially, need to learn how to be true in its fullest, most living, most unpedantic sense. But how true do we think imagination can be? What is its nature? How can we train high school pupils to be as responsible toward the truth of imagination as they try to be towards accurate truth in mathematics and science?

One way could be this: Call up before the mind's eye an image of a flower petal, a rose or a mallow, with its pure, clear color and delicate substance fluttering in the breeze. It is narrow, close to the stem and flares outward, widening into the air and light. And now turn to a different kingdom of nature. Picture a butterfly's wing, pointed where it is attached to the body and widening out into the full, beautifully colored wing of a texture so impalpable that it can glide and float on the wind.

And you say, "See, a butterfly is a flower tossed by the wind!" You have had an *image-i-nation!* What have you really done? You have seen deeper than what first met your eye. You have seen *through* the vivid impressions made by two quite distinct and separate physical organisms, to the invisible laws and forces which informed and built them both, just as the Japanese poet who wrote the haiku:

> See, white petals blow
> Back up to the cherry bough!
> No, a butterfly!

and as Rudolf Steiner, when he wrote:

> Behold the plant!
> It is the butterfly
> Held prisoner by the Earth.

> Behold the butterfly!
> It is the plant
> By the whole cosmos freed!

Now you can understand why William Blake says:

This life's dim window of the soul
Distorts the heavens from pole to pole
And leads you to believe a lie
When you see with, not thro', the eye.

But the lens through which we look in this way is still unformed in many of us and needs careful shaping and training.

Now I think that it is just during high school that people can work at building and developing this kind of eye, an eye that has the power to foresee the consequences of our actions and to look into the invisible laws that create the miracles of intricate plant, animal and human forms. With our physical eyes we see the marvels of these forms and of color, stars, oceans and of people, but they can not see into the world of the invisible forces that create them, or into the inner nature of a human being. Is there really an eye that can do this? And, you see, there is such an eye! Poets call it imagination.

Kinships

A man, to be greatly good, must imagine intensely and comprehensively; he must put himself in the place of another and of many others; the pains and pleasures of his species must become his own. The great instrument of moral good is the imagination.

—Shelley, *A Defense of Poetry*

Imagination has a still further and very particular property which could be of special importance for the world today. It does not only see the very core, heart and whole of what it perceives. It recognizes and fosters the likenesses and kinships among people and in nature. It probes through the altogether different faces and personalities that surround us and glimpses—deeper than what first meets the eye—the archetype of humanity that imbues each member of every race, every nation and creed and makes us all akin. When we are able to recognize this archetype in one another, we no longer need to hate our differences, but are somehow freed to welcome and even delight in the wealth of diversity that these variations provide. We have a new grasp of the unity and wholeness of mankind, of families and of our own invisible core, our individuality.

Through the eye of analysis, by contrast, we see and are able to make sharp, fine distinctions and divisions. To this we owe much of the greatness of our modern civilization as well as an important stage, not to be neglected in the training of clarity and exactitude of thought. But it also leads us to distinguish and too often foster the differences and dividing-walls between races, nations and creeds, the divisions in families and in the subtly interwoven forces that weave the fabric of our own souls. We split the atom and our own identity.

Gazing into nature, imaginative insight, with its love of likening, sees the star form in the vast night skies and again the same form in the faces of daisies in a morning meadow. It recognizes it in crystals and even in crystalline thoughts that radiate star-like into the world. It discovers how the courses that rivers take across countries and continents are mirrored in the boughs of trees, in the veins of leaves, the veins of rocks, in our own veins and arteries. The whole world, we realize, is interrelated in one analogy after another. We are embedded in a meaningful web of laws that weaves the Earth and the heavens, the East and the West into a whole.

Our physical eyes are finished organs, and if there is something wrong with them, they have to be corrected by glasses or contact lenses. But the eye of imagination is never finished, and it is only we ourselves who can build it ever further so that it becomes more and more transparent to the light of reality, so that the curve of its lens grows more perfect and there is ever less astigmatism to distort what we see into fantastic shapes and illusions. We ourselves can learn to focus this lens so that it does not limit us to near-sightedness but gives us broad perspectives and clear views.

A Heightening of Imagination

This organ of imagination can heighten its powers even further if you direct it towards all that is positive. When this happens, like the sun itself, it sees and draws up towards itself all that wants to grow. We have all heard of the "evil eye" that supposedly puts a curse on all it rests upon. But we have also experienced people who have a "good eye." When they come into a room, everything about them seems to brighten and thrive, as a landscape does when the sun comes out from behind a cloud. And conversely, if you look up to the image of what you, in your heart of hearts, would most dearly love to be and look up to it as steadfastly as, say, a dandelion looks up to the sun, you can gradually *become* what you imagine, just as a dandelion becomes a tiny golden image of the sun itself. And so, in this way, too, you can gradually bring about some of the ideals you hold for the world around you and make the world "As You Like It!"—not in any trivial or superficial sense, but as you like it in your truest, most thoughtful self.

"Trust thyself! Every heart vibrates to that iron string."

—Emerson

Inspiration and Intuition

Poets have capacities of still another kind. Homer begins *The Iliad* with the words, "Sing, O Muse, the wrath of Achilles." Even today a poet may tell you, "The poem is not really mine. I heard it." Something higher than his ordinary self has inspired, breathed it into him, and now he in turn can breathe it out again and inspire his listeners.

Inspire! As you recall the cousins of this word, *as-pire, ex-pire, re-spir-ation,* you become aware of what a universal process this breathing is. You can breathe in a thought, an ideal. You can breathe in the very light—the morning-light over a summer meadow or aslant a white birch. You can breathe in the tone of a distant church bell and, still more deeply, the silence upon which it floats. I believe everyone shares such experiences, to varying degrees.

That the awakening of this kind of awareness is part of human progress you realize if you read what Rudolf Steiner has to say in his book, *The Mission of the Archangel Michael.* In ancient times, he tells us, the spiritual was in-spired with the breath strengthened by yoga exercises. Though this was possible in the past, such practices do not now achieve the same result. Air is no longer a bearer of spiritual forces as it was in the past. Light and tone, however, are still so imbued. In a wonderfully subtle way our senses are breathing organisms. When with each sight we see and each tone we hear we become able to breathe in their indwelling spirit, we shall, he tells us, have reached a stage of human cultural development fitting for the progress of humanity today.

In imagination the poet sees with his inner eye. Inspiration allows him to breathe in something beyond himself. With intuition he *becomes* more than himself. Intuition makes possible the imitation of a tiny child and the art of acting. Keats, glancing out the window, felt the dust sifting down through all his feathers. He had caught a glimpse of a sparrow taking a dust-bath.

Shelley has given us three pure examples of these three poetic capacities: of imagination in "To a Skylark," of inspiration in "Ode to the West Wind," and of intuition in "The Cloud."

We began with the Word that was in the beginning: the great, creative artist of the universe. The poet becomes its pupil to the extent that he develops wonder that leads him to Wisdom; a love of language in which he awakens to its native music, sculpture, motion and unique creative nature; and a power of imagination which he shapes into the eye of truth. Then he may gradually become ready to receive, as a gift from the gods, their inspirations and become more than himself, in very deed, a poet.

REFERENCES

William Blake, "The Everlasting Gospel"

Rachel Carson, *A Sense of Wonder*

John Dryden, "Song for St. Cecilia's Day"

Ralph Waldo Emerson, *English Traits*

Dag Hammarskjöld, *Markings*

Vaclav Havel, *Disturbing the Peace*

Jacques Maritain, *Creative Intuition in Art and Poetry*

William Shakespeare, *The Merchant of Venice*

Percy Bysshe Shelley, *A Defense of Poetry*

Albert Steffen, *The Mercury Capital*

Rudolf Steiner, *The Mission of the Archangel Michael*

THE CRISIS OF THE WORD TODAY

All men are poets at heart.
—Emerson

There is an ever-growing concern today to help protect and heal the dying and poisoned landscapes that lie around us. But what of our inner human world with its landscapes of language?

What is happening to its contours and vegetation? We find fast encroaching deserts bare of vocabulary, in which little beside the jaunty cactuses of "O.K." or the limp, ungrammatical weeds of "Like:" "like I said," "like I do," "like I met this guy," can thrive. Where virgin forests, rooted in imaginations once stood, now psychologists and educators have set up reforestations of plastic "studies," their syllable-twigs and branches stapled together with no reference to organic growth; and incomprehensible skyscrapers of legalistic language tower above our heads. In public schools, the times when children used to hear the great language of the King James version of the Bible, on which our poets and farmers were fed for centuries, have been outlawed. Instead, this generation is allowed, for religious inspiration, at most a few minutes of silence, which they are more than likely to fill with their memories of the latest TV commercials or video tapes.

We may well have at least as great a task as that of the environmentalists, perhaps an even greater one, if we take up the responsibility of trying to protect, purify, enliven and redeem the word. But how can we do this? Perhaps, first of all by observing and steeping ourselves in the nature of language itself. How is language related to our life-sustaining activities—to breathing, for instance?

On the outflowing breath, part of us is carried out of ourselves into the surrounding world, mingling with it, perceiving it; and then the fresh air of the world, together with these perceptions, is gathered back into our breasts—inhaled, enlivening and nourishing our inner being. But our breath performs also another function. Upon its outstreaming flow, our words, like tiny boats built of the ephemeral substance of sound, may be "scattered" forth by the enthusiasm, by the "West wind" of our inspirations, like "ashes and sparks … among mankind … to quicken a new birth!"

To the rhythm of one deep breath, our heart pulses four times—pulses unceasingly throughout our lives with the impulse of our individual being. These two rhythms: the one uniting us with the world so as to bring life to the body and wisdom to the soul; the other, the pulse of our very selves who long to love—the waves of these two rhythms, working together in harmony, can wash like refreshing waters about the mechanical beat, and the frozen, pedantic language and thoughts that threaten our culture today.

But how are we to learn and encompass all this? The poets say, "I listened and I heard." Just as it takes the expanse of the night sky to allow the stars to become visible, so all music, all poetry, all dealings with the word require just such a deep and silent sky into which we listen, listen, and still more deeply—listen! Can we, too, create within ourselves such a silence, that hints of the starry voices of spiritual thoughts begin to become audible there?

In his essay "The Poet," Ralph Waldo Emerson writes:

> Poetry was all written before time was, and whenever we are so finely organized that we can penetrate into that region where the air is music, we hear those primal warblings and attempt to write them down, but we lose ever and anon a word or a verse and substitute something of our own, and thus miswrite the poem. The men of more delicate ear write down these cadences more faithfully, and these transcripts, though imperfect, become the songs of the nations....

There is a great public power on which [the poet] can draw, by unlocking, at all risks, his human doors, and suffering the ethereal tides to roll and circulate through him; then he is caught up into the life of the Universe, his speech is thunder, his thought is law, and his words are universally intelligible as the plants and animals....

And Shelley tells us in his *Defense of Poetry:*

The great instrument of moral good is the imagination.... Poetry strengthens the faculty which is the organ of the moral nature of man, in the same manner as exercise strengthens a limb.... Poets are the unacknowledged legislators of the world.

One of these "unacknowledged legislators," one who Goethe said might have become, had he lived, emperor over the domain of literature, is the German romantic poet Novalis (1772-1801). In our battle for the Word today, we can scarcely find a better guide than this extraordinary individuality. Novalis himself seems to describe in his *Christendom or Europe* the crisis that today lies about us in all its actuality:

To a brother I will lead you; he shall talk with you, that your hearts shall open, and you shall robe your withered, beloved expectations in a new garment.... This brother is the heartbeat of a new age....

Old and new worlds are joined in battle; the inadequacy and incompetence of our national organizations have become apparent in terrible phenomena.... It is impossible that the worldly powers should bring themselves into balance. A third element, that is worldly and superearthly at the same time, alone can absolve this task.... From the standpoint of the cabinets, or popular consciousness, no unity is thinkable.... Let neither power hope to destroy the other.

Who knows if we have had enough of war. Blood will flow over Europe until the nations recognize their frightful insanity which drives them vainly in circles; until touched and softened by a heavenly music they step in a motley coalition ... and have celebrated with hot tears a great ... festival of peace, upon the smoking battlefields....

Christendom must become living and active once more and form for itself ... *without regard for the boundaries of nations*, an organism which takes into its bosom all souls who thirst for the super-earthly and which gladly is the mediator between the old and new world....

When and how soon?... Only patience.... Until then be serene and full of courage in the midst of the dangers of the times. Proclaim with word and deed the divine Gospel, and to that eternal, immeasurable faith remain true even unto death ....

We are on a mission. We are called for the fashioning of the Earth.

The world must be romanticized.... Romanticizing is nothing other than a qualitative potentizing.... By giving the commonplace a high meaning, the familiar a secret aspect, the finite the appearance of the infinite; thus do I romanticize it.

What poets have followed in the wake of Novalis? Rudolf Steiner himself spoke and wrote of two of them. He spoke with deep praise of the German author Christian Morgenstern and of the Swiss poet Albert Steffen. Here are creators of healing, of therapeutic poetry rooted in a science of the spirit, such as are needed to combat the powerful attacks of materialism being encountered now in their ever-increasing fierceness and uncanny ingenuity. What poet of this century do we have in the English language who has something of a similar spirit stature? Out of a wide diversity of voices, that of Christopher Fry may perhaps be mentioned, especially as he speaks in his *Thor with Angels* and *A Sleep of Prisoners*. In these, the fullness of his Christianity-imbued imagination is also matched by the power, rhythm, beauty and mobility of his language.

At the opposite pole, however, we find poems written in our time which parallel the physical splitting of the atom in their expression or description of the splittings of the human soul. Surely today something else is needed—something sturdy and true out of the heights and the depths, out of the heavenly and the earthly and out of the "pulse of heart and lung," which has the magic ability to untie them both in the human soul. Are we not now beyond the moans of the schizophrenic soul? How shall we work towards a growing realization of the living, healing power of the Word?

Language

In ancient times, the names of invisible beings were held so holy that they could be spoken only by a high priest into a sacred flame. Gradually the names of the gods were uttered by everyone. Today we still call cultural epochs after great poets and heroes, but the vital, musical pulse and power of the spoken word has long since been cramped into the tiny iron bars of print. Recently it has been drawn further down into the sub-earthly, infinitesimal minutiae of the silicon chip, and the language that we hear and speak has grown poverty stricken, thin, and polluted as surely as the environment in which we live. With each thrust that we make deeper into sub-nature, Rudolf Steiner has called upon us to take a corresponding step higher in consciousness into the realm of the supersensible, and in the arts he has shown us how this can be done and at the same time carried down into the actual techniques of each one, Christianizing them in the light of the New Mysteries.

If it is an archangel who gives each language its character, permeating it and holding sway there, then may it not behoove us to try to become friends with these great beings and to help to bring about a lofty friendship between them? But how can we dare to, how learn to become servants, friends and helpers of such beings? First of all, perhaps, to love language as all poets do, and then to become conscious of the wisdom with which each language has been created and constructed.

If we think only of the intricate and precise nuances of Greek grammar, we realize that no one of us could ever have thought of anything so socially and expressively wise. Yet every Grecian child came to speak it and in so doing was educated by it. The wonderful balance of vowel and consonant in the very sounds of the Greek language—as opposed to the prevalence of vowels in the southern, and of consonants in the northern languages—reflects the balance of nature in the geography of Greece, and this balance of musical vowel and formative consonant both expressed and formed the Greek spirit. In like manner, every tongue is imbued with its own particular wisdom and reflects its place of origin.

Translation

If we set out to search for the essential nature of our work with words, we may come to ask ourselves whether all great prose and poetry, all languages, are not ultimately translations. Are they not all reembodiments of those archetypal thoughts and entities which, growing down to us out of the spiritual world like an inverted tree, rooted in the Word that was in the Beginning, send their shoots and buds down to us here? If so, it was Adam who first caught and incorporated them in speech when he put names to things. As translators, how can we incarnate these thoughts and names in a new landscape, a new language?

As we become more acutely aware of the individual sounds of language, we hear how it can paint with such consonants as *d*—in darkness, doom, dismal, despair; create a special sense with *l*—in life, light, love, lift. Each vowel gives expression to its own music that strikes a special tone or emotion in the soul.

As translators, we recognize that the nearer we approach the realm of poetry, the more each word and each thought must be fraught with subtle, life-giving rhythms and be wrought by the formative powers of our will. We begin to understand how Rudolf Steiner could say that in a mantram each sound, each rhythm is in its proper place. This could easily lead us to despair of ever translating such verses, for in very deed they *are* untranslatable.

In translating from the German language, we have a special advantage in English in that it has one of its roots in the same element as has the German: in their common Saxon heritage. This Saxon root is so vital and alive that even today it still has new word-forming powers and can do what Rudolf Steiner often does in the German: combine words into vessels strong, limber and imagination-imbued enough to hold spiritual thoughts and imaginations. In a poem, "To the Berlin Friends," for example, Steiner speaks of erecting soul houses:

> Built on knowledge
> Upon its iron-firm, light-woven web.
>
> (*Auf der Erkenntnis*
> *Eisenfestem Lichtesweben.*)

It also allows us to use newly such prefixes as *en-* and *up-*, as in *enwarm* and *up-rising* ("up-rising in dying"), leading the language in healthy harmony with its past creatively into the future forms of a new age.

The first great Saxon translator was the cowherd Caedmon, who was fed verses from the Latin Bible and who then put them into Saxon verse, accompanying them with his harp. In describing this, the Saxon historian Bede created my favorite definition of a poet:

> And he, all that he could learn by hearing, mediated with himself and, like a clean animal, ruminating, turned into sweetest verse.

What better way to characterize the poets than to liken them to that animal so long held sacred in ancient times as they take in the pasture grasses of their experience and, slowly ruminating and chewing on their cud of memories, transform them in the glowing fires of their spiritual digestive system, and who then give forth to the world that most wonderfully nourishing of substances—"sweetest verse."

Imagination

We have spoken a great deal about the sounds, rhythms and forms of language, but what of the thoughts they are to embody? What dedicated schooling and firing of our powers do we need in order to grasp the full sweep of clear thoughts? And beyond this, what awakening and training of the eye of imagination?

What is this eye? The eye, Rudolf Steiner tells us, is sun-created. We can understand this somewhat when we look into the little "day's eye," the daisy, as it sends all its being up into its sunward gaze and, in so doing, becomes itself a tiny sun. In like manner the eye of imagination needs to become sun-imbued, warmth-imbued, strong through the might of awe, outbeaming—in order to grasp that spirituality of thought to which it would bear witness in all its wholeness and power. For it is the property of imagination that it unites, sees whole—not in part—does not separate but makes all the world akin through analogy and fullness.

Imagination also needs to work from the heights to extend its vision. We need to toil up rocky cliffs of experience and look down upon the sea of life so that we may see accurately not only the wonder-play of its surface waves but penetrate to the undercurrents and Gulf Streams that are sweeping the waters of the past into new and future trends and directions. We must also cure this eye of astigmatisms—its egotisms and fantastic musings—and turn its gaze starward, till in imitation, it sparkles silica-like with the fine cutting edge of discrimination. Or let it transform itself, raindrop-like, so that it can hold in its tiny sphere the wholeness of the cosmos with all its facets.

This is far too much to ask, you say. Perhaps, but if with Walt Whitman we can creatively "loafe and invite" our souls, we can perhaps at least avoid some of the decay and pedantry of our day, and, with such hints in mind, help to redeem language and wrest it from its desiccation and pollution.

Today we stand in the midst of the crisis which Novalis prophesied in his *Christendom or Europe*, and which Rudolf Steiner told us would come at the end of this century. We even hear that in the future our children may no longer hear song birds. At such a time as ours, shall those who love language remain asleep to the crisis of the Word? Or shall we, with Emerson, strive to "penetrate into that region where the air is music ... and at all risks ... unlock our human doors and allow the ethereal tides to roll in?"

"Our death-dealing civilization has sprung from the God-forsaken Word," Albert Steffen writes in *From a Notebook:*

> Words which once lived have become coffins wherein spirits lie imprisoned. But they are only apparently dead and can be set free. Out of every such shrine of death an Angel shall appear. The poet may not rest in his love of the "Word" which overcame death, until a whole host of living, divine beings stands before him. With them he sets forth to conquer the beast that rises out of the Abyss.

REFERENCES

Ralph Waldo Emerson, "The Poet"
Novalis, *Christendom or Europe,* in *Fragments*
    (translated by Thomas Carlyle)
Percy Bysshe Shelley, *A Defense of Poetry*
Albert Steffen, *From a Notebook*
Rudolf Steiner, "To the Berlin Friends"

Speech As Awakener and Healing Force

Our speech is, with the exception of our gestures, probably the most intimate and revealing expression of what is human and individual in each one of us. As such, it is of central importance to everyone and especially to teachers whose task and art it is to give human individuals the best start in life. Speech expresses, but it also impresses or stamps itself upon those who hear it, especially if they are young and in the most imitative and formative stage of life. Speech is the great conveyor of meaning; it is also a revealer and sculptor of human beings.

How does our own speech and that of those around us help to equip and influence us for life? What are the elements of speech and how does each of them have bearing upon us?

Some Effects of Speech

If as teachers we can make our speech into an instrument for active thinking, our students will hear how this lends a definite ring to our voice and sharpness to our consonants. They will listen to the audible drama of thought in the intonation and phrasing of the spoken sentences as one thought builds and depends upon another, as conclusion answers premise. And they will imitate this clarity, logic and structure both in their own speech and in their thinking.

Teachers in a Waldorf school are particularly concerned with speech. They use the spoken word rather than text books in order to convey what they know, have digested and then re-formed for their students, who in turn form it over once more for themselves in their own notebooks. For teachers, the spoken word is their constant instrument. They know, for instance, that ear and larynx are closely allied, and that the larynx continually imitates what the ear hears, even when one is not speaking. In this way what children hear models their still soft and impressionable speech organs subtly but surely in its own image. The fact that children achieve a foreign accent more quickly and accurately than adults is evidence of this.

The speech organism, however, consists of more than the mouth and larynx. It also includes our breathing and one might even say our whole nature. We have all experienced the sense of suffocation that overcomes us when we are held captive by a monologue that always begins again just when we had hoped it might end. This sense of suffocation is more than psychological. We unconsciously follow the motion of the speaker's breathing with our own. Such people never breathe out fully, but take in the next breath nervously before they are ready for it. Their breathing is not deep, rhythmical or relaxed enough to refresh them. Such experiences can make us realize that breathing is an intrinsic part of speech and that the way in which people breathe when they speak has a definite effect upon us. Without breath we could not speak. It is the river upon which our words navigate on their voyage to other human beings. It is as vital to communication as waterways to commerce. And its tides, shallowness, uncertainties or serenity are of at least as much moment to us as are the waterways of the world. With what a sense of boredom or well-being we listen to lecturers and teachers; and this has as much to do with their manner of speaking as with what they have to say. The phrasings and impacts of the breath are as various as there are people on earth. Through them we mutually affect one another, usually unconsciously, but nevertheless actually.

Children are more sensitive to these impacts than adults. Not only children's speech but their whole manner takes on something of the clarity and fineness, the blunted or sloppy character of the consonants they hear, something of the flow or purity, the harshness, fullness or weakness of the vowels. But they imitate more than these. The hearty relaxation or hesitation, the ease, nervous constriction or hysteria with which the breath of the adults around them comes and goes are like a life-element. The warmth, brutality, thoughtfulness, integrity, artistry, the whole life-attitude of the speaker model the breath, laden it with burden or refreshment, carry it over into the coming and going of the blood, influence the rhythmic and circulatory systems which are such vital centers of physical and psychological health.

If we could picture the strands of speech which are woven in the interchanges and discussions in the classrooms throughout the world during a single morning, we would have before our eyes a fabric in which an immense variety of patterns glistens with color, life, warmth, pales in places to grey, intricate webbing, and becomes in others cold, mechanical even threadbare. This fabric is a formative part of the student's environment.

Vowels and Consonants

It is a slow and difficult process for adults to change their way of speaking; it demands very conscious activity and practice. But it is comparatively easy to influence the speech of children. How can this be done? How can we help them to preserve the wonder of words, the magic of language, and to speak in such a way that they will think more clearly and imaginatively, so that they become more active, adaptable and healthy?

First of all we must, of course, be engaged in work upon our own speech and have a sense of its many possibilities, of its stature as an art. As this art is disciplined and ennobled, so also is that which gives it expression.

The art of speech, like that of singing, movement and acting, uses only one instrument: the human body. It is interesting that these three were once combined as one in the ancient choral dances of the Greek religious festivals and dramas, for instance. This unity is hardly possible or desirable today except in the singing games of small children. The three arts gradually grew distinct from one another. However, if we teach recitation, keeping in mind its early background when drama as a religious, social and moral influence was a great educative factor in the life of the day, producing a catharsis or purification in both artists and audience, we will find that we can strike a deeper, truer note. Such recitation will remain rooted in the memories and capacities of those we teach long after they have forgotten the facts we have taught them.

What practical steps can we take in pursuing the art of speech with young people?

Small children love the sounds of words. They play with them in the same delightful manner as they splash in brooks and fountains. It is important that we do not stunt but direct them in their love of the gesture, life, music and imagination of vowels and consonants. In this the art of eurythmy is a unique help and guide. Through it they grasp the essence of the sounds and experience how "L" lifts and lulls and gives liquid glow and glint to a glitter, ripple, or cloud; whereas "D" leads you down into darkness to deep dungeons, danger and doubt. "Ah" opens the heart in wonder; "UUU" contracts it in awe, coolness and fear. As the teacher leads the children in poems and speech exercises with this as background, they will come to have a delighted sense of how through their sounds many words still remain true to the gesture of the object or process they designate.

"T" and "D" are the thorns of the consonant world, and if you chisel away to make them as thin, strong and prickly as possible, you will have helped all the other consonants to become clearer also. This sharp clarity gives bony structure to speech just as "L" and "R" bring it flow and motion. Small children, by the way, should learn to trill an r, not like a motor with the sides and back of the tongue, but like the whirr of a hummingbird or the high song of an insect, with the least possible portion of the tongue-tip. This will enable them to point the tip of the tongue for the rest of their lives and give it a strong muscle so that their whole speech will be more skillful.

As you lead your students through these exercises, you begin to notice how quick, exact and responsive grow their powers of listening, making distinctions and performing. The precision and agility which the exercises train aid the same qualities in their thinking.

Besides working for clarity and mobility of speech through the consonants, it is also important to free or "un-imprison" the voice wherever it may be caught: in the head in a hard, nasal twang, or in a pompous overweaning breast resonance, or where it is ripped out of the muscles with a harsh, military report. This means working more especially with the vowels. The air is the element upon which speech rides, and the vowels can unfold upon the air just as tiny dried-up Japanese flowers unfold their full beauty when placed in water. This imprisonment of the vowels indicates a certain passivity in the students. They do not rouse themselves sufficiently to project their voices properly, but remain "stuck" in some particular part of their organisms. The teacher must find the means to help bring them to direct their voices away from here and out into the air beyond themselves.

The more precisely and the closer to the front of the mouth the sounds can have their starting point, and the more consciously and perfectly they can be controlled and formed, the lighter and stronger they become. However, it is through the ear that the students should learn. If you make them too aware of the physical placement of the sounds, you will soon hear that the natural flow of the speech is hampered and that it grows mechanical and artificial; for the nature of speech is that it communicates and therefore has its being largely outside of ourselves, just as tone arises from a tuning fork but actually quivers in the air around it.

Speech which starts from the back of the throat is the most physically bound, the most unconscious and most difficult to form. The hard voice soon becomes hoarse and can even injure the throat's soft tissue. The further forward it is possible to bring the point of departure of each sound, the less this holds true. It is even a good exercise to imagine that you form all the vowels in front of the teeth, though later on one learns that differences of placement underlie fundamental differentiation of style. A forward speech is particularly important to cultivate when teaching small children. Speech has not yet settled deeply into their organisms; it still hovers about it—high, musical and pliant. In about the third grade children can be encouraged to bring it down and make it firmer if they have not already done this of themselves.

Choral Speaking

Speech chorus is actually a highly economic means of teaching, for through it, in a short time, a teacher can refresh, enliven, and train each child in a large group and bring to each one simultaneously a variety of valuable experiences.

The pictures in a poem fill a child's imagination; through them a sympathy for the world and an enthusiasm for beauty are awakened. Ears learn to follow the melody of the vowels and the sculpture of the consonants. The children breathe deep with the wonderful surge, swing, skip, or ripple of the rhythm. And these things they learn to appreciate not just with aesthetic passivity but with active artistry. As the poem moves from enthusiasm to despair, from bitterness to joy, their whole inward being becomes more agile, pliable, and lively. The boys soon learn that this is not idle "playing around," but that often every bit of their strength is not enough to fulfill the demands of a powerful passage, and that they must be every bit as active and skillful as on the baseball field if they are to cut the consonants sharply enough and throw them home in just the right dramatic slice or curve.

They learn, too, that art is practice and has definite laws of clarity, rhythm, phrasing, and gesture. They learn that the speaking of a poem is new each time and each time requires new effort and new awareness. So they become a little less apt to expect life to be "easy," to expect things to turn out "right" at the first try, a little less apt to despair when efforts fail. They become interested not only in the final result but in the *process* of achievement as well. Like the violinist, they learn the difficulty and delight of disciplined tempo-change and of dramatic crescendo that, like a wave, mounts, waits and then—at just the right moment—breaks with full decisive force.

It is important, however, to keep a balance between choral and individual speech training, for only when a student speaks alone can a teacher hear and correct speech failings with enough accuracy and attention.

As the children work over and over again to form the consonants exactly and livingly, they grow more alert. As they speak with fuller power and carry a long thought through on one long breath, the diaphragm grows stronger and the circulation stirs. Indeed, good vigorous recitation constitutes one of the best possible "breathing exercises," for it requires a natural deep breathing which strengthens the diaphragm muscles. When students speak out fully through reciting a poem, not only do their lungs grow strong through exercise and fill with freshness, but the soul also "breathes," so to speak, expanding in wonder and courage, contracting in concentrated thought or earnestness; and the "inspired," ideal element of the poem acts as a kind of inner oxygen that quickens their thoughts with life and eagerness.

In this way they learn a good many poems by heart and these become a part of themselves. Because of them, they look at the world with new eyes, with new sympathy and appreciation. Poems learned in early life are dear to us like no others. They belong to us and rise up in us at odd or at critical moments to comfort or to help us see the world in its full color and subtlety.

Recitation and Breath

The reading of poetry is almost a lost art, though there are some recent signs of its revival. It is usually read so that only the meaning is stressed, or if the rhythm is attempted, it falls into a mechanical beat or excited emphasis which puts all meaning to sleep. True rhythm is carried on the rhythmical breath which is as fluid as a wave and overcomes mere beat while it carries the thought easily upon its motion.

Poetry used to live on the voice of bards and minstrels. Today it has almost died into the printed page or, rather, become a disembodied art, living only in "unheard melodies." And though, as Keats says, these are often sweeter than those heard, yet they lack body. By giving poetry expression in the spoken word we bring it from the imagined to the actual and take a step ourselves from the passive to the active, from the observer to the creator.

Let students recite with vigor and enthusiasm and watch their eyes light up, their color change. See how they then have to use their diaphragm and stir the circulation as surely as they would in a swimming race. But the fire in them has a special quality, for it burns up from the fuel of a thought, an imagination or an ideal. Thought, emotion and will to act have been brought to a single focus which expands their lungs and quickens their pulse. This humanizes at the same time that it makes healthy, and it makes healthy more surely than a contrived breathing exercise done with half a heart between book learning. In this way speech acts upon the physical health of the pupils.

The more one speaks, the more awake one becomes. A lecturer or teacher has no trouble in keeping awake; not so the listeners. Even though they may be interested, they tend to yawn and nod. Children become more alert and learn better after they have recited. Their own activity awakens them. This activity comes into play particularly during the out-breath, that part of the breath upon which they speak. The in-breath should come as a natural result of having emptied the lungs.

That which we ourselves produce, our own speech, our own consciousness, is active during the out-breath. We may be more aware of the in-breath in that we notice the life and freshness that flow into us upon it, but we are then, nevertheless, comparatively passive. The teacher can help pupils to sustain the process of breathing out by guiding the force and phrasing of their speech. This will simultaneously strengthen their concentration, their voices and their diaphragms. One can have the students speak sometimes with their full power—not harshly—or can give them from time to time a well-developed process of thought couched in long but well-knit clauses. To recite such sentences will demand prolonged and carefully phrased exhalation.

It might be interesting to digress here to pursue the theme of the breath in another more subtle kind of "breathing" process, disconnected from recitation. Let us say that we become interested in something. We pour out our whole attention into an object or process in all-engrossed absorption; our whole concentration "is in it": *inter-est*. And as this interest becomes more active as is that of a poet, then we, so to say, breathe out into the object, empty our spiritual lungs so completely that now a counter motion takes place, an *in-spiration*. The interest is brought about by our own activity; the inspiration, as all poets will testify, is the activity of the "muse," a gift of the gods. We cannot direct or control this "muse," but we can open the door for her. Through this we see that the quality of the interest—its discipline, intensity, unqualified joy and dedication—is also an educative factor, a factor that belongs to a different dimension of education from that in which facts are acquired and stored up. This dimension is concerned not with nourishing but with exercising, not with increasing knowledge but with increasing capacities for life. Through the quality of interest, students grow more receptive to new ideas, more capable of being inventive or creative. This, too, is a kind of "breathing process."

When we laugh the out-breath is stronger; when we weep, the in-breath. In fear we gasp for new breath before we have quite finished exhaling. This is what stutterers do chronically from subconscious fear, grown organic. But they rarely stutter when they sing or while reciting poetry rhythmically. Why is this? Because rhythm is a basic characteristic of the breath and guides it rightly. It helps to re-establish lost balance. Rhythm is in itself a great healer.

Just as language consists of more than meaning and has a "body" consisting of consonants and vowels, it also, one could say, has a soul as expressed in its musical, rhythmical nature. Children need not only the nourishment of the content which language brings them, they need exercise, motion of soul as well if they are to grow up in a healthy manner. What provides them with this? The spirit of language itself tells us: the soul moves in *e-motion*, in every expansion of joy and love, in every contraction of fear and disgust and in every intervening nuance. The more finely modeled and vigorous these become, the more differentiated, intelligent, and flexible become the child's soul-forces. We are very much absorbed today in the exploration and dissection of the soul; is not the next step to deal with what activates, cultivates and strengthens it?

The strong motions of a poet's soul create and model a whole world of varying rhythms. Through reciting poetry we come to experience and take part in this world. We learn to lift and fall upon its waves, to balance like a dancer on that wonderful, weightless moment between coming and going that is the very essence of rhythm, the third element, the moment of lightness and freedom that no mere beat—which consists only of the two motions of coming and going—can ever afford us, and which has, therefore, disappeared altogether from the dance floor. We grow alert from head to toe to the dip, flow, plunge, change and interchange of tempo; we rise on the crescendo of rhythmic waves now grown into mountain ranges, only to poise in a thunder of silence, fall and catch ourselves in the final firmness of absolute conclusion—or perhaps start over again in modulations as small as those of rippling water. In dramatic speech that awakens us, in epic that strengthens, in lyric that makes us light and malleable, we enter into new regions and disciplines of feeling.

We know that fear, expectation and surprise make us catch our breath and make our heart beat faster. This influence upon the breath is just as true, though less noticeable, of emotions less crude. Emotions play upon the rhythmical motions of the body; and, conversely, when our rhythmic processes are disturbed in any part of the body, we tend to become depressed or annoyed.

In his *Foundations of Human Experience*, Rudolf Steiner makes an important contribution to physiology and psychology when he explains how, just as the brain is the instrument of thought, so the rhythmic system is the instrument to which our emotional life is linked. This can give us new insight into the means of building up both physical and psychological stamina.

Poetry, through its use of imagination and through the musical power of its language, is an educator and shaper of the feelings. When we embody it in the spoken word, we must first exert and tune our own imagination, feeling, and will. These in turn play upon the instrument of our breath and heart beat. By thus activating and strengthening the rhythmic system we help to establish a healthy basis for emotional life.

Though we cannot say that this in itself will make human beings moral, we can say that without something of the kind people will cease to be so. We are at work here upon those processes which are capable of taking up moral ideas and impulses. No such impulses, only coarse urges and violence will flourish easily in the dead weight of stagnant soul-waters or in hearts that are not to be "moved." Unless an idea is felt strongly by an intelligently modeled and activated soul, it remains cold and barren and cannot become an ideal which is the spring of action.

The healing quality of rhythm can be brought to students in many other ways than through poetry, of course. It can even be introduced into the presentation of subject matter. Rudolf Steiner indicates how a whole lesson can be enlivened by bringing about expansion and contraction: by bringing the students close to laughter and to weeping, for example. In this way, and by using other kinds of contrasts, a class can take on a rhythmic form in which the teacher becomes an architect in time. Such a lesson can end in a deep sigh of pleasure, in a sense of deep satisfaction for both teacher and pupil. As we try to put some of these thoughts into practice, we may, perhaps, begin to understand something of what underlies the at first bewildering statement that Rudolf Steiner made in his lectures to the teachers: that one of the principal tasks of the education of the future will be to bring children to breathe properly.

We must return to the subject of recitation, however, especially to what can be done with it in school. Here, face to face with a class, it will soon be driven home to us that exposure to rhythmical verse easily turns the stomach of a teenage boy. And his is a healthy reaction. He cries with Emerson, "Your goodness must have some edge to it, else it is none." I once taught a boy who, at the mere mention of the word poetry would politely avert his face and with pained distaste and elegantly lifted wrist, hold his nose with forefinger and thumb. He actually became one of the best writers in the class and sprinkled his prose with a good dash of unacknowledged "poetry." A boy needs to learn respect for the demands of poetry, respect for its force and its difficulties. He needs to be defeated by it, pit his strength against it mentally and in rigorous discipline of writing in strict form. The strength and skill that recitation requires must be borne in upon him. He probably also needs the anonymity of evolving this skill under cover of choral speaking in order to ease his embarrassment. Yet behind this shield it is good for him to feel that he cannot give a strong poem sufficient bite unless he puts his whole force into it, that his consonants must cut clear, his voice win more power and depth yet not grow tense, nasal, or nervous, that speech requires all he has of manliness. Once he has experienced this, he may be willing to try a lyric, especially if it requires difficult changes.

The girls need to feel the beauty, the rise and fall of the melody and all the range of feeling that a poem can give them, but they will be willing to go along with the boys and wait their turn.

Fire and Form

These boys rightly fear sentimentality, for sentimentality is the weakness not the strength of emotion. It is a kind of shapeless, uncontrolled drooling of the soul and its cure is in fire and form. Students should come to know and to duplicate the various forms of rhythm—the thoughtful iambic pentameter, the harmonious power of dactylic hexameter, the liveliness of anapestic trimeter—and to realize that the four or five meters commonly used today are only a vestige of the twenty-four meters used by the ancient Greeks. (Masefield used some of these in his "Cargoes" and "Sea Fever.")

Metrical rhythm, however, is only one "continent" in the world of poetic rhythm. It is based on the measure and length of syllables. The "continent" of Anglo-Saxon rhythms, on the other hand, knows no such measuring. Out of the slash of the Viking's sword-arm, out of the beat of his blood as he fought against the cold seas arose the alliterated crashes of the weighty syllables, the irregular spattering of the light ones. You have had no impression of *Beowulf* if you have not read it in a translation that recaptures some of this action-stirring surge of language anymore than you can translate the North Sea into a lake and have much left of its native power.

The dangers of sentimentality and subjectivity can be combated by exercises in form. Not only must the consonants and vowels, the rhythm and phrasing be formed as perfectly as possible, but the dramatic gestures must emerge and take on edge and contour. The gesture of thought must become audible. The emotions must now flow through exacting channels and so grow muscular and sinewy. Each thought and emotion requires its own objective form of expression that places upon the reciter its particular demand.

Thought and emotion are no longer enough. The task must be "done." We cannot remain in the passivity of sentimentality. More fire must be added to temper the metal of our speech and weld, turn and hammer it true.

Nor can we remain in the comfortable realm of reflection. Speech that remains merely reflective does not engage the listener. This is one reason why pupils will listen to a story that is told to them more readily than one which is only read. It is difficult for a reader to overcome the rather ineffectual, high tone of the reflective mind. But lay aside the book and engage your whole being in your words, they carry energy, life, and warmth. The vowels no longer turn the voice upward. It is no longer like the quiet, passive waters of a lake that send upward to us their beautiful, shadowy pictures, but now it takes on an active, downward line like that of a down-running brook. This is something that our students need to achieve today. Granted that this reflective quality of mind is one of our most precious abilities, it also has its grave dangers when it becomes overemphasized. A disease from which we have all at some time suffered is that of being caught in the purely reflective world. We have all experienced the agony of being imprisoned in the kind of reflection that cannot break through into action, a torment that can end in schizophrenia if we cannot summon the opposite force of will to balance it. In such moments we see everything as in a world of mirrors that from all sides reflects the world and ourselves to ourselves. We feel caught in a viewless web that holds us paralyzed and from which we do not know how to free ourselves, a web intricately woven by the marvelous grey spider of intellect-divorced-from-feeling. To escape from this Scylla into the Charybdis of feeling which has been bereft of all thought, into an over-preoccupation with sex of which we see so much today, is no solution, for we are only putting one force *beside* another. The solution lies rather in allowing thought to send its light down into the darkness of passion, lifting and enlightening it on the one hand, and on the other in bringing enthusiasm up into the realm of ideas, firing them and lending them life and color.

So in speech we need with enthusiasm to use all the exactness of the intellect, all the formative power of thought and put to use what rises up out of the lower nature by transforming it. In speech the forces of anger and our will to battle are needed and are converted into the ability to hurl out and project the voice; the forces of procreation are, through the alchemy of the artistic process, transformed into the power to create and form the spoken word in a beautiful and meaningful way, to give it life and body and in so doing counteract the tendency to the stagnation of these forces, a stagnation that tends to bring about perversion. The forces of antipathy can be changed into cutting the consonants clear and hard. In this kind of transformation lies health and humanity.

If recitation of great poetry becomes an art, if its fire and discipline move us sufficiently to produce a catharsis in the sense of Aristotle, then passions can become heightened to *com-passion* and our everyday knowledge and science can grow beyond itself to become that *con-science* which Albert Steffen, the Swiss poet, calls "the knowledge of what will harm the ego of humankind."

Speech is an educative force. Through the truth and imagination of its content, through the beauty of its rhythm and music, through the purity and sturdiness of its vowels and consonants, it can feed, activate and form the soul and bring the body alertness, harmony, and health.

REFERENCES

Rudolf Steiner, *The Foundations of Human Experience*
(previously, *Study of Man*)

Poetry: Nourishment and Medicine

Have you ever tried to feed teenagers a moral precept? If they are docile, they will follow it out of a grey sense of duty or fear, but if they are strong, colorful individualities, they will more than likely reject it as puritanical, in favor of what they feel to be "life" and "experience." And somehow we admire, while we ache for these careless, debonair youths. They are not to be moved by formulas and recipes. Unless an idea can take on life, it does not have the force to grip them. When an idea is able to do this, it becomes an ideal, and "Ideals," Rudolf Steiner says, "are the bones of the soul." Without them it is formless and flabby. We suffer today from psychic rickets, decalcification and emaciation of the soul. Young people are too often taught the exact science of vomiting up facts, too hastily gorged, together with bits of unrelated data and vocabulary. Some are starved for nourishing, whole food, well prepared and warmed through by the teacher. Many are crammed beyond capacity with reading that they are given no time to digest.

We are in need of a science of soul-education: how to nourish it and give it strength and stamina; how to teach it to move with fineness and depths of emotion; how to give it form. It is not only adolescents who are in need of this; humanity in general stands in need of more than physical healing. And here I would like to turn to one of the most impractical of all arts, as it is usually conceived, the art of poetry, for practical advice.

Unless ideas can be taken up into the motion of the soul, turned over and over, kneaded and chewed and finally digested in the warmth of the heart, they can neither help us to build up ideals, the bones of our own souls, nor give the milk of wisdom to others. Unless we can cultivate these powers of rumination and digestion we will not develop the strength to confront the problems of our life today nor the capacity to produce ideas which can cope with reality.

Besides nourishment, the soul needs activity and exercise. What better puts it in motion than music?

> What passions cannot Music raise and quell? . . .
> The trumpet's loud clangor
> > Excites us to arms . . .
> The soft complaining flute,
> > In dying notes, discovers
> > > The woes of hopeless lovers . . .
> > Sharp violins proclaim
> Their jealous pangs and desperations,
> Fury, frantic indignation,
> Depth of pains, and height of passion . . .

Thus speaks Dryden in his "Song for St. Cecilia's Day." In "Alexander's Feast" he tells how old Timotheus with his lyre played upon the soul of his emperor, leading him from joy through emotions of triumph, defeat, rage, melancholy, love. All that is rhythmic, all that expands and contracts brings the soul into pulse and motion, from the great ebb and surge of drama to the long and short syllables of the 24 different kinds of verse feet used by the Greeks, only some five or six of which are commonly used today. These waves of rhythm provide the buoyancy upon which our feelings glide, dance, thunder, rise and fall. The syncopated beat of the tom-tom rouses primitive passion as surely as a storm fans fire. By contrast, the monotonous, unvarying tempo of the lecturer who has only purely intellectual information to impart puts us to sleep. Likewise the intellect, when it is disconnected from the heart, imparts no rhythm to language as we hear in a great deal of modern poetry. But between the primitive beat and monotony lies the whole wealth and varied gamut of the rhythmic world. Not only are there endless possibilities of metrical forms, but there are various continents of rhythm. The continent of vigorous Anglo-Saxon verse is based not upon length and measure of the syllables but upon their sheer weight and force. Rudolf Steiner tells us that this is the transformation of the slash of the Viking's sword-arm, the chop of his ax, or the thud of the ale mugs sounded upon the table-boards. Then there is the Japanese island of muted rhythm. Their syllables are only counted like stars or water drops.

If we follow all these rhythmical motifs one after the other, trying them ourselves as a swimmer surfing the waves, our whole being must become agile and pliable; it must sound depths, surge up to shining crests of drama only to plunge, sway and right itself. It will grow in subtlety and strength. In the wake of poets and musicians who follow the motions of the starry spheres we learn harmony; from those who trace the course of human history, compassion. These experiences alone will not make us into moral beings, but they will plow the ground in which moral impulses can grow. Rudolf Steiner has shown us how, just as the brain is the floor of thought, so the interlacing rhythms of heart and breath form the groundwork for our emotional life. The harmonious interplay of pulse and breathing forms a healthy basis for soul life, and in turn, a well balanced soul life works back upon the rhythms of the body and keeps them healthy. It is these secrets that are the elements of the poet's world.

But without form emotions become extravagant. They gush carelessly in a kind of soul-catarrh. Fire and sharpness are needed in order to contain and dry up the flood waters of sentimentality. "Your good must have some edge to it," Emerson reminds us. The metal of your matter must be heated so that its strong girders or delicate spines may be hammered true, subtle and clean-biting.

Consonants in themselves give form. Each has its unique gesture. A "K" cuts and carves, "T" taps, touches and tip-toes, "W" wuthers in windy weather and wave, "R" makes the river run and ripple. The tone form of a vowel must be transparent, clear and ever in movement; it is not to be heavy with selfishness. The starry patterns of lyrics teach us form as does the thought-provoking sonnet, the symphony of a drama, the architecture of the epic. Thought-mass, motion and music must be molded into structure. This at once objectifies, makes firm and heals.

Poetry is not an embroidery of life to be enjoyed by the few; it is a human faculty. "What is more refreshing than light?" asks the old man in Goethe's fairy tale of *The Green Snake and the Beautiful Lily*. "Conversation," replies the gold king. Through poetry we hold conversation with our own higher being in the dawnings of imagination, inspiration and intuition. When all else deserts us poetry is there waiting to befriend and heal us.

When we are oppressed by a weight or ache of soul, the vowels approach as helpers. *AH* opens the cramp that grips us so that we can pour the full measure of our pain into the smooth coolness of *U: AU!* The *U* reaches into the very center of the ache and draws it outward. We hear its impersonal, compassionate tone outside ourselves. We are no longer alone. Together we descend into the pit of the pain to work upon the wound.

Perhaps the cause lies deep. Some injury, ugliness, some evil deed of our own is lodged in the unconscious. Today we go to the psychologist or psychoanalyst. With their aid we dig into the darkness, pry out the worm of jealousy or despair and bring its horrible dragon-like shape wriggling into the light. We are rid of it. We feel better.

But poets have another method. Together with their muse they descend into the slumbering world of the unconscious, and there in a kind of waking dream begin to hum and spin filaments of music in the dreaming dusk. Over and under the strands of music weave, to the tune of long-forgotten star-music. They begin to glint with *E*, glow with *AH*, flash fresh and fiery with *F*, whirr in *RRR*, turn, twirl and touch tenderly with *T*, darken with *D*, thunder, grow powerful and sound out like a trumpet in *U,O, AU*, diminishing, dimming, murmuring, humming into *MMMM*. There in the depths a wondrous cocoon is woven and in the heart we become conscious of the murmurous warmth, a warm brooding, a tranquil, immense dawning, and, at last, in its own due time, a prick, a hatching, a bursting—and there, winged upon words, flies a butterfly, mirroring upon its silken substance the blue heaven, the brown of earth, perfect in pattern from tip to tip, endowed everywhere with eyes, gliding on the light. The worm has disappeared; there is no wound. The poet is not a surgeon but a healer, not a chemist but an alchemist, who has transformed the hideous enemy into musical imagination.

The word contains all human attributes: thought, feeling, will. It forms and transforms. It is medicine and mediator. How shall we teach ourselves responsibility toward words and reverence for the Word? Perhaps by remembering that we ourselves are the poetry of the gods and as such ourselves poets, since we are made in the image of god. As poets it is evident that our first task is to heal, to begin with ourselves and then to bring back into shriveled language the true, the beautiful, and the good.

Albert Steffen is in this sense a modern poet. In the following poem he leads us to the plant world so that we can learn its "blossom-language" (*Blumen Sprache*, a term he often uses). In purity, devotion, innocence the flower gazes up into the sun. Can we learn to gaze likewise with the clear eye of knowledge seated in the heart? Can we, like the blossom, build a cup weaving it out of the music of our memories, welding it with the forces that work restoringly and refreshingly in the deep regions of oblivion? The poet gives us the answer:

> Oh, look within the blossom's cup
> until you know the lore of life.
> You utter so for all the dead
> the word that lets them love the earth,

and to the living give the light
that ripens heaven's wisdom here.
Yet but for Him who woke from death
you fill the blossom's brim no more—
with draught of memory no more—
and never with oblivion's dew.
Oh, learn yourself what flowers are,
Be chalice for the Living Sun.

Today human beings are developed in body and brain but the rhythmic system which should harmonize and unite these is weak. In consequence they are beset within by a kind of schizophrenia, without by the splitting of the atom. Where shall we look for help? Surely to the Word which was in the beginning. But our words have died and become husks. We can revivify them.

Through motion: We can put wings to verse feet and let them follow the rhythm of the breath of life and the pulse of the heart.

Through thought: star-clear thoughts transformed for earth-battle; all the dross of illusion burned away by the fire of concentration.

Through form: We can build, with the gestures of consonants and the colors of vowels, the floors, pillars and doorways of sentences into the architecture of lyric, epic, and dramatic poetry.

Then higher beings can once more dip down into the substance of language and lift it into life. They will teach us the "blossom-language." They will bring us the for-get-me-not, the herb self-heal and the daisy, the little day's eye that forever looks up to the sun. But the Word that was the spirit of the Sun has become the Son of Man. Christ has become the true muse of poetry and true poets ... healers.

REFERENCES

John Dryden, "A Song for St. Cecelia's Day"
Johann Wolfgang von Goethe, *The Green Snake and the Beautiful Lily*

WHY WRITE?

A Few Suggestions and Exercises

Why write? Why write a letter, an essay, a story, a poem? Write a poem because a melody, an experience, and imagination rises and hums in you, and the memory of something you have heard or done or read gives it the sounds, mood, color, the wings to glide out into the air in song or across the paper in silent music. You write because there is a thought, a message, a task, a story that must be told, a game or process to explain. Writing it down crystallizes it into clarity, in fact crystallizes with it the writer's whole being, making it firmer, more structured and awake.

What children have written, be it feeble or clear, disorganized or harmonious, works back upon them in a formative or disorienting way, and in time works back upon the whole class. This is why you take the best of what they have handed in and read it aloud to them: it both stimulates and forms their future efforts. This, too, is perhaps the primary purpose of a school literary magazine: that it hold up to them a goal of clarity, skill and healthy imagination which they become eager to emulate. Likewise, if we want young people to write well, they should hear from their earliest years the language of the greatest writers—Shakespeare, Blake, Burns—or of the King James version of the Bible, which nourished the style of a Lincoln.

Writing is a social art. A vast spectrum of experience needs to pass from one human being to another if friends, nations and races are to understand and live in community with one another. But this the media, with segmented and capsulated impressions interrupted by advertisements, cannot do. It takes literature with its art of conveying the heart and depths of things. Without such communication, there is no community, no circulatory system to keep the soul of our humanity fed, active and refreshed.

What exercises can we give our students in order to awaken and discipline their capacity to write clearly, fully and vigorously?

Describe exactly, in all its fresh detail, a crystal, a dew drop, a young fern in a forest. Describe—only through the eye—the experience of waking up on an early summer morning in the country; next day, the same—through the ear only. Careful observation of the subtle qualities of the sense world can help to guide us away from the "cute," garbled, or psychopathic kind of make-believe too often associated with the word "imagination" today.

Expansion and Contraction

It can be both productive for the students and a real joy to the teacher to invent exercises based upon the principles of contraction and expansion. The combination and alternation of these can activate a healthy circulation in the souls of the pupils and help avoid boredom. You can combine these two principles in a single exercise so that they act with something of the effect of a hot and cold shower. Or you can spend two or three weeks on such concentrated, constricting work as outlines, summaries, précis and the three-part essay, with the strict demands of its first and last paragraphs. Then take the students, for a period, into the expansive experience of developing variations on a single theme, into various ways of developing the central part of the three-part essay, and into all kinds of descriptions. Even here, you will succeed best if you give them set requirements (contraction) as a scaffolding around which they can build a variety of detail with full freedom of choice (expansion). For instance: Let each student write down in class a list of words that picture what groceries, clothes and other assorted objects can do to, from, and with a paper bag, such as: *rip, burst, spill, eject, catapult, roll, hop, spit, splatter, ooze, flop, vomit, straggle, fly, whizz, seep, pour, trickle, meander, ripple, thud, dance, peer, peep, pop, pirouette, undulate, crackle, spurt, etc.* (You have restricted them to a required type of verb, yet expanded the activity of their imagination by appealing to their love of humorous variety.) As soon as someone has ten words, read them aloud and have others add their inspirations. "Now write a paragraph describing how an old woman, desperately gripping her bulging bag, boards a bus, trips over the umbrella of an immaculate matron; and every word must count!" (They are restricted to a particular subject and to the economic use of words: nevertheless, the subject and the words themselves entice them to expansive activity.)

The real success of an exercise depends primarily on whether it is *carried through* into corrections and re-writing, guided, not by long comments, but by the teacher's very specific instructions.

Clear Understanding

Ninth graders may find it hard and meaningless to study what they find difficult and uninteresting, but they do realize readily that friendships can be wrecked or turned sour through lack of clear understanding, and that you cannot refute an opponent effectively unless you know just what he has said, no matter how distasteful it may be to you.

The teacher now explains that she is going to give the class an exercise to develop this kind of accurate understanding. She will read them a paragraph. After each sentence, read only once through, they are to write down what they have grasped of it. How can they best prepare themselves to listen? What is there in nature which has the characteristic of giving back faithfully, reflecting clearly, what is presented to it? Yes—a lake, or better still, a pond. How quiet the water is there, how utterly relaxed and at rest! Nothing of it calls attention to itself, no opinionated little waves distort the truth of what it mirrors. "I loafe and invite my soul, observing a blade of summer grass," Whitman says, his soul as relaxed and self-less as lake water. Yet just at the surface of this deep quiet, there is a slight tension. Here it is that the reflection arises. It is just this subtle and exact attention upon the surface of their un-noisy, relaxed, fathomless selves that they are to call upon.

Now you read them, sentence by sentence, a paragraph from an essayist, then later perhaps from a scientist and a novelist. At the end you ask them what sort of person wrote each one. How pedantic! How dull! Yet the results are infinitely interesting: everything from word perfect to a blank page. You learn things about the students you had never guessed. Gay little breezes caper across a girl's soul and shake the impressions into utmost confusion. Others cannot resist the temptation to go beyond the reflective and either add to or transform, perhaps ever so beautifully, the original thought or image. Still others distort both the facts and the mood. Objects appear that were never there. The important thing is that they realize *which* process they have used without undervaluing either the exact reflection or the capacity to transform the image *while remaining true to its spirit*. Both students and teacher can see where the attention span is short, where the additions are built up not upon the given facts but out of their own preconceived ideas, or where they have not observed the mood and intention accurately but rather expressed their own sympathies and aversions. The exercise may also reveal abilities you did not suspect or, through the very perfection of performance, an over-reflective nature caught too one-sidely or even dangerously in the nerve-sense system.

I have never pursued this exercise for more than a few days, being too cowardly in face of the sanguines, but I believe that if a courageous teacher returned to it consequently over periods of time, it could build up valuable muscles of concentration and faithfulness to truth, the muscles that strengthen the soul, till with full, joyous subjective force it can penetrate into and become one with an objective reality outside itself. Yet, without the loving response of a perceptive teacher, it could, of course, become deadly.

Grammar as a Basis for Style

During class, ask each student to write a sentence made up largely of *adjectival* prepositional phrases, for instance: *The key under the clock, between the boxes, on the shelf, over the table, next to the window, in the pantry, is my grandfather's.*

After a few minutes: "Now another sentence all, except for three words, of *adverbial* prepositional phrases." *Down the hill, under the trestle, through the tunnel, across the bridge, around the fountain, past the statue, into the ball-field, raced the boys.* "When would you use the first kind of phrase, when the other?" It does not take them long to realize that if they want to set a composition in motion and give it drama, adverbial prepositional phrases will do it, whereas the adjectival phrases lend an air of precision and static exactitude.

Another: "You go for a horseback ride in the country; the pace quickens and you are thrown from the horse. Describe this vividly in a paragraph using *simple* sentences only." When some of the class are finished, "Now the same scene again, but all written in *compound* sentences." Lastly, using only *complex* sentences, the same once more. A few will still have time to write down what effect each kind of sentence produces and when they would use each one. Later you can ask them to think of writers who use one or the other predominantly and read them examples which you have discovered in the works of great writers. Here lies a basis for conveying in turn action, flowing narrative and dreamy harmony, or the complexities of intricate thought. This realization could be taken up in various ways in later compositions.

Let a class make lists of *abstract* nouns: *infinity, immensity, loyalty, despair, eternity, courage, hopelessness, nobility.* Is the effect really one of abstract thought, or does it stir the heart with nostalgia for some far, shimmering ideal or plunge it into haunting depths? Look through some pages of Conrad and you will find in his use of just such parts of speech one of the secrets of his magic. Now turn to Hardy, that great dramatist of destinies and master of the *concrete*

65

noun, and lead them to, or let them discover on their own, every imaginable name for a rise of ground: *knob, knoll, hummock, hillock, barrow, boss, mound, bluff, cliff, ledge, ridge, promontory, peak, headland, hogback.* How grandly Hardy sets your feet on the Earth and brings you to grips with every aspect of its architecture!

So, quite objectively, grammar reveals itself as the stylist's basic lumber, the boards and beams with which to build a world.

The Cultivation and Elimination of Adjectives

All through the elementary school, the teacher has been awakening the children's capacities to observe the qualities of things and has helped them to find just the right word for the shade of green in a spring leaf, the crackle, ring or chink of a sound, the smells, chill and warmth of an Indian summer garden. A high school teacher with the good fortune to inherit a class well taught in the art of descriptive writing, gathers in a wonderfully rich harvest of homework. Even the most flighty students see exact, fresh detail and strive to be true to what they observe, using adjectives like fine brush strokes. This can be consolidated in the ninth grade, but by the tenth the boughs of their sentences may begin to hang heavy and droop with ornate adjectives, becoming weak. It is time to show them how to strengthen these by tucking an adjective into a noun—changing, for example, "little geese" into *"goslings,"* or a lovely open space in the woods into a *glade.* Let them reduce "The huge man shouted with tremendous force as he stood shaking on the edge of the great pit" from 18 to 10 words, using no adjectives: *"The giant roared as he teetered on the chasm's brink."* You can invent all manner of delightful sentences to be condensed. Then set them a composition: Describe vividly a scene into which a bevy of brightly dressed children scamper, play about in lively fashion and suddenly disappear, leaving a sense of solitude behind them. *No* adjectives, *one* adverb!

Exercises such as these can be done immediately and in class, but there are others which need to mature like seeds in the dark, to be nurtured and transformed during sleep. They may need three nights, a week—for the poet seven years or several times seven years sometimes. Even though the extraordinary wealth that wells up in the writings of adolescents can scarcely be explained unless one thinks that these come over with them from the past and so have already had more than enough time in which to mature; nonetheless, time has its definite laws and rhythms, and an appropriate span of it helps a theme to ripen. So it is well to assign a real composition a week ahead of time.

Tone Color

In the tenth and eleventh grades, we can make them more conscious of the secrets of such words as *glimmer, glisten, glitter*. What have they all in common? What is it that gives each its special nuance? This must become for them more than a vague feeling. Lead them to hear how the *mm's* build a gentle gloom through which the liquid, shining gloss of the *gl* shines; how the *tt's* sharpen it to a metallic flash; how the *s* in "glistens" lifts like a wisp of mist drifting up from a sun-touched dew drop and vanishes in the twinkle of the single *t*. The sounds speak a language of gesture, light, chill and warmth.

In preparation for a winter composition, let students make lists of words that tell what light and wind do to snow. From these take *twirl* and ask them to develop all its rhymes right through from whirl to pearl and swirl. What is the motion that all of these create? Find all the rhymes for *drift*. What is the underlying gesture here? Rudolf Steiner tells us that rhyme was begun in the fourth century A.D. in order to help make amends for the fall of language, and now we begin to understand why.

Students have already learned what rhyme and alliteration do at the beginnings and ends of words, but now they can discover what poets know: that there is a wonderful echo and repetition of sounds that wander and weave *throughout* the words and lines of poetry and prose and bring mood, color and form into play, as do the keys of music. Let us call it *tone color*. This can be made visible if students copy out some lines of poetry and choose an appropriate color for each of the sounds (*not* the letters) most often repeated. If they do not ink in these letters, but let them shine out strongly in their particular colors, their pages can become a veritable flower garden:

> **By**-*l*ow my **babe** *h*e still and s*l*eep.
> It gri*ee*ves m*e* sore to s*ee* th*ee* w*ee*p

or from Sandburg's "Cool Tombs":

> ….. he forgot
> the **c**opperheads *a*nd the *a*ss*a*ssins….
> **c**a*sh* and **c**oll*a*teral turned *a*s*h*es….

> **P**oc*a*hontas' body, *l*ovely as *a* **p**op*l*ar,
> sweet as *a* red haw in Nov*ember*
> or *a* **p**aw**p**aw in May, did she w*o*nd*er*?
> d*oe*s she rem*ember*… in the d*u*st,
> in the c*oo*l tombs?

Exercises with various verse forms can become a great delight, especially if the students are not allowed to become sloppy in their work. They become flexible in their handling of the laws and beauty of language. If they are not allowed to get away with inverted word order for the sake of a rhyme or with "padding" for the sake of rhythm, but must work to achieve natural word order without sacrificing rhyme or rhythm, they will be proud of the results. They learn that, far from rhyme restricting them, each new one brings a whole fresh possibility of thought and imagery on its wings. The various verse feet create dances and dirges, thoughtful or dramatic moods, and the stanzaic forms teach them the architecture of speech. Now they can handle free verse with a far more musical, rhythmical or structural ability.

Before Writing a Short Story in the Twelfth Grade

The Swiss poet and dramatist, Albert Steffen, has made a suggestion particularly valuable for the building up of a portrait or a character. Look, he advises, for the mineral, plant and animal counterparts of what has formed the body and soul of your subject. We can ask ourselves whether the subject's features are schist- or granite-like. Is the voice tinny, chalk-like, like asbestos or gold? Has it an edge of iron? Are there glints of sapphire, diamond, something of crystal, steel or marble in a girl's soul or complexion?

To what tree, flower or vegetable is a man allied? Does he shelter like a maple? Does a woman stand queenly as a sunflower? Do the children have dandelion or cabbage heads, or pansy faces? I can never forget one student's opening sentences for such an exercise: "My uncle is long and bends like a banana. He is slipping out of middle life and growing pear-shaped." She is writing still.

What lion, fox, elephant or wolf peers or prowls here? What insect or fish darts or flickers, what parrot, chickadee or fawn?

And the background for such a portrait: What colors, housing, landscape is characteristic? Above all, what quality of light illuminates it? A naked light bulb? Fog? The light fluttering down through breeze-blown green? Perhaps a dark room or barn pierced by a narrow shaft of brilliant sun—early dawn or, as in Hardy's *Return of the Native*, a dark moor where the fateful game of two enemies is lit by a cluster of glow worms prisoned under a glass jar.

If you study the first chapter of Hardy's book and know much of it by heart, as my own high school teacher did, if the students have breathed with the changes of sky and heath as the Earth rolls into darkness, following the architectural structure of the moor, step by step, till the whole silhouetted edifice is suddenly crowned by a single human figure, then they will be ready to write with a new command of language, a new rhythm and perspective of spirit, the first page of a novel in which they lay out some vast scene—mountains or seas or city—and finally introduce the first single character against this soul-widening expanse.

Exercises in conversation between young and old, at a bus stop or in a train, can follow. The characters most satisfactory to deal with are either children, whose every motion is alive, or the old, upon whose faces and in whose gestures years of habitual moods, professions and destinies have inscribed themselves. Adolescents, despite what they may think, are altogether unequal to a love scene or poem, and you will actually relieve them of a burden if you say, "Anything but a love poem" right at the start.

Read great short stories with them. One of the most productive themes you can set them is that of "making much out of little," using Gogol's "The Cloak" or Katherine Mansfield's "Miss Brill" as models. Remind them of what repetition can do in such a novel as Alan Paton's *Cry the Beloved Country*. Talk over various ways to begin and end, how to use crescendo and abrupt, dramatic strokes.

Above all, require detail exactly described, faithfulness to experience and to sequence in time. Steer them away from the sultry, the degenerate, the self-conscious probing into the mires of their own souls. Such introspection, to which they are already prone, walls the adolescents in from the fresh air of the world around them. Inwardness is quite another thing and shines best when lit up for a moment between the clearly perceived facts and events of external life. For our aim is to lead the students to know and love that which is other than themselves, so that they will want to act perceptively, compassionately and practically in a large, diverse and evolving world.

REFERENCE

Carl Sandburg, "Cool Tombs"

LITERATURE AND THE DRAMA
OF POLARITIES

Viewed from without, the soul of the adolescent is in a state of glorious imbalance. Adolescence is, in one sense, a disease without which you do not progress as a healthy human being, an abnormality without which you are not normal. The soul is a-flow and a-wash with new, fresh ideals, dangers, dramas and mysteries.

These tides may, in some cases, be dammed up and then all but drown a young person in a seeming apathy. But often the currents are so indomitable that they will break through anything that stands in their way, whether family, established customs, or morality, unless floodgates are thrown open to them through which they can flow. Then, if these adolescents find that the channels now accessible to them lead them in the direction of their deepest and truest longings, they may set to work with an enthusiasm, dedication and industry that is surprising.

One of the tasks of a high school teacher is to help the students—through the medium of imagination rather than through raw experience—to explore these longings, extremes, ideals, dreams and life riddles even further. Here a teacher can have no more effective collaborators than the poets, dramatists and novelists of great literature. Through them, the students come to realize that now they are no longer alone in their world of discovery. These artists plunge with them into depths and delights, and voice their own questionings; and one or another author becomes their friend and guide.

A good English teacher longs to bring students into direct contact with great authors so that from them each young person can learn, as Keats learned from Spenser, Dostoyevsky from Gogol, and Melville from Shakespeare and Hawthorne. All original authors have apprenticed themselves to a chosen master and followed in his footsteps for a longer or a shorter way. How can a teacher bring about a similar apprenticeship? Actually it often requires hours or months of search for just those works or passages that give the essence of a man or a period of literature. Then a significant impression can make its effect in a relatively short time.

However, it is well worth taking a precious half-hour of a morning lesson to allow each student to recite a poem learned by heart. Then ask the others if they can remember any of the lines they have just heard. Give extra credit on a quiz for any volunteer memorization, and it will surprise you how some of them write out ten, thirty, even fifty lines for you! A poem learned by heart will stay with them throughout a lifetime. Learning by heart allows time for the substance, mood and music of a poem to trickle down below the head-knowledge of academic teaching and become formative forces within the life of the feelings and the will, developing powers of compassion and purpose. All this belongs to the "economics" of teaching. Where does one spend, where economize time in order to achieve far-reaching results?

All good teachers know these things as far as literature is concerned, but they often fall short of letting the students learn to write in a similar way—by becoming the authors' pupils. Writers themselves have always done this. But today in school, we ask pupils to write essays *about* what they read, to analyze and criticize them. This sharpens their critical powers and is very necessary and good. But it is one-sided. It strengthens no imagination, no productive ability, encourages no breadth or variety of style.

After reading Chaucer, let the class practice Chaucer's art of portraiture, using his swift, economic strokes and abrupt transitions, sketching like him the most telling articles of dress and character with shrewd humor. Or let them try Hawthorne's Rembrandtesque use of one ray of light in a large darkness, Emerson's sure-footed pace of thought, Hardy's mastery of concrete nouns and Conrad's abstract ones, Melville's splendorous, rolling seas of language and alliteration. This exercises deep regions of their beings. Their imagination grows truer, more concrete and expansive.

But now, soon, it will be time to take them into the opposite gesture of contraction, to have them analyze, make outlines, abstracts and precis.

It is probably in the tenth grade that adolescents feel the changes within themselves and in their relation to the world around them most intensely. Physical puberty comes earlier, but this, now, is a puberty of the soul. Especially at this time, expeditions into literature and the writing of compositions can act as veritable medicine. If, for instance, they read and write about the loneliness which they are sure to encounter—now more than ever before—they can be helped to value it: to realize that just through loneliness one can grow, can come to have a sense of one's own individuality, find companionship with it, and through understanding the loneliness of another, become a better friend.

In their tenth grade study of the origins of Greek drama in the ancient Mystery Schools, they hear, on the one hand, how the neophyte was brought to feel a loneliness so deep that of itself it gave birth to devotion—a devotion to a star, a bird, to some thing or some one other than one's self. What has happened? Loneliness has found its relief and resolution in devotion. Later the students encounter this same soul-transformation and healing in Coleridge's "Ancient Mariner," Byron's "Prisoner of Chillion" and other works. Several times I have had seniors remind me of this transformation in a way that told me that they themselves had tested such a cure and found it valid and helpful.

In the works of Aeschylos and Sophocles, they come to see, on the other hand, how passion reaches its fruition through—as Aristotle puts it—"vicarious fear and pity so intense that it causes a catharsis of the soul." Passion, rightly intensified, spills over into *com*-passion.

A class may well have learned about the form of Greek theater and many of its properties in the ninth grade, but it is a pity that they should not hear of just such motions and resolutions of soul later in the tenth grade, at a time when they are especially ready and in need of them.

Dionysos and Apollo—Chaos and Cosmos

Now we turn to the other root of Greek drama, to the Dionysian dances. The class listens inwardly to the pounding of rhythmic footsteps as the two choruses of young men advance and turn in *strophe* and *anti-strophe* beneath the flare of torches, moving and speaking in resounding unison to the "god within" (our word en-*thu*-siasm stems from this), to the upward-striving, subjective, chaotic god who longs to grow above and beyond himself—*Dionysos!*

Two roots of drama—one fed by the Mystery Schools, the other by the Dionysian dances—are united in Athens by the actor, Thespis, and they form the mighty trunk of Greek drama proper. Through the study of Aeschylos, Sophocles and Euripides, the students see how the poet's relationship to the gods, along with his poetic style, grows steadily more earthly, whereas the sense of human conscience becomes progressively more inward, individual and conscious. A dramatic workshop using scenes from "Antigone" can give special reality and power to this study.

At the same time, tenth graders come to respect the properties of Apollo, father of the nine muses and god of the sun, whose serene regularity, objectivity and harmonious, stringent rays encourage and shape both plant and human from without. It is he whose rhythmic music pervades Greek lyric and epic poetry. One can ask the class to formulate the contrasting attributes of the two gods:

Dionysos: inner fire	*Apollo:* outer form
enthusiasm	serenity
chaos	order
dramatic conflict	musical harmony
aspiring	inspiring
individual	cosmic
subjective	objective

It is these two gods, then, that the tenth grade teacher should also learn to invoke. Dionysos tells us to throw discretion to the winds, let fire and lightning loose, to ride the tides of melancholy and humor. He urges us to explore the depths of longing and all the wonderful subjectivity of the soul. Then Apollo comes to the rescue and curbs both teacher and class, as he curbs the horses of the chariot he guides across the heavens. He discloses the majesty and force of *form* that disciplines all creation and chisels it to beauty.

So, invoking Apollo, the teacher restricts and shapes when giving an assignment. "The homework for tonight is to write a sonnet. Remember, it is written in *penta*meter, not *tetra*meter. You must choose musical sounds and use at least one alliteration; the thought and images must be clear. Don't invert the order of a sentence to get a rhyme; don't pad with archaic 'do's' to keep the rhythm. You must have a metaphor or simile and use color. You must be true to nature and to experience," you tell them, summoning up all your courage and decisiveness. Then, calling on Dionysos, you continue: "Otherwise, you are absolutely free to do anything you want. You can write of the darkest city, the most silent and sunlit mountaintop, of your own soul struggles, whales or dragons—of an old woman. Only start with a mood, a musical phrase, a wonder or longing, an image—and now, listen!" And you read them sonnets by Shakespeare, Keats, Donne, Millay and have them recite the sonnets they have learned till they are fairly soaked in the long, thoughtful line and mighty structure of the sonnet form. "The fun *really* begins when you start to re-work the poems after you have written them," are your parting words. Or, if their gasps have been all too despairing, you read them a stunning sonnet written the year before by an eleventh grader they know, and they leave with the silent resolve to do every bit as well or better—and some of them do.

When the sonnets—one of them written in perfect *tetra*meter despite your warning, some half-tadpole half-frog, but each containing a pearl or grain of pure gold—come in to you, you show them how an "and" here or a "the" there will turn the verse into *penta*meter; how trite words can be replaced by shining ones, gaudy by clear, abstract by musical words. And at last the treasures of some of their deepest experiences—now polished, pruned and clarified—fill you with wonderment.

The two gods help you further. Apollo shows you how to build a lesson as you would write a poem—with structure and an ear for the right kind of repetition, echo, or even a kind of rhyming of your subject matter, allowing the content to ring out in overtones at many levels as do metaphors and similes—and your preparation takes on a new, refreshing dimension that is rewarded by a deeper, quieter, yet more relaxed attention from the students. They begin not only to hear but to *breathe* the lesson in. Dionysos fires you to enthusiasm, temperament, dramatic change of tempo—compassion.

The Influence of Geography on Language and Poetic Form

Rudolf Steiner recommended that the tenth grade history teacher show how geography is a shaper of history "as at this age the students are justifiably materialists." This same guideline has proven enormously productive in teaching the history of literature.

Let us start with the southern stream of Western literature, which originated in Greece, a land where there is a balance between mountains and the sea, between the lassitude of the tropics and the rigors of the northlands. In this climate, the Greeks lived an out-door life steeped in the daily and seasonal rhythms of the Earth and the heavens. Here they could unfold undisturbed their own rhyth-mic nature: the natural harmony of breath and heartbeat, which are neither allowed to grow sluggish from heat nor whipped out of course by the cold. Their gestures, too, took on the large, rhythmic quality of this life. Harmony and rhythm became the criteria for excellence in athletics and in sculpture—as we see in the propor-tions of the human form and the fall of the garment folds. These imbued Greek architecture and the flow of Greek poetry. Homer's dactylic hexameter is the finest expression of the natural relation-ship between heartbeat and breath, so much so that, combined with exercises in curative eurythmy, it helps to cure the rhythmic disturbance that underlies stuttering.

Peoples of southern climes tend in their language to emphasize vowel sounds—the soul-bearing element of language—whereas northern words are built up out of the more formed, consonantic element, sounds imitative of the external nature that human beings must constantly combat. One can hear this shift in our own country when traveling from Georgia to Maine — from the warm, relaxed, welcoming drawl, "how-ahh ya-awll?" to a brisk New England "Hey" or "yep."

The Anglo-Saxons spoke forceful monosyllables stamped with the signature of nature herself: crash, crag, sludge, bridge, growl, stream—often four consonants to one vowel. By contrast, in the Maori language of warm New Zealand, the proportions tend to be reversed, as in *Aoteoroa*, the name for New Zealand itself; *wai nui*, water; and *moana, Waiganui*. In Hawaiian, too, we find a large proportion of vowels. The ancient Greek language keeps a sono-rous balance of consonants and vowels. As the students recite lines from St. John's Gospel or the *Iliad* in the original Greek, they experience this balance, as well as the very stride and spear throw that the ancient warriors carried over into the rhythms and har-mony of their verse.

The study of the lyric takes the student from Sappho up through the Latin to the beginning of rhyme, then to Italy, France, England. They scan and write in a number of poetic forms, ending with the sonnet, which they have followed from Dante to E. B. Browning and across the seas to Robinson and Millay in this country.

In striking contrast to the world of the Greeks is the homeland of the Eddas and Norse myths, of the northern stream of poetry, a land that prepares the class for the study of Caedmon and that wonderful lyricist Cynewulf, then finally of Beowulf. Here rivers ran sluggish to the sea through swamplands and fens, swollen by incessant summer rains, till the mists rose like furnace smoke, crawling the horizon in purple coils, through which Thor flashed his fiery beard. Axe strokes fall in the forest. In winter, ice-blocks sway, crashing between surge and shore; "Fast to the deck my feet were frozen," sings the sailor in the "Seafarer"; beer mugs bang the boards of the mead halls, heels ring on the hard ground, sword strokes cry out through the cold. Face to face with storm, snow, hail and rock, the Anglo-Saxons form terse, vigorous, simple words that echo the elements. The savagery of the weather makes them into doers, attackers. In language as in life, they attack at the start. Their rhyme comes at the *beginning* of the words: "Tempest and terrible toil of the deep," "Grim and greedy his grip made ready." Alliteration is brief, beginning rhyme. There is no time for the lingering echoes of "singing, ringing... lonely, only." Gone is the harmony of Greek meters, in which it is the *musical length* of the syllable that forms the verse. It is now the force, the *weight* of the syllable that counts. It is the axe-stroke, the stroke of the sword that bursts in thunderous verse-strokes from the pent lungs of the scops, or poets, and gleemen, or reciters and singers. Now that they are cramped in the mead halls, they must suppress the customary gestures of their limbs and so give vent to them in a new form in their poetry, and let strong consonants *sculpture* the words.

Rudolf Steiner has indicated this path from axe-stroke to Anglo-Saxon poetic rhythm as a concrete example of how physical gesture is carried over into speech. In a certain sense speech is, in its dynamics, transformed gesture. We can even observe how the way in which a child walks is characteristic also for the dynamics of his speech. In Anglo-Saxon poetry, four weighty strokes fall in every verse. The small syllables, like so many wood chips after the axe falls, fly helter skelter into the air as they will (no time to count them). But it is also the beat of the blood, whipped awake by the north winds, pounding like Thor's hammer, that you hear, and the breath that comes in short gasps as the wind tears the words away from the lips that form them. There is a similar vitality in the *kennings* or metaphorical nouns of northern poetry: the whale-path; swan-road; heather-stepper; word-hord.

After the study of *Beowulf,* each member of the class writes some lines in this same poetic form, using kennings and words of Saxon root, and perhaps learns a Cynewulf poem by heart. Later they will read Christopher Fry's powerful play, *Thor with Angels,* with its gorgeous, Saxon-rooted language, set at the time when Angles, Saxons and Jutes were still at war and St. Augustine came to England.

After 1066, the southern and northern streams of literature come crashing together and mill about in troubled patterns. The familiar song, "Sumer is i-cumen in," is one of the first examples of the union of northern Anglo-Saxon words with southern rhyme and meter. During the centuries from Caesar's inroads into England up to Chaucer, one can trace how various words are picked up and absorbed into the mainstream of Britain's language.

Finally, out of a host of dialects, Chaucer raises one above the rest and moulds it through his genius into a firm trunk of language, broad enough to uphold and nourish the boughs of various new literary forms about to spread themselves abroad in the age of Shakespeare. Now the class learns by heart the first lines of Chaucer's "Prologue" in the original midland dialect and writes verses in royal couplets. They try out the polaric characteristics of Anglo-Saxon and Latin-derived words, discovering the elemental, poetic, almost child-like power or crudeness of the one, and the exact, polished, intellectual deftness or pedantic dryness of the other.

It is in this spirit that one would like to present the study and history of language, not in isolation, but as it came about—an inseparable part of the growth of literature and human history, an expression and pulse of its life blood.

Drama

For this dramatic time of life—the high school years—drama itself is one of the most potent educative forces that can be found.

Rudolf Steiner has given us a key to grasping the problem of evil by separating its nature into two realms: the extreme that carries us away in a glow of unearthly bliss and vague idealism, and the other extreme that contracts, hardens and fetters us in materialism. But the artist in each of us can enter lovingly into both elements and transform them to the uses of creation. We can refine exultant glow to enthusiasm and sharpen the heavy hardness of matter or soul to a fine edge that carves forms and thoughts to clarity. In drama, where we use neither clay nor paint as our material, but only ourselves, all such transformations are particularly effective.

If, in a drama class, you can stir all the unresolved chaos, the subjective fear or fire in students and show them how, with every fiber of their being, to pour these, not into self-expression, but into an objectively formed gesture, exploring with them every dynamic nuance and concrete detail of it with matter-of-fact strictness, enthusiasm, humor and insistence, they come to experience a sense of achievement, relief and joy that enables them to walk with confidence into the next situation that confronts them.

For what has happened? Their subjective natures have each entered fully into and become one with a form outside themselves, an objective form. The walls between subject and object, between self and the outside world, have been broken through, dissolved; and the students discover, at one and the same time, both the world and themselves. In this moment they are no longer *self*-conscious but *world*-conscious and self-confident therefore in dealing with the world. This can be one of the most important experiences in the development of a high school student. But we live in a time when most of the world and its artists do not believe that the gap between subject and object can be bridged, and this inability leads to a widespread sense of isolation that can cause neuroses, paralysis, eroticism and often despair.

Exactly for this reason it is important that we realize, especially in the realm of drama, that the teacher should not use just any method. Rudolf Steiner's insights into speech and drama are needed here, if anything more, rather than less, than in any other facet of education. Yet it is never enough merely to read about an art or even study it for a short time, any more than reading a book on music will make a pianist of you. A thorough training is called for, or at least a teacher who has set both feet on the road to such training.

Art as Balance

Educators and students today are confronted with the fact that academic "head" knowledge does not nourish the whole human being and can often lead to serious problems of imbalance and ill health. After the "nervous" activity of exams, students let off unused emotional steam by indulging in all manner of outbursts that have no relation whatsoever to their studies or ideals. To bring about a balance of knowing and doing, of head and limbs, sports programs or more altruistic and purposeful work programs are devised. But neither of these really succeeds in inwardly uniting and making fully permeable the nervous and metabolic systems. For this, an inner circulation and breathing between two such activities is needed, one that at the same time transforms the nature of each. In the human body, this power expresses itself in the restorative, rhythmic circulation of the blood and the breath. And it is in dealing with just these processes that the artist is trained. Like the blood, the artist is constantly "entering into" the one pole, transforming its properties so that they may be assimilated by the other pole, and then in like manner entering into the opposite field. Moving between polarities, the artist lovingly forms a third creation born of both parents, yet new in itself, uniting idea and deed, substance and form, the inner and the outer, the subjective with the objective, never stagnating in the one or the other, yet entering fully into each. So when literature and drama become artistic activity, then, like breathing and circulation, they give life to the soul and become healing and health-giving forces in education as in life.

Schooling Capacities through the Study of Great Authors

How can ninth graders experience powerful and beautiful language to help offset their continual exposure nowadays to the brittle, desiccated or dismembered corpses of what "was in the beginning" as "the Word"? Where can one find such language and also satisfy their need to experience adventure and daring discoveries? Where better than in Melville's rolling swells, serenities and storms of language, than in his alliterations and oceanic rhythms—and all these combined and intertwined with his strange, savage characters, brotherhoods, lonelinesses and stark dangers.

But should *Moby Dick* be taught in the ninth grade? Surely only a twelfth grader or college student is ready to grasp the depths of its philosophy and appreciate the significance of its drastic yet subtle soul-configurations, dramas and humor. As the first Waldorf teacher to have chosen this book as the center of the ninth grade literature main-lesson block, perhaps I may share my reasons for having done so—although others will surely find different or better grounds for or against this choice.

Awakening a Sense for Language

God came upon [Jonah] in the whale, and swallowed him down to living gulfs of doom, and with swift slantings tore him along "into the midst of the seas," where the eddying depths sucked him ten thousand fathoms down, and "the weeds were wrapped about his head," and all the watery world of woe bowled over him....

83

It was while gliding through these latter waters that one serene and moonlight night, when all the waves rolled by like
scrolls of silver, and by their soft, suffusing seethings, made
what seemed a silvery silence not a solitude. On such a silent
night, a silvery jet was seen far in advance of the white bubbles at the bow....

During my college years, I had been introduced to the marvels of
this book by John F. Gardner, who later became faculty chairman of
the Waldorf School of Garden City. Over the years it ripened in my
memory till I was ready to bring it to ninth graders as a story rich in
vivid description and drama. I challenge anyone to find many other
instances of such death-confronting drama as in "The Chase—First
Day," or such a soul-spiraling use of adverbs as appear there:

The whale—sidelingly transplanted himself... ripplingly
withdrawing from his prey... for so revolvingly appalling was
the White Whale's aspect, and so planetarily swift the ever-
contracting circles he made, that he seemed horizontally
swooping upon them....

So we plunged in: I, cutting, pruning and skipping, leading the
class into the amazing profusion of detail that describes the Spouter
Inn, Queequeg's dress and habits, the ship's rigging; they, some
lagging, others leaping ahead, some insisting after all on reading
the whole book. We were very thorough with most of the first and
last chapters and covered the middle portion through individually
assigned oral reports. We learned passages by heart, working hard
on them each morning, following this with a "log" or review of yes-
terday's lesson, written up by a different student each day. To set
a high standard, the most able pupil was assigned the first one.

Melville's adventure-filled biography started us off. Next day
the students were asked to divide it into three parts by way of review, and on the third day, for homework, to condense his entire

life into three sentences. Such long, convoluted and ungainly sentences as some of these turned out to be (to the consternation of some of the parents) have seldom been seen, although we practiced beforehand in class. But in the process, they had wrestled with, and in many cases achieved, some mastery over the complexities of complex sentences and their interrelationships of noun, adverbial and adjectival subordinate clauses, thus killing two literary birds with one exercise.

Awareness of Human Brotherhood

What breadth of human compassion and variety of outlook, what brotherly wisdom and tolerance are variously illustrated throughout the book, and often compacted into the unspoken eloquence of gesture, as when Queequeg's stance seems to say, "It's a mutual joint-stock world in all meridians. We cannibals must help these Christians!" Our own vision expands and contracts in turn as it follows the unconsciously cosmic soul of little Pip, then Queequeg's earth-centered deeds—the colossus of a crazed Ahab, and then the loyal, single-heartedness of Starbuck. And when the final cataclysm is over, and the all-conquering whale, the whitely arisen spirit of nature, has defied those who would defy him and dragged them down into one common pool

> ... the great shroud of the sea rolled on as it had rolled five thousand years ago.

What then? A jewel, a New Testament of a half-page epilogue.

Who remains? Only he who has taken into his consciousness every other inmate of the ship and—his spirit ever expanding towards the far horizons of the sea and of the soul—describes the denizens of the depths and airy heights. Only he with the most widely-aware, all-embracingly loving faculty of soul now floats "on the dirge-like main among the unharming sharks ... where savage sea-hawks sailed with sheathed beaks." He floats serenely on his drowned friend's "coffin life-buoy," which has been resurrected, "upward burst" to him from the very "center of the all-destroying vortex of the down-sucking spiral of the sea." And now above the ocean-devoured ship he floats orphaned, yet free and orphan-succored upon that selfsame sea.

But still another value emerged from having chosen this book for the ninth grade. I had already started a study of the Concord Group in the twelfth grade, and now I heard from the teacher of tenth-grade Ancient History that teaching the life of Buddha even to a very eager pupil who had come to us from public school was very different from teaching those who had heard Buddha's story told in our fifth grade. The memories of the latter formed a mellowed sounding-board, as it were, which resounded with the over- and under-tones of Buddha's life, with sympathy, color and understanding in response to the now far more conceptual and complex high school presentation.

Therefore it seemed possible that a ninth-grade literature block could well create a similar sounding-board for the twelfth-grade lessons on the transcendentalists. So we widened our view beyond that of Melville, and his all-important friendship with Hawthorne, to walk the roads of Concord, meeting Thoreau, Emerson, the Alcotts, Margaret Fuller, Longfellow and others. We read in "Specimen Days" of Whitman's visit to Concord and his unforgettable impressions of Lincoln and the Civil War. Reading shorter passages from each, we contrasted Melville's turbulent style with Thoreau's clarity of simple speech; the mystery and detachment of Hawthorne's lake-like reflections, as he surveys both beauty and evil, with the deliberate pace of Emerson's sentences and his nugget-like aphorisms—choosing three adjectives to characterize each style. So we soaked up something from one of the finest cultural heritages of the Western world. As twelfth graders, these students were already at home with these heralds of a new science of the spirit and ready to explore their thoughts at greater depth.

Senior Year—Exploring the Range of Human Capacities

Rudolf Steiner wanted the students to leave high school with a sense for humanity as a whole and for human nature in particular. There is a fine opportunity to build some grasp of this by the way in which one shapes the literature study during the senior year. The students themselves have reached a certain maturity and detachment on the one hand, and on the other, they have a newly won identification with their own powers of thought.

There is another special privilege that we teachers enjoy. Whereas as parents we take a few young people through adolescence, as teachers we see, over the years, groups of them progressing through the four high school grades. Through watching this progression and with the help of insights from Rudolf Steiner, we come to recognize stages of development characteristic for each of the four years. Though these may be delayed or accelerated, or obscured by personal gifts and problems, the same general traits continue to emerge.

For instance, after the eleventh and going on into the twelfth grade, a kind of consolidation seems to take place within the students. The self is more focused, more centered; and from this more consolidated center they are able to look out at the world around them with a somewhat greater detachment, a more mature perspective. As a senior once put it to me, "We are more sure of ourselves this year, and so we are more tolerant of each other and enjoy our differences."

At the same time, their thinking undergoes a change in quality. They can now walk around their thoughts as around tables and chairs, feel their weight, test their reality, pit themselves against them and experience them more intimately. In a sense they are now ready for the first time to think for themselves, to have their own thoughts. But what does this mean? Thoughts, after all, are hardly our own. Each one is thought by thousands. A new thought appears possibly once in a decade. Isn't it only the clarity, love and intensity with which we experience thoughts that make them ours? Now the students welcome them as guides to help point towards directions in life problems, help them find their friends and themselves. Thoughts like Emerson's that have a vigorous grip on truth bring troubling questions into the light and help make them transparent and permeable to solution.

With this new firmness in thought, seniors feel a growing certainty and self-reliance. This is the time—when they are themselves experiencing new perspectives and a new power of self-direction—that they are especially ready to interest themselves in the perspectives which great pioneer natures can open out to them. It is a time when they can respond with an almost musical enthusiasm when they open the pages of Emerson's "Self-Reliance" and read there the words:

Trust thyself; every heart vibrates to that iron string.

With Goethe's *Faust,* who is the archetypal modern human being, as the central focus during the winter months, one could well start in the autumn with the cooler, thinking and observing pole of human nature: the "seeing man," the "eagle," of whom Emerson and Thoreau are prime examples, and follow this with the cosmic and human breadth of Whitman. Then, after *Faust,* they would be well prepared for the soul-searchings of Ibsen, and finally could plunge into the warmer region of human nature, into the large, surging heart-forces of the Russian, Christward-striving soul.

Not all of what is outlined here can necessarily be given during the same year. One or another element can be added or omitted. I do not mention the completion of the poetry course, the writing of a short story, nor time devoted to the fairy tale. For these, as for grammar, essays and book reports, it is necessary to have continuous "run-through" periods as well as the main-lesson blocks.

The Transcendentalists

If you can study one of Emerson's essays—perhaps "Character" or "Self-Reliance"—paragraph by paragraph, you can help lay a foundation for Goetheanistic thinking. Rudolf Steiner says of Emerson that he—in contrast to Woodrow Wilson—was among the American thinkers able to overcome the forces of the "double," to which the West is so particularly exposed, and that the key to the difference between these men is to be found in the style of each.

Send each senior searching through the works of Emerson, Thoreau and Whitman for examples of the tenets of the transcendentalists: the relationship between matter and spirit, between quantity and quality, the whole and the part, art and science, and for the transforming forces of metamorphosis. Have the students give oral reports on one of Emerson's essays of their own choosing, and you will be amazed at the nobility of language and thought with which they do so. They discover that in the seeming cold of Emerson's thought burns a hidden fire. Strike into his steely activity and the sparks fly. He is shockingly radical: *"Whoso would be a man must be a nonconformist."* He has the drastic trust in his readers to expect them to take him at his best meaning and not to misinterpret him. He answers some of the deepest, though hardly yet formulated, questions of young people's hearts and spirits.

Emerson's great aphorisms, learned by heart—as many as they can—will stand young people in good stead when they write essays for college and later throughout the whole course of their lives. Let them follow these by more of Thoreau's as they study *Walden*. The passage in "Spring" that starts with the description of a thawing railway bank is strewn with them. Let them experience how his mild lucidity of style grows sharper in *Civil Disobedience* and can have the cutting sting of a whiplash in "Slavery in Massachusetts."

Whitman opens out a whole new, vast world for both teacher and pupil to explore—a world of warm, compassionate will and intuitive perceptions. It is like entering a virgin forest to track down the most magical passages from his longer poems, not forgetting "Passage to India." Let them discover "A Noiseless, Patient Spider" and the hush of "When I Heard the Learned Astronomer" and of "Come, Lovely and Soothing Death"—then see how he condenses a fearful Civil War battle scene told in prose to a single short serene stanza: "Look Down Fair Moon."

Later in the year, even a brief acquaintance with Ibsen will bring a breath of the North into the classroom and a confrontation with the knots of social and soul problems. In *The Wild Duck*, you have the embodiment of two evils; first in the idealist whose cold rigidity and lack of human insight lead to disaster as surely as do, on the other hand, the comforting lies and leniency of the philanthropist. And who keeps to the healing path between these? A seemingly minor character, but she is there to be discovered.

The Russian Soul

Through the surges and fluctuations of the Russian soul, the seniors' own lives of feeling are stretched, deepened and broadened; and amidst the darkness and dualities into which they are plunged, they can find—especially if the teacher is aware of it—an intense search for Christianity, like a single shaft of light in the rich gloom of a Rembrandt painting. This search is so individual that it leads Dostoyevsky, the confirmed atheist, into the heart of the orthodox church, and brings about Tolstoi's excommunication from it. These two giants were able to weld passion into compassion—that heart-substance without which there can be no genuine social life, and which lies at the basis of the true Russian's ideal: human brotherhood. They explore the borderlands of consciousness in illness, crime, atheism—even insanity—and follow the poor and downtrodden. Almost always these men are seeking for the redeeming spirit in the essential nature of human beings. For example, Dostoyevsky, in his famous "Pushkin Address," leads nationalism past its limiting barriers, over into what is universally human, when he says, "To be a true Russian is to be the brother of all mankind."

Through Tolstoi, who reaches out in his correspondence to Gandhi in the East and to Henry George, Edison and William Lloyd Garrison in America, one is able to give the class a broad world-view of ideas and personalities. One can also give an impression of how a cycle of culture develops by taking the Athene-like birth of Russian literature with Pushkin, its youthful phase in Lermontov and Gogol, the golden age of Tolstoi, Dostoyevsky and the Westernizer Turgenev, and then the twilight period of Chekhov—all in a single century! Meanwhile the work of Pasternak and Solzhenitsyn, especially the latter's *Nobel Lecture*, can be woven into the course. This is a great deal to cover, but actually, if the teacher gives a sense of Russia as a whole through the fascinating lives of the authors, touching on the highlights of their works, and the students present lively oral reports of the novels they have been reading during the winter and the summer before, it is surprising what a rich and vivid impression can result.

So through the literature periods, the students can see how a culture develops a cycle in time, and how great ideals express themselves in one part of the world more through the nature of the keenly observing head and in another more through the impulses of the heart or intuitive will. Thus they may take with them, as they leave school, a world-panorama and an appreciation of the breadth, depth and diversity of human capacities. In so doing they have exercised, stretched and strengthened these very same capacities within themselves.

REFERENCES

Fyodor Dostoyevsky, *Pushkin Address*
Ralph Waldo Emerson, "Self-Reliance"
John F. Gardner, *American Heralds of the Spirit*
Herman Melville, *Moby Dick*

BACKGROUNDS FOR RUSSIAN LITERATURE

With Special Emphasis on Soloviev and Dostoyevsky

PART I

Soloviev was a forerunner. And one of the most interesting tasks for a teacher—or for anyone, for that matter—is to seek out those great pioneers of modern and future thought who are to be found in almost every country and culture; and then to explore the inner landscapes they provide, climb the crags of their rocky conceptions and breathe the high, clear air and large perspectives of their insights. If we are to stir the imagination of the younger generation, give transparency and mobility to their widening powers of vision and toughen their mental grip, we must find examples for them, great figures who can help to nourish and exercise young people's capacities.

Such creative spirits need to be found, moreover, in countries other than our own. Interestingly enough, once one comes to know one of these forerunners, one discovers that they have already found out others of their own kind, have spun threads of friendship across the seas, built indestructible bridges of insight between peoples, and links from their own time to our own. In some respect these pioneers are more contemporary now than they were in their own eras. Goethe, Carlyle, Coleridge, MacDonald, Emerson, Thoreau, Tolstoi, Dostoyevsky are some of these.

Soloviev is another. Margarita Voloschin, a Russian painter who worked on the first Goetheanum,[1] writes in her book, *The Green Snake*:

---

1. The building for the international center of the Anthroposophical movement, designed by Rudolf Steiner. After the first building was destroyed by fire, Steiner drew up plans for the second Goetheanum on the same site in Dornach, Switzerland.

The people whom I came to know in the spring of 1910 in Moscow belonged to a circle that had a strong connection with Soloviev. The philosopher himself had been dead for ten years, but his spirit was livingly present in various groups in Moscow. There was alive in these friends of mine a certain Apocalyptical mood and a sense that there might now be possible a new revelation, a spiritual knowledge, a concrete, esoteric Christian way. It was interesting to see how the mystic Soloviev connected some of these friends to the Goetheanum. According to their point of view, natural science should be permeated with Christianity, while at the same time spiritual science should be pursued with the same exactness of natural science. Most of these people were highly cultivated and broadly educated members of the academic world. Soon after, the greater number of them came to Anthroposophy.

One of these was Assja Turgenev Bugayev, a niece of Ivan Turgenev, the novelist, later to etch the glass windows for the present Goetheanum. For years one saw her in Dornach, a quiet, independent figure with her pale green, Slavonic eyes and broad cheek bones, sitting in a corner of the Kantine drinking coffee and smoking endless cigarettes. Her husband, B. N. Bugayev, whose pen name was Andrei Belyi, has been called the most profound exponent of the Russian symbolist poets. His work appears in almost every collection of modern Russian poetry along with poems by Maximillian Voloschin, husband of Margarita, and those of Alexander Bloc. All three men were acquainted with the work of Rudolf Steiner.

It is not only for Russians that Soloviev can kindle a new sense of knowledge, but it was perhaps only in Russia that he could have been born. If we are to understand him and his significance, it will be necessary to gain an insight into the nature and potentialities of the culture that gave him birth.

The Task of Russia

Just as we, today, have the task of developing that consciousness of soul by means of which we can look at nature and at ourselves objectively, just so, Rudolf Steiner tells us, is Soloviev's philosophy a seed for that of the next historical epoch to be centered in Russia, when people will become capable of receiving a higher, more social member of their being than is the consciousness soul, which we are now maturing. This *spirit self* will enable a greater sense of brotherhood and community to come about. It is interesting that Steiner does not use the word *develop* but the verb *receive*. And it is one of the tasks of the Russian folk soul to cultivate a vital receptiveness. In order to do this, certain powers of soul needed to be kept untouched, virginal. How have the wise forces of history worked to bring this about?

For centuries Russia was isolated from Western intellectuality by the Orthodox Church, which allowed only the Gospels to be printed, and by the hierarchical form of society which kept most of its population in serfdom under the rule of her noblemen, the Boyars. Russia was turned inward and Eastward, the waters of her spirit dammed back into a great reservoir of latent power. At the same time her deep love of her Mother Earth, the Cosmic Father and the blessed Child was sheltered and kept alive. This love pervaded the fields, the very air, the sunlight that glanced off the green and golden domes and glistened in the snow; it rang and boomed in the tones of the bells that pealed out over towns and cities. It was on the lips of every nobleman and peasant as they greeted and blessed one another and called out joyfully on Easter Day, "Christ is risen!" It sent out its tiny sparks across the snow-bound steppes from the candles lit below the icons in lonely huts, and permeated the color, the baking-fragrance and drama of countless saints days and festivals. Russia was kept long in her pictorial, receptive childhood, protected from the awakening prick of the intellect and gathering her own force. Since the rise and fall of communism, all this has been wiped out, but it still lives for us in many of the great works of Russian literature.

The Russians, Rudolf Steiner points out, have greater mobility of soul than the average Westerner and can grasp the spiritual with greater ease, but they do not penetrate down into the physical world as deeply nor yet have so sharp a realization of the ego. They tend to live in a dream-like atmosphere, but with great intensity. They are waiting their time.

One who reads Russian novels cannot fail to be impressed by the richness of their emotions, the depths of soul of which they are capable, nor by how difficult it is for the ego to take a firm, directing hold on the dramatic gamut of the Russian temperament. Few nations are at once so kind and so cruel; none so capable of realism and idealism in the same breath, so torn between nihilism and religious conviction, so quick to acclaim their great writers nor so swift to exile them. Duality is rooted deep in their nature.

In their fairy tales, which deal not with a single hero but with many, and in their novels, which describe clusters of characters of almost equal interest, there is already evident their feeling for the collective community it seems their future task to bring to fruition.

It was Peter the Great who flung open for them the door to the West. He broke the hold of the Boyars, imported skilled foreigners, made French the court language and introduced Western thought, techniques and luxuries. Catherine carried this trend further. From now on, despite a number of attempts to close the door to the West, Russia was to be exposed to its materialism and intellectuality. She could no longer foster the forces of childhood only; but she still had great resources of vitality and receptivity.

And now, like Athene springing full-grown from the head of Zeus, Russian literature emerged in all its youthful stature in the person of Pushkin. In a little over a century's span, the first wave of Russian literature, in one powerful sweep, rose through Gogol, Lermontov, Turgenev, reached its peak in Dostoyevsky and Tolstoi and plunged into Chekhov's twilight, breaking in the foam of

Andreyev and sinking to the lower depths of Gorki, while a new wave was preparing to crest in Pasternak and Solzhenitsyn.

In her book, *Memories of Rudolf Steiner*, Assja Bugayev records Steiner as saying:

A folk is an ordered organism. Russia has already achieved such a living organism. It has a nervous system—that is Gogol and Dostoyevsky; it has a muscular system—Tolstoi. However it has not yet a skeleton. For other European peoples natural science is the skeleton. For them it is right that it is so, for they can school their thinking upon it. The Russians, however, have a feeling that they must save their thinking for something else. For them natural science is poison. Only spiritual science can be a skeleton for them and to this Goetheanism is the way.

At another time she quotes Steiner as saying:

Tolstoi and Soloviev are two spearheads pointing to the future of Russia. Through them will come good impulses for the future. They are both characteristic for her. In the West, people always think they must do something. For Tolstoi the not-doing is much more important than the doing.... He tried in his *Calendar* to bring cosmic rhythms into life. That smacks of the future. His conception of not resisting evil by force is an important striving toward a new Christianity, but Tolstoi has not yet found a fully active relationship to Christianity and evil. That I have shown in my statue in its forward-striding effective presence of the Christ that has in the gesture of the arms nothing battling or aggressive.

Once when Steiner was speaking to Margarita Voloschin of Tolstoi, she asked him whether it was not Dostoyevsky who was the more significant representative of the Christian impulse in Russia; whereupon he answered:

> Tolstoi's idea of brotherhood is more forceful, powerful, and will persevere. Dostoyevsky stands as a penitent before Christ for all mankind.

Soloviev's Early Years

Only in Russia could Soloviev have found the qualities which he needed in order to develop his own capacities and the substance of his thoughts. How and when did he enter into such a folk? What were his inheritance and his childhood like? What manner of man was he and how have Russia and the West responded to his work?

In 1900, in a preface to Soloviev's *War and Christianity,* Stephen Graham wrote, "Vladimir Soloviev is Russia's greatest philosopher and one of her greatest poets, a serene and happy writer.... He was a seeker and also a seer, a thinker and also a singer." Solzhenitsyn mentions him in his *Nobel Lecture.* Still, he is little known today. Even those who are well acquainted with Dostoyevsky may know little or nothing of his indebtedness to Soloviev.

It is difficult to find much by or about him in the library in America—or even in Russia now, says Sonia Tomara Clarke, a distinguished journalist who has often lectured on Soloviev. She remembers well how as a girl in her native Russia she was allowed to attend meetings of the Soloviev Society in the home of one of her relatives.

Vladimir Soloviev was born prematurely on January 16, 1853, into a cultivated Moscow family. His mother, a "Little Russian," had a deeply religious nature and claimed a philosopher in her ancestry. His father, a well-known professor at the University of Moscow, wrote the first exhaustive history of Russia, in twenty-nine volumes. He had traveled and studied in Europe. Influenced by Hegelian thought, he endeavored to show how history reveals the organic evolution of humanity. The household was filled with an atmosphere of significant, hearty conversation and of reading aloud. Distinguished guests came and went. "There was nothing of the cheap wit and mental meanness that so often sterilize the creative intelligence of otherwise wonderful children," wrote Stephen Graham. All of his brothers and sisters achieved distinction in life and letters.

His grandfather, a priest, consecrated Vladimir at the age of eight to the service of God. From an early age he had prophetic dreams and felt a mystical reverence for nature. Everything about him was animated by his fantasy; he named his friendly pencil, Andrew. He read the lives of the saints, loved poetry and learned folklore from peasants with whom he felt happily at home.

Soloviev reports that when he was nine years old, a little girl whom he loved was indifferent to him. In a lonely moment during mass, the world around him vanished; the blue of the sky was all about him and in his soul. Through this blue he saw a vision of Eternal Womanhood, *Sophia*, woven of the azure ether and holding in her hand a flower grown in no earthly country. She nodded, smiled radiantly and disappeared in the mist. His soul became blind to worldly things.

But not for long. His disposition was naturally sunny and outgoing. He was full of animation and an infectious hilarity. He made friends with his father's visitors, many of them full of Western ideas. These fascinated him. At fourteen, after reading the life of Christ by a Western author, he proclaimed himself an atheist, made Socialism and Communism his ideals, and threw the family icons out into the garden. When he went to the University of Moscow, he turned to the study of natural science and Western philosophy. But his innately religious and thoughtful nature remained unsatisfied; he experienced an emptiness in natural scientific thought.

While studying Spinoza, he became convinced of the total spiritual unity of the world; a living sense of God's reality grew upon him. At eighteen he underwent a religious crisis and returned to the Russian Orthodox Church. However, the powers of reason which he had applied in his studies he did not reject. At twenty-one, having passed through the University, he joined the Theological Faculty. At this time he published *The Crisis of Western Philosophy* in which he maintained that it was possible to approach Christianity through reason:

> My true mission is to work at the theoretic aspect of evolving Christianity. Christianity has been destroyed in its false form by the development of science and philosophy. It is time now to re-establish true Christianity, to bring eternal content into rational form. The practical fulfillment of Christianity lies in the far future....
>
> My aim is to justify the faith of our fathers by raising it to a new level of intelligent consciousness.

It was after reading this book that Tolstoi wrote:

> My acquaintance with Soloviev added very little that was new to my knowledge, but it ... caused a philosophic ferment in me and confirmed many things, in clarifying thoughts of paramount necessity for the remainder of my life and for my death, thoughts that were of such comfort to me that, had I the ability and the time, I should try to pass on to others.

A few years later, Tolstoi passed through what his wife called "the terrible years," a religious crisis which changed the course of his life and work. This came to a head about the year 1879. Out of it emerged the book *My Confession*. Everything he was to write and do from then on was to be tested in the struggle for his individual conception of Christianity. This he approached through thought and his consuming love of truth, and so independently that he was to be excommunicated from the Church. In this battle for Christianized thinking, he had responded to Soloviev as to a kindred spirit.

Because of jealousy and intrigue at the University, Soloviev was sent, in 1875, to London to study medieval philosophy and mysticism. He had already explored spiritualism and, though himself a good medium, had rejected it. Now and for some years to come, gnosticism and theosophy became his chief studies.

In the British museum, the same building in which Karl Marx had worked upon *Das Kapital*, Soloviev bent over a book and once more experienced how the walls around him melted into azure mist, out of which there formed the radiant face of Sophia, the "Virgin of the Rainbow Door." This time she said to him: "Be in Egypt," and disappeared.

So to Egypt he traveled, ostensibly to study Arabic. His tall thin figure draped in a long black cloak, a high black silk hat on his head, he went into the desert, only to be captured by Bedouins, who understandably took him for the devil himself. Reassured by his mild manner, they withdrew and left him alone, surrounded by the distant howling of jackals. There in the desert he had his third and last vision of Sophia, of whom he was to write later in his *Lectures on Godmanhood*.[2] Of this experience he wrote:

> My steadfast gaze embraced it all as one;
> The seas and rivers sparkled blue beneath me,
> And distant woods and mountains clad in snow.
> I saw it all and all was one fair image
> Of wondrous beauty, holding all as one.
> The boundless was within its form enclosed;
> Before me and in me is you alone.

He returned to Moscow but soon left the university because of disputes involving the Slavophiles. Though he had once been one of their number, he now combated their narrow-mindedness. He spoke of three social forces: a tendency to socialism—which had been exaggerated in the East by the Muslims; a tendency to

---

2. Currently translated as *Lectures on Divine Humanity*, Lindisfarne Press, Hudson, NY, 1995.

individualism—found to an extreme in the West; and the tendency to respect God in other individuals and societies—which should be realized by the Slavs. One sees here Soloviev's understanding for the social polarities that we struggle to bring into relationship today and his sense of Russia's future task. His views actually contented neither Slavophiles nor Westernizers. In 1877 he moved to St. Petersburg and remained with the university there until 1881.

Dostoyevsky and Soloviev

When Soloviev was twenty, he met the fifty-one-year-old Dostoyevsky. The novelist—arch explorer of the borderlines of consciousness in insanity, crime, suicide and illness—was already a world-renowned figure who had written all of his important works except for *The Brothers Karamazov*. A distance was widening between him and some of his closest friends, and Soloviev's engaging, deeply religious nature was a welcome refreshment. Almost penniless, Soloviev gave away money and even clothes to the needy. He loved animals and was full of good-natured jokes and puns. He had just broken his engagement at this time. Though several times deeply in love, he never married.

In 1878, Dostoyevsky suffered a tragic blow. His little son, Alyosha, two and a half years old, was stricken with an epileptic fit. After three hours he died. Dostoyevsky loved the boy dearly, and he had to watch him die of the disease which he himself had bequeathed him, a disease which he attributed to the drunkenness of his own father, the boy's grandfather. On the surface he bore the blow quietly. Only his wife realized what a devastating effect it had upon his inner life. She recommended that he make a pilgrimage to the famous monastery Optina Pustyn, where the holy man, Father Ambrose, lived. Gogol and hundreds of others had been confessed by him. Soon Tolstoi was also to visit there on foot. Furthermore, she suggested that Dostoyevsky take Soloviev with him for companionship.

Optina Pustyn lay much further off than the two men had realized. Their travel together by carriage stretched itself out over a week's time. Perhaps this was one of the most important intervals in the lives of both men. What must have been their conversations, their exchange of ideas! Soloviev may have spoken in an especially living way about his ideas on the Christian state, the Antichrist and the Three Temptations. It was then that Dostoyevsky confided to the other the vision he believed he'd had of Christ, and his plan for the Karamazovs.[3]

Of their meetings during the winter in St. Petersburg, E. H. Carr writes in his biography of the novelist, "The exchange provided mutual inspiration for both, and Dostoyevsky seems to have derived from these conversations the definite religious, even ecclesiastical train of thought which scarcely appears in his earlier works but emerges into prominence in *The Brothers Karamazov*."

At the monastery Dostoyevsky had two private audiences with Father Ambrose, who was to appear in *The Brothers* as Father Zossima and gave expression there to convictions which had been maturing in the heart of its author: "Love every man, even in his sin; love every leaf.... Choose humble love and you will subdue the world ... walk around yourself and see if your image is a seemly one."

Now Dostoyevsky visited, for the first time in many years, the scenes of his childhood. He remembered some happy years on this family estate, but it also brought to mind the cruel murder of his father by his own serfs, whose bitter hatred he had earned. Dostoyevsky brooded over the death of his son. He saw the walls of the monastery before him, and the new work which he had already begun to plan grew in his mind. His dissolute father, Father Ambrose, his own former atheistic self were all interwoven there. His hero, a figure akin to but far more self-possessed, healthy and effectual than Prince Myshkin of *The Idiot*, he named Alyosha after his little son. But Alyosha's sunny, lovable, religious disposition in

---

3. An account of this vision is reprinted at the end of this article.

the book belongs to Soloviev. Father Zossima sends Alyosha "from the monastery out into the world."

"It is time not to run away from, but to go out into the world," said Soloviev in one of his twelve *Lectures on Godmanhood*, which he started to give in the spring before the journey to Optina Pustyn. They were difficult lectures, beautifully prepared and enthusiastically received. Both Dostoyevsky and Tolstoi attended them. In them he set forth with great clarity the duality inherent in the being of Christ and dealt with the three temptations. These lectures probably embody much of the substance which led Rudolf Steiner to write in *The Mission of Folk Souls:*

> Soloviev's philosophy is more deeply permeated with the Christ idea than any other outside of Spiritual Science.... He recognized the dual nature of Christ: the human and the divine. We must understand the two natures of Christ and the union of both at a higher stage. As long as we have not grasped this duality, we have not understood Christ in His fullness.

Some themes from Soloviev's lectures pervade both "The Grand Inquisitor," a story told in *The Brothers Karamazov*, and *Antichrist* by Soloviev. One is struck by how they both emerge from the same background of thought. "Christianity was given to men as a morally historical task to be accomplished by their free efforts," wrote Soloviev. Freedom and its relation to the three temptations form the central theme of both stories.

In *Antichrist* the reader is confronted with a superman: brilliant, handsome, virtuous. "But he loved only himself." The account of the moment when he is literally taken possession of by Antichrist is a stroke of dramatic genius. Immediately after this everyone is struck by his exalted appearance, and he writes with extraordinary ease and speed *The Open Way to Peace and Prosperity*. Here we have an example of how, as Steiner has pointed out, the force of evil can appear as an author. He is elected President of the United States of the World; then becomes Emperor. Acting on the basis of the three temptations, he gives the people economic security and, as head of the church, issues, in a miraculous manner, pardons of sin to all people. He unifies them under his rulership, asking in return for these three "blessings" only that he be acknowledged as the supreme temporal and religious authority. He gives everything but freedom.

Only a small group of Protestant, Catholic and Orthodox Christians is able to see through these temptations and resist him. After external defeat and banishment, they unite forces and finally, in the desert, a union of all the Christian Churches (Soloviev's great goal) is achieved. Antichrist is at last overthrown by the Jews and by a great natural catastrophe; whereupon the united Christians and the Jews are joined by the souls of all whom the Antichrist had executed, and all reign together with Christ.

In *The Brothers Karamazov*, the coldly intellectual brother Ivan, Dostoyevsky's doubting, atheistic self, tells his brother Alyosha a story which to him is a devastating denial of Christianity; but to Alyosha and for Dostoyevsky it is just the opposite. In the tale Christ appears after one of the *auto da fé* of the Inquisition.

He moves among the crowd; and as a little coffin passes Him, at the request of the mother, He raises from the dead the little girl who lies there. At that moment the Grand Inquisitor appears. The people draw back in fear, and despite their gratitude to Christ they allow Him to be led away to prison. There at night, by candle light, the old Inquisitor visits Him. During the entire story Christ never once speaks. The Inquisitor tells Him how he now serves a great intelligence, the wise and Dread Spirit, but always in Christ's name. The Dread Spirit is the one who had the inconceivable genius to formulate the three temptations. He offered to Christ the power to turn stones into bread, to enslave the people's absolute belief in Him through performing a miracle, and to rule over the entire peaceful and prosperous earth: "A unanimous, harmonious, universal ant-heap." Christ—says the Grand Inquisitor—has mis-judged humankind. He thought people strong enough to come to Him out of their own activity, voluntarily and uncompelled. He loved only the few strong members of humankind. But he, the Grand Inquisitor, loves them *all*. He will not weigh them down with the terrible burden of free choice, but will take upon himself all humankind's sins, make them happy, give them bread and unite them all in peaceful harmony. Christ dare not come again and undo what he, the Grand Inquisitor, has done in His name. "To-morrow I will burn Thee!" The Christ only gazes mildly upon him and then kisses him on his thin lips. The Inquisitor flings open the door of the prison calling out, "Go, and never return." And the Christ steps out into the night.

"And the old man?" asks Alyosha.

"The kiss glows in his heart, but the old man adheres to his idea," are the last words of the tale. And so the Grand Inquisitor becomes cursed with the split soul, the gap between heart and mind which afflicts so many of us today.

In both stories the devil appears as a Great Intelligence of cosmic proportion, contemptuous of the human being as weak and passive. In both, are offered happiness: bread, forgiveness of sins and "universal, harmonious unity" at the expense of active, responsible self-development. And in both, freedom appears as the price and purpose of withstanding the three temptations of the Great Intelligence. Again and again Soloviev stresses freedom.

The purpose of universal history is that the bond between man and divinity become wholly conscious and free. Cosmic oneness must not weigh on the individual in a mechanical way nor as something organically determined. It must be morally offered up by the individual as his own purpose, as his own good.... True unity is not posited from outside, but is reached by free effort, by the persistent and many-sided ac-tivity of mankind itself.

Soloviev and Dostoyevsky must also have spoken often together about Russia, about patriotism and nationalism. In his *Morality, Legal Justice and Politics,* Soloviev writes:

> A nation has a moral duty toward other nations and mankind as a whole.... Different nations are different organs in the body of humanity.... Nationalism in its extreme form ruins the nation that succumbs to it, making it the enemy of mankind.... In renouncing exclusive nationalism, a nation does not lose its independent life, but discovers its true, vital task.

In Soloviev's era nationalism had not yet produced the cruelty and suffering that has become so devastating today. In 1880, in his Pushkin Address, Dostoyevsky kindled a "new spirit" in the Russian people when he told them that "to be a true Russian is to be the brother of all mankind." These words came from his heart with an artist's eloquence to a body of people who acclaimed and loved him, but the thought was forged together with Soloviev.

A few months later, Dostoyevsky was dead. Thirty thousand people followed his body to the grave. Soloviev was one of those who spoke there. During the next years he wrote three essays in memory of Dostoyevsky, calling him not only the great novelist, but the great prophet and Christian leader of Russia.

PART II

Soloviev, Poet-philosopher, and His Ideas of the Christian State

Poetry should have the bloom and radiance of spiritual forces.... It incarnates in images the high meaning of life.... Its source is eternal ideas.... It should tell the truth about nature and the universe.... Poetry is a service, a sacred performance.

So Soloviev wrote in his essay "Poetry," and we see something of this ideal and his search for it embodied in the following poem:

In morning mist with wavering steps, I went
Towards a mysterious and wondrous shore;
Dawn was contending with a few last stars,
Dreams were still hovering, and possessed by dream;
My soul was praying unto unknown gods.

In the cold, white day I tread, as once
Before, a lonely road in an unknown land.
The mist has lifted—clearly sees the eye
How difficult the mountain track—how far,
How far away, all that I saw in dreams.

And until midnight, still with fearless steps,
I shall walk on towards shores of my desire
To where upon a hill beneath new stars
My promised temple, all ablaze with light
Of victory, stands awaiting me.[4]

Soloviev as a poet is hardly thinkable without the insights of Soloviev the philosopher, just as Soloviev the philosopher would have been impossible without the poet's comprehensive imagination. Each enhances and gives breadth, depth and truth to the other, yet they are two facets of a single power. Poetry colored and enlivened all his thinking, and his love of invisible realities gives his poems their soaring spirituality. The writer Arsenyev says of him:

He possessed a gift of artistic expression which obliterated the demarcation between poetry and prose.... His poems are not only the history of the inner life; they possess a peculiar charm. At times they call forth an unaccountable sadness; at times they offer flash-like glimpses into the infinite distance of the future.

---

4. A translation by H. Havelock modified by C.B.

The poems in his single slender volume of verse deal chiefly with supersensuous experience, yet sometimes break into bursts of joyous humor.

Besides being himself a poet, Soloviev published a number of essays on other Russian poets, on Pushkin, Lermontov and more. Soloviev can give vivid expression to dark imaginations, but he can also lift one into the flowing glow, the breath-taking inner lightness and transparency of the following poem:

The Shining Eyes[5]

When by day I go free, or at midnight arise,
We are two...Then there ray
Deep into my soul thy crystalline eyes
In the night, in the day.

The pale ice is breaking, dark clouds are dispersed,
The spring blossoms are blowing;
In the soundless transparency, in stillness immersed,
Thy reflection is glowing.

There is shed from the soul, sin older than time.
Through a crystalline sheen,
Not the grass of the earth, not the hiss in the slime,
Not the earth's rocks are see —

Only light and the water...and in the clear blue,
The shining eyes seeing,
As of old the clear dewdrops in the oceans of dew,
All the days of man's being.

---

5. Heard repeatedly by Floyd McKnight as declaimed in Russian by Regina Stillman and put into an English version by him.

At the time of Dostoyevsky's death, Soloviev was probably enjoying the most outwardly successful years of his life. His *Lectures on Godmanhood*, followed by *Spiritual Foundations of Life*, had brought him distinction; he won wide acclaim through his *Critique of Abstract Principles;* and he was teaching at the University of St. Petersburg. Because he was "so tall and alarmingly handsome," his friends called him the Angel. This was the period during which he devoted himself to theosophy, the knowledge of God. His *philosophy* occupied the center of his strivings.

Soloviev the Philosopher

Soloviev is generally recognized as the first to create an original Russian system of philosophy and lay a foundation for the whole school of Russian religious and philosophic thought. At a time when there was general indifference to metaphysics, he drew attention to eternal questions by his fearless and fiery assertions of the ideas he served. People were struck by the clarity with which he spoke of the invisible. He wanted to reveal the organic synthesis of science, philosophy and religion and to unite the form and logic of the West with the fullness of the spiritual intuitions of the East.

> What is unusual in Soloviev and most fundamental is his world-wide interest, his universalism. Russian life of the second half of the nineteenth century shows no other instance of a personality concerned with Russia, humanity, the world's soul, the Church, God.... Dostoyevsky's assertion that the Russian is primarily a universal man is applicable to Soloviev. The problem of uniting Orient and Occident in a Church of universal humanity was his main problem which he pursued all his life.

So wrote the well-known Russian philosopher, Nicolai Berdyaev.

As Berdyaev intimates, Soloviev was a man whose vision soared to heights from which he was able to gaze out over wide perspectives and grasp a universal whole of grandiose dimensions, at the same time that it reached into the innermost of human nature. Through these two views he came to a conception of Christianity which Rudolf Steiner speaks of, in his *Gospel of St. Luke,* as the most advanced outside of Anthroposophy. Those who have read this book of Steiner's may be especially interested in Soloviev's ideas.

He realized that our understanding of Christianity is only at its very beginnings. He recognized the dual nature of Christ, the human and the divine, and much of what took place when the Christ entered into Jesus of Nazareth.

His own words will best convey a few of his thoughts:

From *Lectures on Godmanhood:*

> Man is a social being, and the highest work of his life, the final end of his efforts, is not confined to his personal destiny, but is to be found in the social destinies of mankind as a whole.
>
> When we turn aside from the phenomenal, clearly defined content of our outer and inner life—not only from our impressions, but also from our feelings and thoughts and will—impulses—and we gather all our forces in a single center of our direct spiritual existence, in the positive power of which are contained all the deeds of our spirit and which determines the whole circumference of our life; when we plunge into that silent and immutable depth whence the turbid stream of our day to day reality springs forth, not disturbing its poetry and rest—in this primeval fountainhead of our own spiritual life—we inwardly contact the primeval source of universal life; we in essence know God as our primordial origin and substance of all, we know God the Father.

CHRISTIANITY:

Christianity is within us and yet it is manifested outwardly; it grows in mankind and in the whole world through a certain objective organic process, and it is also taken by a free effort of will.

In the divine organism of Christ, the acting, unifying beginning ... is the Word or Logos.... On the other hand, the produced unity, the expressed, realized idea ... bears the name of Sophia.... Logos, differing from Sophia, is eternally connected with her. Sophia is God's body, the matter of divinity, permeated with the beginning of divine unity. Christ, who realized that unity in Himself—universal and at the same time individual—is both Logos and Sophia.

Jesus Christ from being the center of eternity becomes the center of history. Godhead and Manhood are joined together in Christ not by confusion of substance but by unity of person. After the Fall a new unity must be striven for.

MAN:

In man the world-soul for the first time unites with the divine Logos internally, in consciousness. Only one out of the multitude of phenomenal beings in nature, man, has in his consciousness the capacity of conceiving all (or the internal bond and meaning [logos] of all that exists; and thus appears, in idea, as the all) and is, in this sense, the second all-unity, the image and likeness of God.

Man not only possesses the same internal essence of life—the all-unity—which is possessed by God; he is also free, like God, to desire the possession of it, may of himself desire to be like God. Initially he has that essence from God.... But, by virtue of being unlimited, he (or the world-soul in him) is not satisfied with that passive unity.

He desires to possess the divine essence of himself.... And in order to have it not only from God but also by himself, he asserts himself as separate from God, outside of God, falls off or secedes from God in his consciousness.

THE WEST:

In order to unite with the "unconditional beginning," one must first separate from it. The West falls away from divine being and tries to base all on self. This is bound to fail; then self-denial awakens, which leads to free reunion with spirit. When the West becomes convinced by facts that self-assertion is the root of evil, it will turn to religion. One nation cannot realize two universal ideas. The task of the West is a negative transition to the future.

DEATH:

As a natural being, man exists solely in the interval between physical birth and physical death. It is only possible to admit that he exists after death if it be recognized that he is not merely a being which lives in the natural world, but is also an eternal intelligible essence. In that case it is logically necessary to admit that he exists not only after death but also before birth, since an intelligible essence is from its very meaning not subject to our temporal forms which apply to appearance only.

Aphorisms from *The Spiritual Foundations of Life*:

Humanity and the cosmos form a complete and living organism. Every power which does not represent the truth is an oppression.

Equality, freedom and brotherhood are reached by self-denial. You cannot deny self unless you first have it.

The moral limit of egoism is not the egoism of others.

If man has love for God and his creatures, this will eventually lead to a bestowal of immortal life upon Nature as a whole, which is now in a state of death and disruption. Nature must be united to man as his living body.

Love and self-sacrifice are only possible in relation to what stands above man.

*   *   *

After the murder of Alexander II in 1881, Soloviev exhorted the Czar in a public lecture not to use capital punishment but to set an example of forgiveness for humankind. At this same time Tolstoi wrote to the son of the murdered man whom he had so deeply revered, begging him not to seek revenge but to pardon his enemies. The murderers, however, were executed. Soloviev had forfeited his position at the university; he was not invited back. Soon after, he resigned from the Science Committee and other responsibilities in the academic world.

This was a turning point in his life. He lost many of his Slavophile friends. He took up the life of an independent writer. In his own words he became "an eternally wandering pilgrim seeking the heavenly Jerusalem." Many friends offered him hospitality. He published his three essays on Dostoyevsky, in which he spoke of him as Russia's great mystic, humane artist and powerful realist, who like himself looked to the Church as embodying the idea of brotherly love. For the next few years he was absorbed in the problem of the social order. He wrote *The History of the Future State of Theocracy* and the *National Problem of Russia*. During this period his *theocracy* became the focus of his efforts.

The Idea of the Christian State: Marx, Gandhi and Thoreau

In 1847, Karl Marx issued his Communist Manifesto, in which he maintained that the fundamental motive for all human actions is economic, and that the history of all hitherto existing society was the history of class struggle. Upon these conceptions he based his revolutionary social reforms.

A year later, in a small New England town, a lecture on social reform was delivered to a handful of rather unimpressed towns-people. It made no stir. America was not to consider it worth re-printing as a separate work until 1928, and then only in a small edition. It did, however, find its way into the hands of Gandhi and was later to become the inspiration of freedom strikers in the United States and elsewhere. Thoreau, in his *Civil Disobedience*, took a step far more radical than that of Marx, for Thoreau challenged the whole conception of humanity that would place economic motives first, considering such a view unworthy of true human nature. He refused to base his social ideas on economic needs, although he paid strict practical attention to them. The peaceful non-support of evil which he advocated was an idea which Tolstoi and Gandhi shared with him. Toward the end of his essay, Thoreau says:

> No man with a genius for legislation has appeared in America. They are rare in the history of the world.... For eighteen hundred years, though perchance I have no right to say it, the New Testament has been written; yet where is the legislator who has wisdom and practical talent enough to avail himself of the light which it sheds on the science of legislation?

Thoreau did not live to know of the man who did just this in conceptual if not in actual form; that is, if we take the word legislation in its broadest sense. Indeed Soloviev took a stride still more revolutionary than Thoreau's, turning Marxism on its head. In his *Lectures on Godmanhood* he wrote:

> If the root of social untruth consists of egotism, then social truth must be based on the opposite of egotism; that is to say, upon the principle of self-denial or love of others.

114

Soloviev recognizes socialism as historically justified in its efforts toward the equalization of material welfare, since such a great inequality between classes has arisen in the world. But striving for material welfare "is but a natural inclination," and so in his eyes socialism cannot be the supreme moral goal it wishes to be. Again from *Lectures on Godmanhood:*

> Even if we admit that the demand for economic equality on the part of the non-possessing class is a demand for getting what justly belongs to it, even then, that demand cannot have any moral value in the positive sense; for to take one's own is only a right, and in no way a merit. In its demands, even if they be admitted to be just, the working class rests evidently upon the legal but not upon the moral point of view.

This, then, would have been his answer to Marx. And what does he say that would throw light on his relation to democracy? The following is taken from the chapter "The Idea of the Christian State" in Soloviev's book *Morality, Legal Justice and Politics.*

> Only when all realize truth, can the will of all be moral for me....
>
> This power [of good] can be manifested in a majority as it does not depend on quantity; however, true solidarity is not the good of the majority, but the good of all and each without exception. It presupposes that every element of the great whole, besides having a right to exist, has an inherent value of its own which does not permit its being made use of as a mere tool.... Christianity, in recognizing the infinite value of every human being, ought to have completely altered the behavior of the state.... The Pagan state had to do with enemies, slaves and criminals. These had no rights whatever.... In a Christian state the foreigner does not lose his civic rights, the slave acquires the right to be free, the criminal has the right to be morally healed and re-educated....

Christianity was given to men as a morally historical task to be accomplished by their own free efforts. *My Kingdom is not of this world.* But the fact that Christ's Kingdom is not of this world by no means implies that it cannot act in the world.... In accordance with sound logic, it follows that just because it is not of this world but from above, it has a right to possess and govern the world. Societies that call themselves Christian must harmonize all their political and social relations with Christian principles.... This is precisely in what Christian politics consist.

In chapter ten of his book *The Mission of Folk Souls*, Rudolf Steiner compares Soloviev's state with that of St. Augustine:

In Soloviev's State, Christ is the blood which circulates in the body social, and the essential point is that the state is envisaged as a concrete personality.... There is, perhaps, no greater contrast than the eminently Christian conception of the State which hovers as a great ideal before Soloviev as a dream of the future ... and the Divine State of St. Augustine, who accepts, it is true, the Christ idea, but whose Divine State is simply the idea of the Roman State with Christ incorporated within it.

In Soloviev's State we find also hints of what Rudolf Steiner later developed in his *Threefold Commonwealth*, in which the cultural sphere, the sphere of rights and the economic sphere, as separate entities, work freely together to form a unified social organism. T. J. Gerrard, in his Introduction to *A Russian Newman*, sums up Soloviev's conception of a threefold society in this way:

The necessities of existence imposed on man three kinds of societies; an economic society for the utilization of the material world, a political one for the ordering of relations between man and man, and a religious society for the due subordination of man and God. Thus there is established a free theocracy. By this term Soloviev meant a knowledge of the divine prerogatives, a consequent love of them, and a free acceptance of them which alone could bring real liberty.

As far as Russia was concerned, Soloviev saw her task as in no way a political one, but one of an essentially inner leadership. There was no reason in his mind to believe that she would produce public institutions, science, art, philosophy or even literature in a purely worldly sense. Her task lay elsewhere. He ends one of his most powerful poems, "Ex Oriente Lux", with the stanza:

> O Russia, in prevision lofty,
> You are by a proud thought enticed:
> Which is the East at which you aim,
> The East of Xerxes or of Christ?

His Later Years

The censors forbade the publication of the last two volumes of Soloviev's *Future State of Theocracy*. He had become increasingly preoccupied with the problem of the reunion of the Churches. In 1882, he had begun a thorough study of Church history. Formerly he, together with Dostoyevsky, had considered the Roman Catholic Church more or less as an expression of the Antichrist. Now he wished to bring about a unification of the Roman Catholic and the Russian Orthodox Churches, that together they might become the expression of the central impulse of Christianity. The Eastern Church, he said, was inclined to neglect the human being, while the Western tended to forget God. This plan naturally caused consternation.

For six months the police prevented him from leaving Russia, but at last he managed to circumvent them. In 1886 and '87, we find him lecturing on the Russian Church in Paris and making friends with a circle of Jesuits. There in '89, he published *Russia and the Orthodox Church*, written in French. This met with a hostile reception at home. The Holy Synod forbade him ever again to write upon religious topics.

He drew up a proposal for the reunion of the two great Christian Churches and, journeying to Croatia, presented it to a bishop there. Finally it was brought to the attention of the Pope, who dismissed it as "a beautiful idea but, short of a miracle, impossible to carry out." This was a severe blow to Soloviev. The concentrated efforts of several years had failed. In 1890, an unsatisfactory love affair came to an end. He was filled with despair and underwent a major spiritual crisis.

But despair can lead to a depth out of which the forces of transformation arise. Soloviev entered upon a new period of productivity, which may be called the period of his *Theurgy* ("the mystic art of creating new life according to divine truth"). He refused to give public lectures and from now on published only outside of Russia. He came to the conviction that the Eastern and Western Churches had never severed their mystical bond.

To achieve reunion of the Churches, no outward union is necessary and might be even harmful. I am as far from the narrowness of Rome as from that of Byzantium.... The religion of the Holy Spirit which I profess is wider ... and fuller in content than all particular religions; it is neither their sum nor their extract, just as the whole man is neither a sum nor an extract of his particular organs.

... The Church has failed to carry out Christ's chief commandment: Love thy neighbor. This, however, inspires unbelievers who champion freedom and social justice, and they are thus disciples of Christ.

A year before the coronation of Alexander III, Soloviev had a prophetic dream. He dreamed he was in Moscow, where he asked a Catholic priest for his blessing. It was refused. But when he pointed out that the mystical unity of the Church had not been shattered by the apparent disunity of the two halves, the blessing was given. A year later at the actual coronation, he asked the blessing of a Papal Nuncio who had come to the occasion and was refused and then blessed under exactly the same circumstances as had appeared in his dream, even into such details as the surrounding houses, streets and persons.

In 1896, he was received into the Catholic Church by a converted priest, who was arrested next day but fled and reported the occasion to the Pope in Rome. This conversion is, for many Roman Catholics, proof that he came to acknowledge their Church as the supreme expression of Christianity; but in view of what has been quoted above and the fact that an Orthodox priest gave him his last confession, one may also draw the conclusion that he simply saw no contradiction, rather a reconciliation, in belonging in spirit to both "halves of the Church" and thus to the Spirit which was their common well-spring.

During this period, from 1890 until his death, he wrote *The Meaning of Love, Justification of the Good* with its supplement, *Moral and Legal Justice, The Tragedy of Plato's Life*, written after translating Plato, and in 1900, just before his death, *War and Christianity or Three Conversations*, in which his *Antichrist* appears. Valary Busop writes of Soloviev:

> Toward the end of his life a sort of special power and intensity of perception seemed to show itself in his work. The poet and thinker approached the most sacred problems of contemporary man.... Everyone was listening to the powerful voice of Soloviev as to the words of a master; his right to judge was acknowledged.

He spoke of dreams as "windows into another world." In dreams, he said, he conversed with the dead and saw visions, sometimes prophetic sometimes fantastic. Even in waking moments, he sometimes sensed happenings at a distance.

Soloviev made a sharp distinction between hallucinations and visions. The former, he said, arose from bodily disease, which should be medically treated. They were phenomena of the subjective, morbid imagination. However, he alluded to his visions as to any other objective reality. In a poem written eight years before his death,[6] he described his earliest childhood vision of Sophia.

There is a story that one summer's day, as he sat on the veranda, regaling a skeptic with tales of the devil, each one more definite and concrete than the last, there rose from the floor a column of thick, brownish, smoke-like vapor. As it almost touched the ceiling, Soloviev pointed and shouted out, "There he is; there he is!"

For all his greatness, Soloviev was also a man of human contradictions, weaknesses, struggles, as well as of ever renewed growth and transformation.

"He was a strange man all his life," writes Sonia Clarke, "a mixture of the prophet and visionary, of extreme religiosity, mysticism, eroticism, scientific discipline and irony about himself and his emotions. Rudolf Steiner said of him that he had a powerful ego but an astral nature that he could not control. When he was young and for a long time, he did not think that evil was a real force, a real being. Now, in his later years, he begins to know that it is. Formerly he had written that sexual love is at the bottom of all creative spirit; now he demands chastity."

Andrei Belyi sketched the following portrait of the philosopher shortly before his death, one which shows us the shadow side of his nature:

---

6. Reprinted in Part I of this essay.

Enormous, bewitched eyes, gray; a hunched back, powerless, long arms; a beautiful head with strands of gray hair, a large mouth as if torn asunder, a prominent lower lip, wrinkles.... He was a giant with weak arms, long legs, a short trunk, spiritual eyes and a sensuous mouth, the talk of a prophet....

Belyi had known Soloviev years before. The philosopher had often been a guest in his father's house. It was Vladimir's brother, Michael Soloviev, who suggested to the poet that instead of his own name, Bugayev, he use the pen name of Andrei Belyi in order to protect himself from the attacks of the academic and literary worlds.

Soloviev became increasingly concerned with the problem of evil. "Something is preparing; someone is coming; by someone I mean Antichrist," he said. He had returned to Russia and was already conscious of the not too distant image of death. One summer's day in 1900, he was taken ill in Moscow. A philosopher friend took him into his home on a near-by country estate and cared for him lovingly. The local Orthodox priest was called in. Soloviev confessed to him and from him received the last rites. He died on July 31st.

In her book, Assja Turgenev Bugayev reports Rudolf Steiner as saying to her that:

> ... in death Soloviev has grown great, much greater than he was in life. After death the individuality grows, enlarges itself, and Soloviev has grown far out into the spiritual world and has become more significant. However, still greater than he is, he could have been, should have been. The Russians are naturally gifted with spirituality, but they have difficulties, restrictions. Soloviev stood at a stage of spiritual development upon which a man is in duty bound to orient himself altogether and exclusively in accordance with the purely spiritual. He, however, did not quite do that. This worked in an inhibiting way upon his development. A certain sultriness [*Schwüle*] in his world conception—the Russians are unharmed by it, but it constitutes for other Europeans a certain danger.

Whatever may have been his shortcomings, Soloviev remains a giant, a universal man, a magical poet, a wanderer sure-footed in the regions of the spirit, and a thinker who brought to birth within his soul the clearest conception in his day of Him who "has become the center of history:"

Emmanuel[7]

The night had faded into darkness of past centuries
When tired from the wickedness and anguish,
The earth, asleep, had fallen into the arms of heaven,
And in the peace was born Emmanuel.

Today no longer miracles are seen.
The kings no longer look into the heavens,
And shepherds do not listen in the desert
When angels speak to them of God.

But the eternal which that night was manifested
Cannot by time be ruined or destroyed;
The Word born long ago under the manger
Is born anew within thy soul.

Yes, with us is God—not in the tent of azure
And not beyond the borders of uncounted worlds,
Not in the wicked fire, nor in the stormy breathing,
And not in sleeping memory of centuries long past.

But He is here in midst of daily life
And in the murky stream of petty worries.
Thou hast in thee the joyous mystery:
Powerless is evil, we are eternal, God is with us!

— Vladimir Soloviev

7. Translation by Sonia Tomara Clarke.

. . . .

A Vision in Wakefulness (A Fragment)
by Fyodor Dostoyevsky

Being extracts from a letter dated 1880, and written to S. P. Katkov

NOTE: The following is an extract from a letter Fyodor Dostoyevsky wrote to a life-long friend, S. P. Katkov, editor of The Russian Messenger *(Russkaya Missyl). The letter was written in November 1880, only a few months before the author's death. It was published in a Russian newspaper, along with some other extracts from Dostoyevsky's letters, in 1900, with the permission of Dostoyevsky's widow. The whole letter was not published, but it may be regarded as genuine, inasmuch as other letter extracts printed in the same article can be verified. The interesting thing about it is that when Dostoyevsky's widow in 1913 prepared the final, definitive collection of Dostoyevsky's books, letters and notebooks for publication, this particular extract was not included in that material. It has been so far impossible to trace this letter any further, or verify it any more exactly. However, this fragment from the pen of Dostoyevsky is of such unique nature that it seems almost impossible to believe that it could have been written by anyone else. Apparently certain parts of the original letter were omitted from the publication, perhaps because of the censorship, or because they may have not been pertinent to the subject.*

… The experience which I relate to you may not be judged as men judge things. It belongs alone to those happenings of the Spirit which 'are foolishness with men.'…

I take courage to tell you this, believing that you will feel an interest in what I have to say. You have often expressed an interest in my life, and have been more than once kind in what you have said about my work.

In your last letter you asked me about the state of mind in which I found myself during those days in which I planned the writing of *The Brothers Karamazov*.

I feel that this book tells so much of my life purpose, and is the result of an experience so unusual, that I am even now moved by the force of it.…

It was in the late autumn of 1876 that one day I lay down for a little rest in the late afternoon. To this moment I am not certain that I did not fall asleep, yet the state of my mind was so clear that I believe truthfully I was awake. Yet, I cannot say positively whether my experience was one of dream in sleep or vision in wakefulness. All that I beheld stood before me clearly and sharply—no part of it was indistinct, as is so often in dreams....

I saw a great space before me: a great void. At once great loneliness passed before my soul....

Everything stood balanced between heaven and earth, and a feeling of timelessness hung over all....

Earth there was, but in an unearthly sense. I could find no place I had ever seen before. Only emptiness and loneliness....

I remained in this condition for a long time, and I felt then a loneliness and a longing I have never experienced before, even in my darkest hours. Yet, a sweetness and love filled this place too, which made it, otherwise unbearable, at least endurable for me....

When I was completely lost in contemplation of this strange place and the silence of it had nearly carried me away by its own invisible power, I became aware of an onrushing breath—a warmth which came from far away. It did not come all at once with force, but gently and softly, it swept about me, rising ever more and more. I was wrapped in it, and felt it warm upon my face. But nothing in it changed the feeling of loneliness, which grew stronger....

The light grew brighter now, ever broadening and rising within itself, dividing and subdividing—breaking forth all about me. Then I *felt* all round me, but did not hear, those words of earliest divine direction, 'Let there be light!' —and for the first time I knew majesty and the depth in the meaning of those words....

Fresh music sounded from the space now, while the light grew ever brighter. I was bathed in tears which flowed freely down my face. Yet I did not weep with sadness, but with strange joy. I saw the purposefulness and the insufficiencies of my life, and the destiny of my soul....

Bright Beings stood before me, and in their midst was One with fair face and clear gaze. The face shone with light from within, while golden streams poured from the eyes. The eyes held me, for with pity and wonder and wisdom infinite they gazed far beyond me upon the world of men....

In that Face was a warmth of wonder, a glow of love, a beauty fresh with a freshness to which nothing earthly can be compared.

All at once, without words to tell me, I knew, *This is the Christ!* And with this knowledge the music I heard sounded forth with pure, unearthly beauty....

The vision stayed with me clearly for a long time, then faded gently from my sight. To the last, those wonderful, miraculous eyes looked out through the rising and falling light, with expression of sorrow and joy mingled....

Then all disappeared, and I was left alone....

*   *   *

I frankly say, my dear friend, you may not understand all of this. If you say so, I shall answer you that I do not understand it either.

Why did this experience befall me? What was its meaning for my life? I cannot tell. God alone, in His infinite goodness, can answer these questions....

From this experience I arose restored in body and freshened in mind. And in this freshness I was able to write the Conversations....[8]

As I wrote, all that came from my pen flowed from my soul as a clear expression of something which I saw in the eyes of Him who stood before me in my vision....

To my last day I shall never cease to recall those glowing Eyes and the light that streamed from them. The pity and the love they shed upon me flows afresh in my heart as I write this....

---

8. "Conversations of Father Zossima," from *The Brothers Karamazov.*

*   *   *

Although this happened over four years ago now, I have never spoken or written a word of it to anyone except to Vladimir Sergeyevich [Soloviev]. Soon after this experience, he and I made the trip to Optina Pustyn, as you know, and it was then that I told him of my plan for the Karamazovs and of this vision. He spoke of the latter in a very beautiful and moving way....

Vladimir Sergeyevich felt this was a thing of the Spirit, and we never spoke of it again. Therefore, I am reluctant even now to write of it....

REFERENCES

Nikolai Berdyaev, *The Russian Idea*
Assja Turgenev Bugayev, *Memories of Rudolf Steiner*
Fyodor Dostoyevsky, *The Brothers Karamazov*
—— *Pushkin Address*
T. J. Gerrard, *A Russian Newman*
Vladimir Soloviev, *A Story of Anti-Christ*
—— *The Crisis of Western Philosophy*
—— "Ex Oriente Lux"
—— *Lectures on Godmanhood (Lectures on Divine Humanity)*
—— *Morality, Legal Justice and Politics*
—— "Poetry"
—— *Russia and the Orthodox Church*
—— *Spiritual Foundations of Life*
—— *War and Christianity* (with preface by Stephen Graham)
Rudolf Steiner, *Gospel of St. Luke*
—— *The Mission of Folk Souls*
Henry David Thoreau, *Civil Disobedience*
Lev Nikolayevich Tolstoi, *My Confession*
Margarita Voloschin, *The Green Snake*

II

ADAM BITTLESTON

SUSAN DEMANETT

L. FRANCIS EDMUNDS

URSULA GRAHL

A. C. HARWOOD

HUGH HETHERINGTON

EILEEN HUTCHINS

LINDA SAWERS

DORIT WINTER

ISABEL WYATT

The Future of the English Language

Adam Bittleston

T HERE is an old story which in different countries takes different forms. Told by Geoffrey of Monmouth and others as an
historical event, it became the theme of King Lear. As a fairy story
it appears in Germany as The Princess at the Well; in England, in
one of its forms, as Cap O'Rushes.

Three daughters of a kingly father are asked to express their love
for him. The first two do so in extravagant terms: the third will
only say, in Shakespeare's words:

> Good my lord,
> You have begot me, bred me, loved me: I
> Return those duties back as are right fit,
> Obey you, love you, and most honour you.

Or, in the fairy story:

> I love you *like salt.*

The father drives his third daughter away with bitter anger; to
him her words mean nothing.

In this story part of the mysterious tragedy of human speech is
contained. Not only do we fail to understand other languages than
our own; within the same language, we fail to receive each other's
meaning, to recognize the full human reality behind the other's
words. This failure is deeply interwoven with human history; but

we can see it happening in a particularly critical sense at the present time.

Far into the past it was already a problem how to find words by which some part of the wisdom of the Mysteries could be told outside, to help human beings to find their way through life. There has always been the risk of arousing anger by saying something that would not be understood; and yet sometimes this risk had to be faced. The third princess, in the fairy-story version, uses Mystery language, speaking of Salt as it was understood by the Rosicrucians; and she meets what is described in the Sermon on the Mount: "Cast not your pearls before swine, lest they turn and rend you." Those fully satisfied with the earthly consciousness, looking only for what will help the earthly mind to fulfill its own aims, may well reject with intense irritation a spiritual knowledge that is born of suffering. And so the princess must go into loneliness. In the Grimm story she is described as weeping tears that turn into pearls. But she is not wrong to have made the attempt, for eventually she is understood.

Cordelia uses ordinary human words to express the personal mystery of her own feelings; and is just as violently rejected. What we want from another human being, we can understand without leaving the comfortable familiarity of our own minds; but to understand what the *other* really thinks and feels, we have to venture out into the cold, into the storm—and Lear is not yet ready to do this. For each of us, another human mind is a supersensible reality. And as human minds, with developing individuality, are coming to be less and less only the products of a particular status and environment, each human being will present us more and more often with the problem of listening to a mystery which we have still to learn.

In all this, the development of human language plays a significant part. For language is not simply a convenient code, which we may or may not be able to decipher. It has had from the beginning an *inner* relation to all that it describes. To pronounce the name of persons or things in earlier times was at the same time to possess something of their innermost being. Language was a ladder that led directly back to heaven. Only through many ages, and many changes, did language come to be regarded as if it were a trivial formula for the appearances of things, and no true revelation of their Divine meaning.

Plato describes in his dialogue *Cratylus* how it is possible to dispute between these two ways of regarding language: those who still see its ancient divine wonder, on the one hand, those concerned only with its practical, conventional, apparently arbitrary usefulness, on the other. The last claim that language is arbitrary, since apparently any sequence of sounds can be chosen for any meaning. The first say that there is always heavenly wisdom behind the choice of particular sounds. Both can bring forward powerful examples. But for good reasons the argument is inconclusive. It is just as when two people discuss a man they know, and one continually brings out his faults and weaknesses, while the other only remembers the good fundamental purposes of his life.

Earthly language, like the human being on earth, lives in the tension between reality and illusion. When Cordelia speaks to Lear, or a poet to the reader, or an Apostle to the struggling, uncertain soul, language is both a miraculous help and a baffling hindrance.

*   *   *

We can try to look at particular languages from this point of view. And in the English language today we meet problems more acute in this respect than there have ever been before. Rudolf Steiner, out of his profound, intimate insight into the history of language, sometimes expressed this drastically. If such remarks seem indigestible, we should not turn and rend him. They are never meant to *finish* the subject—but to call our attention to some part or other of a problem deeply rooted in our history, which we can only gradually hope to grasp.

For example, in a course of lectures on social and educational problems (Stuttgart, 13 July, 1919), Rudolf Steiner said that the terms of the Versailles Treaty were unclear because the operative text was not in the former diplomatic language, French, but in English. And he goes on to say that English has the peculiarity "that in it everything which should be comprehended spiritually cannot be expressed immediately, as is given, if one takes the language only as it is there today." And later: "In the Anglo-American language there is no longer that living relationship of the human soul with the element of language which existed in ancient times. Language has separated itself from the human being: it becomes, as language, abstract. If one hears English spoken, certain turns of speech, particularly sentence-endings, always give the impression of a tree in which the outermost shoots and twigs of the branches have withered. The language allows the soul element which filled it to die away."

Our first reaction to such statements may be an indignant protest that modern English is in fact one of the richest and subtlest means of human communication that have ever existed. But further thought may show that this does not really contradict what Rudolf Steiner says. Just because its *own* life as language has ebbed, modern English may be amenable to extraordinarily varied, subtle, and individual uses. If we take as an outstanding example the English poetry of the last forty years, we can see how violently the normal habits of the spoken or written language are transformed in order to provide an instrument for each poet. "If one takes the language only as it is there today"—poetry could not be written at all. Certainly poetry has always used something grander and richer than ordinary everyday speech. But what it has used has been recognizably close to the source from which the general life of the language flowed. Now it is as if the poet had to breathe a quite individual, characteristic life into something that would otherwise be empty.

Or we can take a single example from another field. Recent tests have shown that very few young people today, even including those who have made active efforts to understand what Christianity is, can find in the word "Grace" any definite meaning. With many other words central to Christian teaching, it has become like a piece of empty nutshell, an indication that a kernel once existed.

In ordinary life we can observe how many things we say do not mean much. Perhaps we are only giving reassuring signs that we are going to behave normally, however strange our inner weather may have become. Or when we do want to make a signal from our innermost selves, only quite conventional and apparently irrelevant words may come to our lips.

Here we approach the heart of what Rudolf Steiner has to say about the English language. He does not regard the process of "withering", of which he speaks, as a misfortune for the world; on the contrary, it is very necessary that English, which tends to become the nearest we have to a world language, should be in this condition. In the same lecture, he says that this is a thoroughly healthy thing for humanity. "In the future, it will not be possible to reach mutual understanding in English without developing an immediate, elemental, intimately felt understanding between man and man, which does not itself live in what is spoken, but will give to language a new life." Something like a true thought-reading must be achieved; what is *said* must be regarded only as a signal, calling us to attend to the other's thoughts, which the speaker cannot fully express. This will call for a new attentiveness to the other's invisible being; it will be healthy that we have to make the effort to meet the speaker on a level higher than that of spoken words. This effort is something that all of humanity should learn to make; the need to do so will be particularly evident wherever English is spoken.

* * *

We may be able to deepen our understanding for this if we consider the mysterious place that English has in the history of languages. A general picture of those language groups belonging to the Indo-European family, which were significant for Europe in the first millennium B.C., can be drawn somewhat as in the first diagram (below).

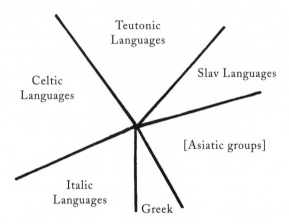

Through the defeat and submergence of the Celtic-speaking peoples, who had reached far across Europe (and indeed into Asia Minor), a far wider contact between the Teutonic languages and those derived from Latin came about than would have existed otherwise. What happened can be pictured as in the second diagram.

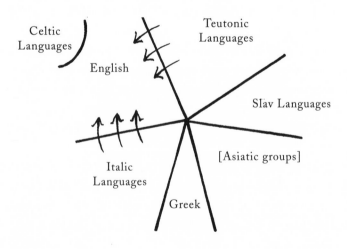

English developed in the space left by the retreat of Celtic languages, itself built up almost entirely from Teutonic and Latin elements—a meeting of languages in character and history very different from one another, the noble intermediary having withdrawn.

We may regard this simply as one of the accidents of which history seems to be made—or ask for reasons. Why did the Celtic nations go under? It is not an easily answered question on any level. Much fascinating work has been done on the rise and decline of civilizations and their relationship to one another; but in the end there does not seem to be any tangible answer to such questions as this. Why could not the Celtic peoples have adopted what was useful in Roman civilization for purposes of organization and defense, and retained their own languages and traditions? To a considerable degree the Teutonic peoples were able to do this.

So long as our vision is limited to the external world, we cannot find real answers. Just as the unity of a person's life is truly to be found only in a supersensible being, so the unity of a nation or a civilization can be found only in the Spirit that inspires it. And such Spirits, like human individualities, go through processes comparable to incarnation, and the withdrawal from incarnation; entering, and withdrawing from, the organization of a nation or civilization, just as we put on and lay aside the earthly physical body.

When he spoke particularly of this, in his lectures at Oslo in 1910, Rudolf Steiner especially directed our attention to two such Spirits: one inspiring the Greek civilization, and one standing behind the Celtic peoples. Both these Beings, he says, went through a great transformation of the way in which they worked, in order to serve the deed of Christ.

The Spirit of Greece ceased to work directly through the Greek nation and the civilization depending on Greece; this Spirit became instead the guiding Being of exoteric Christianity. The Christianity which spread widely through the world—using at first indeed mainly the Greek language—and which established itself firmly in Europe, received inspiration from this Spirit, who served Christ by giving form to the thinking and the life of the Christian Church through the centuries. Greece itself declined in political and cultural influence because its guiding Spirit had taken so wide a task—which continued long after the Greek language ceased to be used in Western Christendom, though every age found fresh understanding through the Greek New Testament.

Meanwhile the Celtic Spirit had gone through what we may regard as a still more drastic change in the manner of its work. At a time when Greece had already flowered, the Celtic peoples seemed still young, with great dormant potentialities. But at this stage the Celtic Spirit, who had given them their ultimate unity, undertook a new task. It became the guiding Spirit of *esoteric* Christianity, working not through wide masses of people but among little scattered groups, to deepen among them knowledge and experience of Christ in ways that could not be those of the Church in general—groups thought of as heretical, or those who inspired the tradition of the Holy Grail, or the true Rosicrucians.

The Gospels transcend the distinction between exoteric and esoteric; and they themselves indicate the kinds of knowledge which belonged to the esoteric realm by describing little groups of people to whom it was entrusted. The Star-knowledge possessed by the Magi; the knowledge about destiny and reincarnation given to those disciples who share in the Transfiguration; the knowledge about the future of the world given to a similar group of disciples early in Holy Week—all these are esoteric, even if some words about them are there for all to read. The Spirit who was formerly the leader of the Celtic peoples now comes to be the protector of little groups which can rightly value and preserve such knowledge, or find it anew when it has been lost.

This is a most wonderful key to European history. It helps us to understand the defeat of the Celtic peoples, first by Rome, then by the Saxons and their successors. It illumines the flowering and the apparent failure of what the historian Arnold Toynbee calls the "abortive North-Western civilization," the Christianity of Ireland and Iona. It explains the fundamental continuity, through the Middle Ages and on into modern times, of movements widely scattered in time and space, which can often do little to make their purposes comprehensible or acceptable to the world around them.

Without the deed of the Celtic Spirit, sacrificing an evident historic mission for the sake of a more hidden one in the service of Christ, there would have been no English language as we know it today. If we take this thought with full weight, we may begin to see certain consequences following from it.

English results from the fusion of languages that were at a different stage of development, and had been subject to very different influences. Linguistically, Anglo-Saxon has gone through a further development, the first consonant-shift, which Latin and Greek have not made. But culturally Greek and Latin are of course infinitely richer. The origins of their culture lie in the Mysteries which were for the most part outside Europe itself. When speaking to Waldorf school teachers about the history of language, Rudolf Steiner said of Greek and Latin:

> Through all sorts of foreign influences, which have worked in another way than in Europe—influences from Egypt, from Asia, these languages have simply become the external clothing for a culture brought to them, largely a Mystery culture. The Mysteries of Africa and Asia were brought to the Greeks, and to a certain extent to the Romans, and the power was found to clothe the Mysteries of Asia and the Mysteries of Egypt in the language of the Greeks and Romans. Thus these languages became external clothing for the spiritual content that was poured into them. This was a process through which the languages of Middle and Northern Europe had *not* passed....

The Anglo-Saxon language had qualities of soul, a certain warm maturity; the words of Latin origin that streamed in, becoming a flood in the sixteenth century, brought with them echoes of Egyptian Mysteries, and a long history of legal and ecclesiastical organization in the Roman Empire. Was there any power that could ensoul this mixture completely, and make it a clear medium for spiritual truths?

We come here to great riddles. Looking back, we see this language developing in the space once occupied by the influence of the Celtic Spirit. If it is to be fully ensouled, the help of this Spirit is needed. But it is at work in a realm *beyond* that of ordinary human language, in the guidance of esoteric Christianity. It is guarding a knowledge which cannot be fully expressed in ordinary speech—particularly in the time of which we are now thinking, the sixteenth century.

But there is a great teacher, concerned with the life of esoteric Christianity, who incarnates more frequently than ordinary individualities, Christian Rosenkreuz. Directly and indirectly, during the second half of the sixteenth century and the early years of the seventeenth, he inspires qualities of soul in the English language, through which the diverse elements can be fused into a transparent instrument for the spirit.

In the polemical religious writing of the time, language was misused to whip up indignation, and if possible to stun the opponent by sheer weight of invective. Each writer tended to become the prophet of self-righteousness; and the element of tranquil, genuine observation was in danger of being trampled to death among the sects. Those influenced by Christian Rosenkreuz were concerned to rescue this element, by transcending in one way or another the religious divisions of Europe. Thus in Shakespeare's work a world of strongly-marked, widely varied human beings appeared, not constructed to fit neatly into the categories of "righteous" and "sinful," and whose author did not seem to be arguing any kind of a case. The Authorized Version of the Bible rendered the Hebrew and Greek originals scrupulously in a form which did not serve any sectarian purpose, but sought to narrow as little as possible the fullness of their meaning. Behind the Version stood supporters of Richard Hooker's profound desire that Christianity should not be thought of as imposing a single pattern of mind and human conduct, but as including and sheltering a wonderful diversity.

Hooker himself wrote, on subjects usually treated in the most arid polemical style, in generous, humane English, which illustrates in yet another way how the language received a new inspiration at the time. As his work is comparatively little known, a brief example may be given. Hooker is here defending the use of music in churches:

> Touching musical harmony, whether by instrument or by voice, it being but of high and low in sounds a due proportionable disposition, such notwithstanding is the force thereof, and so pleasing effects it hath in that very part of man which is most divine, that some have been thereby induced to think that the soul itself by nature is or hath in it harmony. A thing which delighteth all ages and beseemeth all states; a thing as seasonable in grief as in joy; as decent being added unto actions of greatest weight and solemnity, as being used when men most sequester themselves from action.... In harmony the very image and character even of virtue and vice is perceived, the mind delighted with their resemblances, and brought by having them often iterated into a love of the things themselves. For which cause there is nothing more contagious and pestilent than some kinds of harmony; than some nothing more strong and potent unto good.

In the eighteenth century the danger to the language came no longer from religious narrow-mindedness but from a prosaic formalism, which had Hooker's dignity without his heart. A second time it was defended and enriched, this time by writers who felt their kinship with the Bible and with Shakespeare—but also with those of their contemporaries all over Europe who tried to serve true Imagination. Writers who saw that real knowledge is a creative activity, using all human faculties, not only sense perception and reason, became something like an informal European society, with manifold shared enthusiasms and energetic dissensions—a movement much too practical, earnest, and conscientious to be described simply as "Romantic." Through Goethe, Schiller, Novalis and many others, the German language achieved its first great flowering, comparable to that in Shakespearean England. Often in close contact with German idealism, though in reaction against its more ponderous products, Wordsworth, Coleridge, Shelley and Keats made English the instrument for music of a new subtlety and complexity, even when they intended to be simple.

While in general the traditional religious life, on the one hand, and rational understanding of the visible world, on the other, had fewer and fewer positive, living mutual contacts, these writers did all they could to build their thoughts into a golden bridge between earth and spirit. There streamed into them inspirations from a realm where, as Rudolf Steiner has described it, heavenly powers were making great preparations, so that spiritual knowledge should be achieved on earth, during the age that was approaching, in abundance and daylight clarity.

Thus Rudolf Steiner, as the first great teacher of this spiritual knowledge in the twentieth century, could link his work with Goethe's, and use much of the German idealists' vocabulary, with increased precision and simpler construction. Speaking and writing with a characteristic austerity and selflessness, he could make German a wonderful means of expression for Christian spiritual knowledge. Very much that had been esoteric he could make public, guarded by the language he chose so carefully against misunderstanding and misuse. Nevertheless, he had to meet bitter ridicule and every kind of hostility from those whom Blake called "the ignorant hirelings at court and university."

140

If we read Rudolf Steiner's work in English translation, we are generally made aware, in spite of all the conscientious work that has gone into these, that the clothes do not fit. Of course the German does not fit altogether either; but a master hand has been at work with the material he received from masters.

*   *   *

May it not be that English still waits for the full use that can be made of it, until towards the end of this century another great wave of spiritual teaching pours into the world? Once English was threatened by a fanatical religiosity, and later by a pedantic rationalism; now the dangers are greater still. Innumerable anonymous voices, in every continent, use English for commercial and political purposes. Behind such words there may be no discoverable person who stands by their meaning; only someone who knows what effect these words are meant to produce. On the one hand, where the transmission of genuine meaning is intended, as in scientific periodicals, there may be an attempt to deprive language of any human character for the sake of appearing objective; the kind of formulation is sought for (and this may develop further in the near future) which could be fed with the minimum of alternation into an electronic "brain." On the other hand, an extreme subjectivity can be let loose in the arts, where instincts can express themselves without any necessity of conveying a definite meaning at all.

Such tendencies all drag language into sub-human realms, and very great impulses are needed to counter them. They are indeed held in check by human common sense; but all the time they are exhausting words, knocking them about, reducing them to worthlessness. Those with insight today already point out that we are entering the most critical period in the history of the English language, in which the heritage of the past can be lost, and, for the great majority of those who speak English, communication on the deeper levels may break down. But to turn back and deepen our appreciation of the past, though this is necessary, is not enough.

The first great step into the future is to strengthen, through the many disappointments that must come, a mutual understanding *beyond* the level of language, as Rudolf Steiner has described it. We have to accept the immense, the awe-inspiring differences between our minds. We need to build up an atmosphere of unhurried reverence for and interest in one another and in the matter that is being considered, restraining ourselves as far as possible from immediate assent or dissent. What matters first is to *see* each other's thought, free of any words. A half-born imaginative picture, a swift clear dream, moves in the other's mind; sharing in it, we weave in spiritual light, from which words receive real meaning.

The attempt to do this is a training in selflessness which prepares us for the realm of Christ. There is the temptation, for all who speak or write often, to fall too much in love with their own thought-processes. And these then hinder us. The patient and active listener has more freedom to feel, wherever a real meeting of minds is going on, the great presence of Christ. And it is through His presence that language can be redeemed. Wherever real Christian sacraments are celebrated, with selfless speaking and hearing, something of this redemption happens. But what lives at such special moments must work into all the regions where human mutual understanding is needed.

Interwoven with human history, there work the souls who have shared deeply in the development of Platonism, both in its original and in its Christian forms. They are among the greatest lovers of thought, and artists in thought. If we look, on the one hand, at the development of the modern world, and consider, on the other hand, the picture of human history given by Rudolf Steiner, we may be led to think that some of these souls, within the coming century, may be concerned, with others more Aristotelian in character, in a renewed consecration of the English language—

through which even trivial words will receive a flame that fits them to be bearers of a new revelation of Christ.

Externally our language may indeed appear, by the end of this century, a dry, brittle tree. Words may seem at best capable only of describing external facts; when they attempt to express inner things, this may only seem to open up fathomless uncertainties. But there will be those who can observe the flames that glow along branch and twig, a fire that does not destroy, but gives the dry words infinite fresh life.

No genuine word is too external or too trivial to receive this power of redemption. Perhaps a very strange-seeming example may be ventured. Even such apparently neutral, colorless words as the conjunctions once had qualities of soul, warmth and cold, about them. And when language is used in the future in the Christian sense here meant, they will begin to acquire these qualities again. We may take the simple word "and." There are worlds of difference where it is used in the sense of dead accumulation, thing upon thing without sense:

"Tomorrow, and tomorrow and tomorrow...."

in the mouth of Macbeth or of a cynical modern—or if we hear with our whole being the word of Christ:

"I am Alpha and Omega."

In *all* its uses, the word "and" can convey something of the faith that the people and events of the world complete one another, that there is harmony and meaning in bringing them together—*or* that the whole business, by which we are linked in time and space, has no real sense. Every word, and words in their relationships to one another, can be consecrated.

Perhaps we who try in our different ways, with something of spiritual knowledge alive in our minds, to speak or write English today, might compare ourselves to cleaners in a palace that has been left almost empty, beginning to sweep and dust in preparation for the Court that is soon to come, of which the Ruler asks that He be loved "like salt."

REFERENCES

Richard Hooker, *Ecclesiastical Polity*
William Shakespeare, *King Lear*
—— *Macbeth*
Rudolf Steiner, Lectures in Stuttgart, July 13, 1919
   and December 29, 1919

LITERATURE IN THE UPPER SCHOOL

L. Francis Edmunds

Adolescents of fourteen and fifteen have particular difficulties to live through. They are beginning to develop a "mind's eye," to grow *objective*, to range and order their experiences. They swing between outer inquiry and inner searching: beat back and forth between enigmas without and doubts within: are subject to sudden impulses, strange moods and feelings, unexpected thoughts. Question after question forms itself, rising to startling clearness out of dim worlds of feeling. "How am I related to my parents, to the people around me? Do I accept their authority? What is death? Is there a spiritual world? Is there immortality? What do my teachers really know?" And the great underlying questions that we all seek to answer: "What am I as a human being? What is my task in the world?"

Moreover, young people at this stage can feel great loneliness and uneasiness. The ordinary world today can give them no satisfactory answers to their questions. Too frequently they grow up, therefore, to feel themselves unhappy strangers in the world, isolated and unable to relate themselves to their environment or to their historic past. They stand as uncomfortable onlookers, feeling about helplessly for anchorage.

Human beings can find their true position in the world only through a right knowledge of human evolution; and amongst all the evolutionists today, whatever their position may be, Rudolf

Steiner has taught the evolution of the whole human being. He has taught how we can experience our full humanity only by understanding how we are related in every detail to our environment; how we and the world are one and have always been one; how changes in the outer world have accompanied changes of consciousness, and how the world today and human consciousness today are one stage in a great organic development.

For the adult it becomes a task to unlearn and to relearn; to labor, often with difficulty, out of one's own accustomed thinking life, slowly to gain freedom and begin anew.

Adolescents of fourteen and fifteen are still to a large extent free in their nature and can receive directly, without prejudice, what the adult can acquire only through great effort. True knowledge lives in every human being; it has only to be awakened and brought to consciousness. The teacher standing before a class knows that the students, in their inner nature, are wise, wiser perhaps than their teacher, and less spoilt. Present the facts rightly, and the students will themselves from inner necessity seek out the right connections. There may be individual questions and difficulties, but the chief task is to try and represent, in a series of powerful pictures drawn from life, some aspect of human development down to the present day; the students will seize on the truth of the narrative through the knowledge that is already there in their unconscious lives. Their inner problems, as yet only beginning to grow conscious, will find answers in the light of this world development, and they will gain assurance in life and a feeling of security in the world.

In a literature course it becomes a question of selecting a number of characteristic works, beginning with the ancient epics, which are the first great literary compositions, following the transition into drama, which already implies a stepping out upon the earth, and leading over into later forms of literature nearer the present day.

Homer

We will begin with Homer's *Iliad:*

> Of Peleus' son, Achilles, sing O Muse,
> The vengeance, deep and deadly; whence to Greece
> Unnumber'd ills arose; which many a soul
> Of mighty warriors to the viewless shades
> Untimely sent....

Is this invocation merely literary? Is the story that follows the fruit of a single man's inventiveness? Or is it true that through the poet we enter into a real world of past human experience?

We speak of a poet's originality, based on a unique experience of the world. We do not question its integrity. We delight in the manifold uniquenesses to be found in any anthology. It stimulates and lights up our own life experience. But what if the poet should describe experiences for which we have no parallel in our own lives? Occasionally there are such poets. For many the Irish poet, A. E., is one. For years he practiced the art of matching words to thought, of giving true and noble utterance to his experiences. He describes a world of imagination behind the world of sense, a greater majesty, splendor, beauty than anything the physical eye can behold. He tells how the light of day is darkness to the brilliance of that other light.

What do critics say to such descriptions? They are divided in opinion, perhaps speak with respectful reserve. No one doubts the "reality" of A.E.'s experiences for himself, but do they arise out of his nature or are they related to an objective world which he perceives with an inner eye?

That which Homer describes was felt to be true by many generations; it was the life pulse of a great civilization. The Greeks enter history out of a world of "Myth," but right through their historic period this world of myth is for them very truth; it is the substance of their daily life; their being echoes to the wonder of it. The events of the epics had long preceded historic Greece. It is indeed at the entry of Greece into outer history, when consciousness of these events was fading into memory, that Homer gathered up into his soul those great imaginative experiences and wrote his epics. Greek Art, taken as a whole, is homogeneous. The Greek Gods and Goddesses stand clear in the imagination of the Greeks; they are the same for all Greeks, and they are for all Greeks as they were for Homer. What is the picture of the Greek world in the poems of Homer?

Below is the world of human beings, and above, in the upper atmosphere as it were, dwell the Gods grouped around Zeus (Jove). Sensible and supersensible, physical and imaginative consciousness merge into one. Humanity is not only surrounded by objects, it is everywhere surrounded by beings. Human thought, feeling and will is penetrated by this world of beings. The Gods and Goddesses appear in their own form; in human likeness as friend or foe; or they speak through signs and tokens and dreams. They are favorable or adverse; protect or injure; have human offspring and fosterlings—that is, mortals on earth in whom is incarnate a portion of their being; group themselves round chosen heroes who carry with their leadership the fate of communities or kingdoms; are inseparable from the warp and woof of human fate and action. Some people see them, know them, converse with them, are guided or misled by them.

A young race in the ascendant is opposed to an old race in marked decline. Achilles, young, proud, impetuous, extreme, preferring a short memorable life to a long easy one, stands opposed to Hector, also young, but wise with the experience of his race, temperate, constant, loving life and friends, but heroically submissive to fate. The Gods, according to their attributes and tasks, are ranged on the one side or the other; Apollo with the Trojans; Athene and Hera (Minerva and Juno) with the Greeks. Homer has an epithet for each, a specific epithet, expressive of their whole being; by their natures they are impelled to enter the field of human action, to play their part through human beings for the fulfillment of world destiny.

Jove alone is free. He alone does not appear amongst mortals, though he watches and directs all. He alone is impartial, for in him there works a deeper law. He can enter the inner sanctuaries of existence and understand the wisdom of fate.

> Expect not Juno, all my mind to know,
> My wife thou art, yet would such knowledge be
> Too much for thee; what I in secret plan,
> Seek not to know, nor curiously inquire.

He holds the scales; in his will is cosmic law. A higher knowledge makes him free among Gods and mortals:

> While yet 'twas morn, and wax'd the youthful day,
> Thick flew the shafts, and fast the people fell
> On either side; but when the sun had reach'd
> The middle Heav'n, th' Eternal Father hung
> His golden scales aloft, and plac'd in each
> The fatal death-lot; for the sons of Troy
> The one, the other for the brass-clad Greeks;
> Then held them by the midst; down sank the lot
> Of Greece, down to the ground, while high aloft
> Mounted the Trojan scale, and rose to Heav'n.
> Then loud he bade the volleying thunder peal
> From Ida's heights; and 'mid the Grecian ranks
> He hurl'd his flashing lightning; at the sight
> Amaz'd they stood, and pale with terror shook.

Nothing in the *Iliad* is by chance; everything, great and small, is ruled by wisdom. Love and hatred, sympathy and antipathy, play themselves out in human souls, not merely personally but with a human mission. It is not a personal destiny that sets Hector against Achilles. Each knows, or half knows, his own fate and the fate of his opponent. They stand opposed on earth by a greater destiny. So, too, with the Gods. For mortals the drama is of life and death. For the Gods there is obedience to cosmic laws by which they live. As the planets are now in conjunction and now in opposition, so do the Gods group themselves according to their natures and the script of the heavenly constellations.

Often it is difficult to follow their actions, to grasp their moral nature:

> All night in sleep repos'd the other Gods,
> And helméd warriors; but the eyes of Jove
> Sweet slumber held not, pond'ring in his mind
> How to avenge Achilles' cause, and pour
> Destructive slaughter on the Grecian host.
> Thus as he mus'd, the wisest course appear'd
> By a deluding vision to mislead
> The son of Atreus; and with wingéd words
> Thus to a phantom form he gave command:
> "Hie thee, deluding Vision, to the camp
> And ships of Greece, to Agamemnon's tent:
> There all, as I command thee, truly speak.
> Bid that he arm in haste the long-hair'd Greeks
> To combat; for the wide-built streets of Troy
> He now may capture; since th'immortal Gods
> Watch over her no longer; all are gain'd
> By Juno's pray'r; and woes impend on Troy."
> He said: the Vision heard, and straight obey'd;
> Swiftly he sped, and reach'd the Grecian ships,
> And sought the son of Atreus; him he found
> Within his tent, wrapp'd in ambrosial sleep;
> Above his head he stood, like Neleus' son,
> Nestor, whom Agamemnon rev'renc'd most
> Of all the Elders; in his likeness cloth'd
> Thus spoke the heav'nly Vision—

Can it be that Jove must stoop to deliberate deception, that he must lie in order to bring Agamemnon and the Greeks to disaster? Can moral necessity take such a form? Or is it that Agamemnon, by the misuse of his kingly prerogative, has weakened his nature and so laid himself open to the forces of delusion? There, where he is weak, he is seized upon by the Vision, that a wrong committed may find adjustment. Jove, perceiving the necessity, allows the consequence to come about according to the nature of the circumstances. He is no judge punishing the offender. Agamemnon, although in error, is still his representative on earth.

> … while in the midst
> The mighty monarch Agamemnon mov'd:
> His eye, and lofty brow, the counterpart
> Of Jove, the Lord of thunder; in his girth
> Another Mars, with Neptune's ample chest.
> As 'mid the thronging heifers in a herd
> Stands, proudly eminent, the lordly bull;
> So, by Jove's will stood eminent that day,
> Mid many heroes, Atreus' godlike son.

So it is with all things in the *Iliad*, till the conviction grows that it is patterned everywhere on cosmic law. Day follows day evenly. The narrative proceeds as steadily and as inevitably as the sun through the sky. Nothing is hurried and nothing is delayed; nothing is overstressed, and no detail is neglected. The story is grandly human, we accept all or none, it stands in the realm of art as a sublime mountain range in nature.

The feeling grows that in the past there lived a human race whose "real" was not our "real." Space and time, life and death, what they felt as their environment, were different. It was an age when imagination was an objective experience, common to all. The world of objects stood revealed as the shadow picture of a world of being. It was a golden age in which the spiritual was manifest outwardly in daily life and human beings inherited a knowledge of their divine origin.

The question might be asked, was asked indeed, "Do you then believe in these Gods and Goddesses and in their existence? Where are they then?" One may believe in the reality of the Greek Imagination. To that Imagination the Spiritual world of beings and facts appeared in mighty pictures, as described in the Homeric epics. For centuries people shared this common experience. They discussed these higher facts as we discuss the weather. As they changed, this experience changed; slowly it withdrew from outer consciousness and was drawn inside to live as vitalizing force within the subjective real of today. When we overcome the tyranny of self, then, with God-inspired eye we will know that world again.

Norse and Germanic Epics, Beowulf

To other cultures, in other times, according to their natures and their mission in the world, the spiritual world appeared differently. They had a different Imagination of it.

We will now turn to another epic, the *Volsunga Saga*.

This epic, too, had been recited for centuries before it was written down. Here, too, a world experience is gathered up around a particular race, around the last of that race, the mighty figure of Sigurd. The inspiration of an age-endeavor pours itself into the grand imagination of the slaying of the dragon. There is the brooding of an even higher world in this story, profound preparation, a universal sacrifice. The epic speaks of an approaching darkness, a world death. It is as though something of the deepest consequence is offered, is longed for, and recedes; as though something had been prepared but could not, for that time, be given. That which lived in Greek imagination actually descended into earthly life; filled a mighty epoch of human history; brought to earth an era of art, religion, science. That which lives in Norse imagination seems only to have reached down to the outer hem of human existence, to have lit up a strange wonder and longing in human souls and then to have faded away before their gaze; it is as though a Being of the highest wisdom and grace hovered above them but could not find entry and was lost to them. Everywhere in this epic there is the pain of parting, of being sundered, of sinking out of light into darkness. As they look the sun of the world appears to be setting forever. Strange contrast with the sun-filled vigor of the *Iliad!*

There was a dwelling of Kings ere the world was waxen old;
Dukes were the door-wards there, and the roofs were thatched with gold:
Earls were the wrights that wrought it, and silver mailed its doors;
Earls' wives were the spinning women, queens' daughters strewed its floors,
And the masters of its song-craft were the mightiest men that cast
The sails of the storm of battle adown the bickering blast.
There dwelt men merry-hearted, and in hope exceedingly great
Met the good-days and the evil as they went the way of fate:
There the Gods were unforgotten, yea whiles they walked with men,
Though e'en in that world's beginning rose a murmur now and again
Of the midward time and the fading and the last of the latter days,
And the entering in of the terror, and the death of the People's Praise.

It is strange that this mood should find an echo in a poet of the early twentieth century, A.E.:

We dwindle down beneath the skies
And from ourselves we pass away:
The paradise of memories
Grows ever fainter day by day.
The shepherd stars have shrunk within
The world's great night will soon begin.

When the story of Sigurd opens, the glory of the day is already nearly by. The Gods have withdrawn, all but one, Odin, the greatest and the last to remain. He still comes in rare moments to give or to end a mission.

Then into the Volsung dwelling a mighty man there strode,
One eyed—and seeming ancient, yet bright his visage glowed;
Cloud-blue was the hood upon him, and his kirtle gleaming grey
As the latter morning sun-day when the storm is on its way;
A bill he bore on his shoulder, whose mighty ashen beam
Burnt bright with the flame of the sea and the blended silver's gleam
And such was the guise of his raiment as the Volsung elders had told
Was borne by their fathers' fathers, and the first that warred in the wold.

Out of ancient past he brings once more the mission of the race, the sword for the slaying of the dragon. Sigmund alone can wield that sword; his son, Sigurd, fulfils the mission. He passes from the world like the last golden beam of a setting sun. Death descends like night on that race and generation. It is the death of the ancient imagination. The curse of something misbegotten is the cause of that ruin. That curse descends indeed into earthly history; it is the curse of a phantom treasure on earth and leads to a universal forgetting of the spirit.

154

The world of the epic dissolves away and humanity sinks more and more into the sense-perceptible, the physical. What was darkness before is now the only light.

The last descendant of the heroes is Beowulf. In the story of Beowulf there is also contained a world experience. In this story, however, a cosmic Heaven has shrunk to a blue sky, a flaming sun-hero to a grim warrior fighting for truth. The eye of imagination, almost blind now, still perceives dimly something of the grandeur in human life; sees in the gloaming of the gathering soul-night the last faint rays of a spirit sun gleaming round the helmet and glancing along the sword-edge of the fighting figure.

Beowulf wrestles with the first dragon at night, in the place of human habitation. He lays aside all external means, and fights with his hands alone, with his mighty grip, his will.

The second dragon, the fiercest and the mother of the brood, he can only reach in the murky depths below earth existence. He descends into the water to fight below the surface. His companions are left above on the shore in the daylight. There below the surface—that is, in the imaginative worlds, for so only can one understand the story—he fights the doer of evil on earth; and he fights with the weapons of that world, for the sword with which he slays the monster is taken from her hall and melts at contact with her blood.

The third dragon he kills in the sight of men. This dragon's fury is roused by a man stealing its treasure. Beowulf alone, in his old age, dares go to meet it, and of all whom he has helped and befriended in his long life, one alone stands by the hero in his last conflict. The rest dare not approach. They keep their distance, and when dragon and hero are dead, rush for the treasure and receive its curse.

With Beowulf's death half the world's history comes to an end. People sink into despair, for their last hope and support seems gone—but already something new is approaching. It is woven curiously into the story of Beowulf itself like a message of unfamiliar sound borne across great distances.

The following passage comes early in the story:

There was the sound of the harp, the clear song of the minstrel. He who could tell of men's beginning from olden times spoke of how the Almighty wrought the world, the earth bright in its beauty which the water encompasses, the Victorious One established the brightness of sun and moon for a light to dwellers in the land, and adorned the earth with branches and leaves; he also created life of all kinds which move and live. Thus the noble warriors lived in pleasure and plenty, until a fiend in hell began to contrive malice. The grim spirit was called Grendel, a famous march-stepper, who held the moors, the fen and the fastness. The hapless creature sojourned for a space in the sea-monsters' home after the Creator had condemned him. The eternal Lord avenged the murder on the race of Cain, because he slew Abel. He did not rejoice in that feud. He, the Lord, drove him far from mankind for that crime. Thence sprang all evil spawn, ogres and elves and sea-monsters, giants too, who struggled a long time against God. He paid them requital for that.

Later occurs the following phrase:

The truth has been made known, that mighty God has ever ruled over mankind.

And what a mingling of something old and something new is in the following:

Then the sword, the battle-brand, began to vanish in drops of gore after the blood shed in the fight. That was a great wonder that it all melted like ice when the Father loosens the bonds of the frost, unbinds the fetters of the floods; He has power over times and seasons. That is the true lord....

The wave surges were all cleansed, the great haunts where the alien spirit gave up his life and the fleeting state.

Beowulf, lying wounded, calls for a sight of the treasure:

Then he spoke, the aged man in his pain; he gazed on the gold. "I gave thanks in words to the Prince, the King of glory, the eternal Lord, for all the adornments which I behold here, that I have been able to win such for my people before my death-day. Now have I sold my old life for the hoard of treasures: attend ye now to the need of my people. No longer may I tarry here.

A few lines later:

The prince of brave mind took from his neck a golden ring, gave to the thane, the young spear-warrior, his helm bright with gold, his ring and corslet; bade him use them well: "Thou art the last of our race, of the Waegmundinges. Fate has swept all my kinsmen away to their destiny, earls in their might; I must needs follow them."

That was the last word from the old man's thoughts, before he sought the pyre, the hot, fierce surges of flame. His soul passed from his breast to seek the splendor of the saints.

The substance of the story is old, yet the language declares the presence of something new. As people sink finally into the sense world, they are greeted there, on the floor of the world, by a new teaching. Beowulf, at the last, has perhaps caught a glimpse of an approaching new day. Christ has walked this earth. The moment of greatest loss becomes the moment of greatest gain.

Anglo-Saxon Poets

Small children do not stand and contemplate Nature, but live directly in what is going on around them. They draw no great distinctions between the living and the lifeless. Trees and flowers, birds, animals, sun, moon and stars, rocks and streams, the winds, all converse with one another and with them. They find nothing strange in spirits, in gnomes and fairies; things of the senses and things of the soul make one world. They frequently dream of angels, and night dreams mingle with day dreams, for this waking life is also a dream.

Among simple peoples who have preserved the forces of childhood, much of this still persists. Folk tales and legends are evidence of a life of soul that modern scholarship treats lightly. The learned of our day class all these things as superstitions. At the same time, those who still have these experiences feel uneasy at the sight of books; they feel that books kill the eyes of the soul, that the black printed letters are little devils leading them away from God.

Close and loving observation shows how the children, as they grow in years, emerge slowly from this life in nature and awaken to a sense of self. The changes go on subtly below consciousness; inwardly they feel how they are separating from the world of nature, how they are losing their state of innocence, and a mood of sadness fills them of lingering farewell to what they may never know again in life, of apprehension of this world of thinking adults and defined objects. For under modern materialistic conditions, in which the life of thought is so abstract and remote from child experience, the world seems cold and comfortless. From having been one with nature they become spectators, an outsider in a sense, alone in a separate being. What later is to be the conscious experience in thought of subject and object, world and self, is here, in its beginning, a delicate mood of soul, a feeling of being sundered from the world of one's first loves, a sinking from spiritual worlds into the world of the senses.

The children have this experience because it is a past experience of the human race; it is the experience of the Fall. The epics are memories of this past. To listen to them was once an education of the soul. The process of sinking into physical nature continues, however, through the centuries and the epics become remote from human life. As people grew dead to the realities that produced the epics, so now they grow dead to the epics themselves—but this growing dead brings a mood of desolation. Outside in space the world grows clearer; they concern themselves more with external details, with agriculture, trades, vocations. Within, the soul is plunged in darkness; and in the darkness there is longing for what has been lost, there is a growing fear of death, a universal death, and there is no comfort to be found. The bard stands in the pagan hall, but the fountain of song is almost dried up and yields little joy. Men are no longer lifted to their feet with mighty impulses of will. King and warriors sit round the board; there should be worlds to gain, but listlessness creeps over the soul.

One day there enters into the pagan hall a Christian monk, a missionary. He tells in simple language the story of Our Lord, of the Fall and Redemption, of God made flesh, the Passion, Death, and Resurrection. "Your gods are dead," he tells them, "they lead the way to death. The living God, the Christ, suffered death that death might be overcome, and the soul be saved."

It is always surprising how readily kings and chieftains received this teaching. English history tells how these first missionaries traveled from hall to hall winning converts everywhere. People listened with eager hearts. Here at last were the good tidings, new wine to cheer the heart and rouse the soul. Once again the halls resounded with song and verse; singers struck new epics from the trembling lyres, "Genesis," "Exodus," "Christ." Once again tales were sung as of old, but the heroes were new: St. Guthlac; St. Elene, Andreas the Apostle.

The story of the poet Caedmon, who died in the year 680 A.D., is remarkable. It tells how the gift of song came to him overnight, how it burst from him in his old age with torrential might, an ancient power set free to serve new ends. With what ecstasy of soul he begins his narrative of Genesis.

It is very right for us to praise with words and to love in our hearts the Lord of Heaven, the glorious King of Hosts. He is fullness of power, Head of all exalted creatures, Lord almighty. Beginning or source was never wrought for Him, nor shall an end come now for the Lord everlasting, but for ever in high majesty He shall be mighty above the thrones of heaven.

Death has been overcome, the human soul is saved forever, that is the burden of the new song.

Cynewulf in the eighth century wrote a long epic, "Christ," in which he quotes the Gospels thus:

Be joyful in heart. I shall never leave you, but ever continue my love towards you, and give you power, and abide with you for ever and ever, so that by my grace ye shall never feel the want of God.

What comfort for an emptied soul, the promise of life eternal, of goodness beyond pain, of light beyond darkness, of Christ Himself at the end of all human traveling.

In this same poem, though, Cynewulf is much preoccupied with the question of sin and the judgment to come. Again and again he warns about the time of the final sorting. Not the fear of universal death grips people now, but the fear of eternal damnation. Can they resist the temptations of this earthly paradise? The victories of the epics must now be re-achieved within each soul. The promise is there at the end, but can one reach that end? Thus a new struggle begins, the struggle between soul and body, between heavenly aspirations and earthly ambitions.

Two great processes meet in the human soul.

The epics told of experiences once common to all. People knew their truth, for the evidence lay hidden in their own souls. But the time of forgetting came, and the process of growing more worldly that went with it. This process continues ever farther. People grow more and more engrossed in external everyday affairs, they feel themselves well-grounded citizens of the earth, dependent on their toil for bread, anxious to secure daily shelter and comfort.

There now approaches them the new teaching. Their souls are virgin soil to it. The longing that still lives in their hearts makes them receptive to it, it has fashioned the ear with which they listen to the messengers, the gospel bearers. Their own personal experience of spiritual worlds is fading away, but the new teaching stands ever before them to recall them to the spirit, directing them to think more of their souls and less of their bodies, more of the life hereafter and less of their day to day interests.

As time goes on they learn to regard the Church as a necessary institution to which all must belong. They accept the seven sacraments as they do the hours of the day, something that takes its own course in life and is self-evident. They recognize the need for priests and pay their tithes to the Church. They believe that by special prayers and intercessions they can help the soul after death. Beyond that, though, increasingly they put from them the thought of death and keep busily occupied with the affairs of the living.

In the past people had not feared to die; it was the manner of death that was the more important. Achilles preferred a short life and a glorious death in battle to a long life and a peaceful death in bed. Now, however, death itself is felt as an evil. Put off the thought of it as long as you may. Churchgoers still preserve an instinct for the immortality of the soul, but they fear damnation at least as much as they love salvation, and for the most part prefer the world they are in to the world to come.

Thus we proceed through mediaeval times to the thirteenth, fourteenth, and even fifteenth centuries.

Fifteenth Century: Everyman

Everyman is a play belonging to the end of the fifteenth and beginning of the sixteenth century. In this play Everyman has grown so much a part of matter that only the experience of death can serve to remind him of his soul. God sees that but for death he would sink into utter beastliness. He sends death as his messenger to summon Everyman to a reckoning before it will be too late.

DEATH: Lo, yonder I see Everyman walking;
Full little he thinketh on my coming;
His mind is on fleshly lusts and his treasure,
And great pain it shall cause him to endure
Before the Lord Heaven King.
Everyman, stand still; whither art thou going
Thus gaily? Hast thou thy Maker forgot?

Everyman has accounts of business to settle, he is not disposed to be hindered just then, does not recognize the voice of Death and, even when he does, cannot take it quite seriously.

EVERYMAN: Oh, Death, thou comest when I had thee least
    in mind;
In thy power it lieth me to save,
Yet of my good will I give thee if thou wilt be kind,
Yea, a thousand pound shalt thou have,
And defer this matter till another day.

The thought of death dawns on him and comes as a shock in the midst of life. Everyman begins to realize his helplessness. Surrounded by friends he experiences his utter aloneness.
Fellowship is the first to forsake him.

EVERYMAN: It is said, in prosperity men friends may find,
Which in adversity be full unkind.
Now whither for succour shall I flee,
Sith that Fellowship hath forsaken me?

Next come Kindred and Cousin, gushing but indifferent. Lastly his worldly goods, his life's treasures, appear as paltry tinsels that have ensnared his soul.

GOODS: Therefore to thy soul Goods is a thief:
For when thou art dead this is my guise
Another to deceive in this same wise.
As I have done thee....

Everyman is now stripped of his connections with the outer world and must do what all his life he has fled from doing; he must face himself. The world in its affairs and interests appears in all its transitoriness. His soul is all he has, and that is a stranger here. But how dare he face that other world? In his life he finds little comfort.

EVERYMAN: I think that I shall never speed
Till that I go to my good deed,
But alas, she is so weak,
That she can neither go nor speak.

As the body falls away, the soul grows stronger; deep qualities appear that have lain smothered under the illusions of the senses. Knowledge awakens in Everyman that has been deeply buried all through life, knowledge as to his true nature, as to the spiritual foundation of the world and his dependence on God. It leads him to the confession of sins and to repentance, to the realization that through the Christ we live and in Him we die.

From now death is no longer a terror; life indeed grows irksome. But the process of death must take its course. One by one his faculties fail him. Even knowledge that has guided him so far must forsake him at the end. Good deeds alone can go with him through the portals of death.

GOOD DEEDS: All earthly things is but vanity:
Beauty, Strength, and Discretion, do man forsake;
Foolish friends and kinsmen that fair spake,
All fleeth save Good Deeds, and that am I.
EVERYMAN: Have mercy on me God most mighty;
And stand by me, thou Mother Maid, holy Mary.
GOOD DEEDS: Fear not, I will speak for thee.
EVERYMAN: Here I cry God mercy.
GOOD DEEDS: Short our end, and minish our pain;
Let us go and never come again.

EVERYMAN: Into thy hands, Lord, my soul I commend;
Receive it, Lord, that it be not lost;
As thou me boughtest, so me defend,
And save me from the fiend's boast,
That I may appear with that blessed host
That shall be saved at the day of doom.
In manus tuas of mights most
For ever commendo spiritum meum.

In Everyman we have reached the zero point in the individual soul. Forgetfulness in life is balanced by awakening at death. In the moment of death, through the Christ, life and death are made equal and the soul proceeds onward.

THE ANGEL: Come, excellent elect spouse to Jesu;
Here above thou shalt go
Because of thy singular virtue;
Now the soul is taken the body fro;
Thy reckoning is crystal clear
Now shalt thou into the heavenly sphere,
Unto the which all ye shall come
That liveth well before the day of doom.

Up to this point Everyman is still to some extent protected. There is something in his soul that makes it possible for him to accept the authority of the Church easily. He rests on the Church. The struggle between soul and body is also the struggle between Church and State in both of which he has a share. The world pulls him one way, it has grown increasingly attractive to him through the life of the senses; the Church pulls him back—through the Mass and the sacraments it holds sway in his soul, and through the instrument of confession it seeks to check unlimited excesses of living.

The Renaissance and Christopher Marlowe

This protection ceases with the Renaissance. People are no longer engrossed in otherworldly interests as was Everyman; they are enthusiastic for the outer world. They roam land and sea, agog to know and discover. For the first time there awakens the power of independent thought. The Church is felt to be a tyrant, the priest a meddler, the old traditional knowledge a fable. People's thoughts follow their senses; the life of soul itself is not yet questioned—indeed, dare not be questioned on penalty of death—but it has grown pale and inward.

This awakening to an intensely thoughtful interest in the world of nature is to be compared with the awakening of thought in adolescents after puberty. Hitherto they have lived immersed in their life of feeling, as in their first years they had lived immersed in their bodily nature; now, however, they have achieved something of freedom in their feeling life, and this is accompanied by a second stage in the development of their thought life. They begin to form personal judgments, to live more in the element of thought.

At this time young people really experience the "enlightenment" of the Renaissance, with its release from Mediaevalism and dependence on authority, and enter now into our "modern" age. They are experimental, wishing to weigh and compare what this one says and that. They are provoked to rebellion by any attempt to force their judgment. Their confidence in adults around them is severely tested. They are apt to grow skeptical about religious questions and to be easily influenced by popular scientific notions of the day. Environment begins to have a very strong appeal.

Behind this intense outer interest there is in the soul a mood of tragedy; inwardly the soul feels baffled. The tragedy of this period is expressed in Marlowe's life and writing. Between the time of Everyman and Marlowe there is less than a hundred years. Marlowe felt the awakening of new powers of soul; so free in thought was he that he was about to be arrested as an atheist at the time of his death; but he could not find the way to inner freedom. Inner powers might give him dominion in the outer world, but this seemed only a trap for the soul; along this path the soul must lose its way.

In Doctor Faustus we have an Everyman who has come to the end of all that the outer world can offer him. He has studied Law, Medicine, Philosophy, Divinity, and has achieved fame in all: "Are not my bills hung up as monuments?" Yet with bitterness he has to learn that in his soul he is as powerless as any other. It is power he wants above all else. To exercise powers divine, to win past the limits of mortality, control and order the elements themselves, move cities, raise mountains, divert rivers, transform kingdoms at will, this power outer knowledge cannot give him. His ambition to be more than man awakens the darkest forces of his soul, and, being man and therefore a spiritual being, this can lead him to nothing less than the invocation of the enemies of light. He turns to necromancy.

FAUST: All things that move between the quiet poles
Shall be at my command: emperors and kings
Are but obeyed in their several provinces,
Nor can they raise the wind or rend the clouds;
But his dominion that exceeds in this
Stretcheth as far as doth the mind of man.
A sound magician is a mighty God.

The egotism of Everyman is balanced through the Church. Faustus disclaims the Church. Self-knowledge makes nonsense of all learning and reveals him a mere drudge and weakling, and in his disappointment he falls an easy prey to the temptations that await everyone seeking freedom.

Be thou on earth as Jove is in the sky,
Lord and commander of these elements.

The problem of Faustus lies in the nature of human freedom. Should he be free to go the way of damnation if he chooses? "I am free," says Faustus. "I wish to sell my soul to the Devil. It is *my* soul. I choose eternal damnation as the price for twenty-four years of unlimited power, it is *my* choice." He has to learn that the power the Devil can give him brings him only shadows and semblances; the knowledge the Devil can bring him shows that human beings know better than the Devil.

FAUST: Tell me, who made the world?
MEPH: I will not.
FAUST: Sweet Mephistopheles, tell me.
MEPH: Move me not, for I will not tell thee.
FAUST: Villain, have I not bound thee to tell me anything?
MEPH: Ay, that is not against our kingdom; but this is.
Think thou on hell, Faustus, for thou art damned.
FAUST: Think, Faustus, upon God that made the world!
MEPH: Remember this! (Exit)
FAUST: Ay, go, accursed spirit, to ugly hell.
'Tis thou has damned distressed Faustus' soul.
Is't not too late?
(Re-enter good angel and evil angel)
E. ANGEL: Too late.
G. ANGEL: Never too late, if Faustus can repent.
E. ANGEL: If thou repent, devils shall tear thee in pieces.
G. ANGEL: Repent, and they shall never raze thy skin.
(Exeunt angels)
FAUST: Ah, Christ, my Saviour!
Seek to save distressed Faustus' soul.

He sees through the shallowness of Mephistopheles, the dark spirit of the senses, and in that moment recognizes God.

But is he not damned? Has he not sold his soul? For the moment the question is in balance, but there comes a second, more powerful, tempter in Lucifer, who beguiles his soul with visions and promises of self-indulgence.

(Enter Lucifer and Mephistopheles)

FAUST: O who art thou that lookst so terrible?

LUC: I am Lucifer,
And this is my companion-prince in hell.

FAUST: O Faustus, they are come to fetch away thy soul!

LUC: We come to tell thee thou dost injure us;
Thou callst on Christ, contrary to thy promise;
Thou shouldst not think of God: think of the Devil,—And
  of his dam too.

FAUST: Nor will I henceforth: pardon me in this,
And Faustus vows never to look to Heaven,
Never to name God or to pray to him.
To burn His Scriptures, slay His Ministers,
And make my spirits pull His churches down.

LUC: Do so, and we will highly gratify thee.
Faustus, we are come from hell to show thee
Some pastime: sit down, and thou shalt see all
The Seven Deadly Sins appear in their proper shapes.

Temptation follows temptation in this and the coming scenes.
As someone, waking from drugs, feels greater misery than before
and plunges back into them, so Faustus wakes from time to time
to realize with full bitterness the worthlessness of his bargain, for
his soul remains hungry as ever.

OLD MAN: Ah stay, good Faustus, stay thy desperate steps!
I see an angel hovers o'er thy head,
And, with a vial full of precious grace,
Offers to pour the same into thy soul:
Then call for mercy and avoid despair.

Can he turn back? He cannot till he has gone the full length of
his venture:

FAUST: I do repent; and yet I do despair;
Hell strives with Grace for conquest in my breast.

Even as he speaks Mephistopheles appears, threatening and at the same time proffering further allurements.

The time comes when Faust has sampled all temptations; there is nothing the devil can offer him more. The clock is striking the hour. He is at hell's mouth, and in that moment only sees salvation, but it is too late.

> FAUST: See, see where Christ's blood streams in the firmament!
> One drop would save my soul—half a drop; ah, my Christ!

The downward path into materialism has brought him below his zero point. To Marlowe, standing at the dawn of an age of untold ambition for power, dominion, knowledge, luxury, it seems that Christ himself can no longer save humanity.

Shakespeare

In Shakespeare we pass from Everyman, the common type, from Faustus, the representative human being, to the world of many human beings, swayed by all the different passions of the soul; love, jealousy, envy, vanity, suspicion—there seems no end to them. Actor after actor comes upon the stage to bring some attitude of soul to life and reap the consequences. Some laugh, and laughing weep; in others, tears are turned to laughter. The hero of great exploits today will start at a shadow tomorrow. What, then, is the human being? All in their own way, through their own suffering, gather a grain of self-knowledge, often when it seems too late.

> MACBETH: (aside) Come what come may,
> Time and the hour runs through the roughest day.

Macbeth's ambition is to become king; yet is it *his* ambition, or some flaw in his nature that life has seized on to bring him to destruction? When does he act from himself and when from outer circumstances? Did the thought arise first in him or in the witches? And why should all things contrive to make the murder easy? Why should Duncan decide to stay at Macbeth's castle? Why should nature play this trick to tempt his weakness further? What is human action? What are its true consequences?

Macbeth, contemplating the murder of Duncan, says:

> MACBETH: That but this blow
> Might be the be-all and the end-all here,
> But here, upon this bank and shoal of time,
> We'd jump the life to come.

Let me but succeed in this life and I will risk the life to follow. This sentiment is not Macbeth's alone; it has grown very general even down to today.

Does he succeed? Yes, he kills Duncan: to learn, though, that action does not stop at itself, but leads on from act to act, a fatal thread that runs through dismay, ruin, every horror, to death itself, nay, beyond death, for death yields ghosts to haunt the living. And what of the dead, what is their state? What is human conscience, the conscience that will not rest, against all reason?

> MACBETH: Methought I heard a voice cry "Sleep no more!
> Macbeth does murder sleep"—the innocent sleep,
> Sleep that knits up the ravell'd sleave of care,
> The death of each day's life, sore labour's bath,
> Balm of hurt minds, great nature's second course,
> Chief nourisher in life's feast —

If only he could sleep at will, but he cannot. Even the dead have tongues to rouse a knocking in the world that drives to suicide or madness. The very laws of nature are reversed. How else should he see ghosts? Why should Lady Macbeth reveal in sleep the secret she has guarded all day waking?

MACBETH: How does your patient, Doctor?
DOCTOR: Not so sick, my Lord,
As she is troubled with thick-coming fancies
That keep her from her rest.
MACBETH: Cure her of that:
Canst thou not minister to a mind diseas'd,
Pluck from the memory a rooted sorrow,
Raze out the written troubles of the brain,
And with some sweet oblivious antidote
Cleanse the stuff'd bosom of that perilous stuff
Which weighs upon the heart?
DOCTOR: Therein the patient
Must minister to himself.
MACBETH: Throw physic to the dogs, I'll none of it.

Lady Macbeth dies. Macbeth stands alone now. His ambition is a mere wraith. Nothing in poetry expresses more the weariness, the greyness of a purposeless life.

MACBETH: Tomorrow, and tomorrow and tomorrow
Creeps in this petty pace from day to day
To the last syllable of recorded time,
And all our yesterdays have lighted fools
The way to dusty death. Out, out, brief candle!
Life's but a walking shadow, a poor player
That struts and frets his hour upon the stage
And then is heard no more; it is a tale
Told by an idiot, full of sound and fury,
Signifying nothing.

Why, then, does Macbeth go on? All is lost, there is no hope or joy left for him. He is steeped in blood; every word he utters reeks with the misery of it. Yet he goes on.

There is one thing left. He will die a man, will pursue his end. He is indifferent to life, to death; he has survived all horrors. He is stripped of his last illusion, the last of the witches' baits. But he fights on and dies fighting:

MACBETH: Though Birnam Wood be come to Dunsinane,
And thou oppos'd, being of no woman born,
Yet I will try the last: before my body
I throw my warlike shield: lay on, Macduff;
And damn'd be him that first cries "Hold, enough!"

Macbeth defeats the purpose of his own part. At the end, instead of horror he arouses sympathy. We pity him. That is Shakespeare's genius. No man has gone deeper into the horrors of life. By these very horrors he redeems life. We pity Macbeth, we pity Lear, we pity Othello.

What is human destiny? Shakespeare does not say. He shows instead that there is no end to life's horror, but there is also no limit to human compassion, love, forgiveness. The human soul at the end is full of charity, without a thought of criticism.

PROSPERO: Bear with my weakness.

This crowns the life of Prospero. He has achieved learning and wisdom, has conquered the elements to let them go again, knows all sacrifice, knows forgiveness to the last drop, is a sage at the end of life. "Bear with my weakness," he says to young Ferdinand. That is the sum of wisdom, of Shakespeare's wisdom—or is it the wisdom of all ages come to life again in Shakespeare?

Is this the end, the final harvesting of all the fruits of human generations? It cannot be. The soil of human wisdom has been ploughed and turned and harrowed. Much sorrow has been poured out upon it. The light of destiny has played upon it. Prospero is but that soil prepared, carrying within seeds of an ancient tree. In him is the first faint stirring of those seeds to life.

Shakespeare's world is a world in time. He begins with waking dreams and ends with waking dreams, and in between is the hard reality of middle life. His first dreams are of childhood, where laughter and tears chase each other by, like the light and shadows of a fairy world. In *A Midsummer Night's Dream* we dream. In *Romeo and Juliet* we have torn the veil of childhood. In *As You Like It* we are threatened with a waking day. In *Twelfth Night* we face a hard grey morning. And now the day is upon us. In the histories we first step into life, a life that rocks and turns to water beneath our feet. We stumble on in the heat of the afternoon, wading, floundering, and now darkness descends, and in the tragedies we are immersed and all but lost. But stripped of everything, mere wraiths of our own being, we yet have something left; we re-emerge, grey-haired wizards of the night—with the hallowed hearts of little children. And now life begins anew for us. As little children we dream again, but this time from out of the future, dreams that are faint premonitions of another dawning day, the first shy vision of a distant promise. To Prospero the hard reality of middle life is itself a passing dream now; his present dreams are more real, but the way is long. He has seen what he himself will never reach; Miranda may.

Keats and the Romantic Poets

Shakespeare, from the summit of his latter days, looks back across the abyss to the peaks of childhood. He has crossed the abyss, the lowest point; he has achieved what to Marlowe seemed impossible. His victory will serve others, has done so. He was the inspiring genius of young Keats, roused his soul to a fever of creative ardor, stirred vision upon vision within him, brought his heart to seek the great heart of nature so that he could see the ancient worlds unfold in the human breast, feel the present, and turn his longing aspiration to the future.

> An ocean dim, sprinkled with many an isle,
> Spreads awfully before me. How much toil!
> How many days! what desperate turmoil!
> Ere I can have explored its widenesses.
> Ah, what a task!...

We have come, with Keats, to the time of the Romantic poets. They were all so different one from another, yet one great Genius stood behind them all, the same that had stood behind Shakespeare through all his days, the Awakener of the human soul, the great guiding Genius of the whole human race. The progress of night continued in their time and swept over them, but in their souls they knew themselves to be Children of Light; each sought to realize the true nature of human freedom. So Coleridge came to know it as something that may never be achieved by outward means, but as springing from within the human soul.

> ... on the sea-cliff's verge,
> Whose pines, scarce travelled by the breeze above,
> Had made one murmur with the distant surge!
> Yes, while I stood and gazed, my temples bare,
> And shot my being through earth, water, air,
> Possessing all things with intensest love,
> O liberty! my spirit felt thee there.

REFERENCES

Beowulf
Caedmon, "Genesis"
Cynewulf, "Christ"
Everyman
Homer, *Iliad* (Trans. Lord Derby)
Christopher Marlowe, *Doctor Faustus*
William Shakespeare, *Macbeth*
—— *The Tempest*
Volsunga Saga (trans. William Morris)

In the Footsteps of Dante

A Journey of Hope and Transformation

Linda Sawers

"Tutto a te mi guida"
— Everything leads me to you —

In the summer of 1264 a bright comet with a magnificent tail swept the sky over Florence. People marveled at its brightness and pondered its meaning as the comet continued its appearance for nearly two months. Some claimed the comet was a sign that a great genius had been conceived and would be born in the city.

Thus was foretold the birth of Dante Alighieri, the man Florence regards as her greatest citizen. This is no small honor in a city that can claim as her sons a host of writers, artists and thinkers. By one accord Dante stands above them all as the man who brought astounding newness to poetry — in content and form and, most important of all, in poetic language itself. This singular honor, however, was not born of an easy relationship between the city and her favored son; it was born of pain, bitterness, injustice and exile. Through this tension of creative genius and adversity, Dante's life and the content of his opus, *The Divine Comedy*, continue to be a source of inspiration today.

While there is no question of Dante's importance or standing in Florence, his place in the high school curriculum is not always so assured. And yet, especially for the eleventh grader, *The Divine Comedy* can be an effective piece of timeless literature.

175

Dante and his journey speak powerfully to students at a critical time in their lives.

In the opening of *The Divine Comedy* Dante awakes to find himself lost in a Dark Wood; gone astray from the right path, he must find his way out. Here, in this gloomy and frightening wood, begins one of the greatest journeys in the world of literature. In this beginning we can see a parallel with the condition of eleventh graders. During this tender year they undertake an invisible journey of the inner life, and for some it is a most unsettling time. For many the world of adulthood looms larger on the horizon than the world of childhood they are leaving behind. This in-between stage can be a time of outer sociability and inner loneliness, a time of coming to terms with the past while struggling to imagine the future. Often, what was once a familiar course turns to a chartless sea. None of these struggles is necessarily overt, but if we serve our students well, they may go through an inner transformation that prepares them to meet the world with confidence. There are no better teachers for this time of life than Dante, his guide Virgil and his Divine Muse, Beatrice.

Dante's journey is mirrored in the inner explorations of the eleventh grade student. The sense that the world is changing rapidly—too rapidly to keep up with—can be a source of anxiety, but this is not as upsetting as a lack of vision for the future. It is here, in *The Divine Comedy*, that Dante shows not only the "lost" but also the "found." There *is* a way out of the Dark Wood.

This journey, so eloquently told, takes root in Dante's own life story. It is perhaps through his biography (what we have of it) that the students make their first connection with the poem. Dante's struggles with injustice are moving as well as instructive, for here is a man who triumphed over doubt and adversity to live as if reborn.

While Dante's early years were marred by the death of his parents, his boyhood was an important time for the poetic genius developing within him. His destiny as a poet was set in motion at the age of nine by his legendary meeting with Beatrice at a May

Day party. From that moment on he devoted himself to her with a fervor that never waned. During his adolescence his love for her found expression in poetry which he dedicated to her, and which he wrote in Italian, not (as was the fashion for poetry at that time) in Latin. At eighteen he met her again in the streets of Florence, where she rebuked him for embarrassing her with his "vulgar" poetry, for Italian was then known as the "vulgar tongue." Chastened, he obeyed her wishes and stopped writing about her for quite some time. At twenty-seven he finished "The New Life." Dedicated to Beatrice, the poem revealed his maturing voice, but he vowed not to write about her again until he could understand the meaning of her place in his life.

In these events the cycle of nine becomes evident. Likewise the number three is also inextricably bound up with the design of *The Divine Comedy*. During this time Dante's understanding of Beatrice was deepening and this would be given full voice in the *Purgatorio* when she becomes his guide:

> My soul—such years had passed since last it saw
> that lady and stood trembling in her presence,
> stupefied by the power of holy awe—
>
> now, by some power that shone from her above
> the reach and witness of my mortal eyes,
> felt the full mastery of enduring love.
>
> The instant I was smitten by the force
> which had already once transfixed my soul
> before my boyhood years had run their course. . . .

Dante's dedication to his muse, Beatrice, was paralleled by his serious pursuit of a worldly life. He lived in the most exciting and prosperous medieval city of Europe, and he entered into the mainstream of this life easily, while continuing to write in the Italian vernacular. He married Gemma Donati, had children and, through his talent for diplomacy, rose quickly in the political power structure of Florence. By the age of thirty he was a popular figure in political life. It was not long before he was elected to the prestigious position of Prior—one of six who served as magistrates for the city. This was a supreme position to which many aspired but which few attained.

However, this success signaled the beginning of adversity. Within six months of his election as Prior, Dante was handed the burdensome tasks of banishing from Florence his best friend, the poet Guido Cavalcanti, as well as his hot-tempered brother-in-law, Corso Donati, for their part in the riots that had swept the city. Their exile, however, did not prevent further violence and intrigue, which eventually overturned the government.

At the time when the Florentine government fell to the opposition, Dante was away from the city, and he remained abroad to see what would transpire. Soon trials were held to purge and eliminate all previous office holders. During his absence, Dante was falsely accused and convicted of graft. A heavy sentence was finally issued: banishment from Florence and burning at the stake if he returned. With this crushing blow he felt that all was lost; all he had achieved was gone. Exiled from his beloved city, his family and his friends, Dante was doomed to wander from city to city for the rest of his life, accepting the patronage of others. He was thirty-six.

Dante's exile from Florence, then, coincided with the closure of his fourth cycle of nine years. In the symbolism of medieval numerology, the number four indicated completion. In a sense, Dante's life had come to an end and it was time to begin anew. However, over the years something had been maturing within him that no foe could take away: his knowledge, his poetry, and his muse. Examining the nature of true choice and of all that had happened to him, he began to understand his task in life. Indeed, his life had led him astray from the "right road" into the Dark Wood.

The result of this self-examination was *The Divine Comedy*, a story which begins with one man and ends with quite a different one—a man who transforms bitterness into love.

In many ways Dante's life and work parallel the transformations that he describes in *The Divine Comedy*, a story which begins in the Dark Wood and soars into the heavenly heights. Taking advantage of his experiences, rather than being defeated by them, he brought something entirely new into the world. For the first time a national language—Italian—was used legitimately for epic poetry. While other writers followed his lead, few achieved his perfection. He carefully created a literary scheme based on the trinity. The Books of *The Divine Comedy*—*Inferno, Purgatorio,* and *Paradiso*—are each divided into thirty-three cantos, plus one of introduction. The number of cantos, then, adds up to one hundred, or one, the symbolic number of God. *Terza rima*, a rhyme scheme which Dante created consisting of three intertwining rhymes turning through three-line stanzas, reinforces the superstructure of the poem. The number three is also reflected in the auspicious timing of the story: it is Good Friday, the vernal equinox, and full moon. In these forms Dante sounds a clarion call for the development of individuality that will shed old ways of thinking and speak with a new voice.

It is interesting to observe the students' initial reactions as they follow Dante's footsteps through the invisible realms. At first the students may react to the "injustice" of the *Inferno*, yet they are soon taken by its terrible logic. *The Divine Comedy* is one of the greatest examples of clear thinking in literature, and students very quickly overcome their aversion to the grim and fearful events and begin to ponder the deeper concepts underlying the story. In a world fraught with confusion about what is right and wrong, students receive the clarifying power of Dante's objective judgment with relief. Dante, they discover, is not a moralizer, but a thinker who sets out to solve problems in human existence. All of human existence is a matter of deed and consequence, Dante asserts, and this is the fulcrum of *The Divine Comedy*. Dante's scheme takes on a new meaning as the students discover the difference between judgment and judgmentalism. In pondering the concept of consequence, the students may feel a new freedom—the freedom of sound judgment.

While Dante's story is ultimately about redemption and forgiveness, it is necessary to explore the lower depths of the inferno as a first step. The proper exercise of human reason is the cornerstone of Dante's theme, and this is the first to be taken up in the *Inferno*. The theme of human reason and its obstacles is pictured symbolically in the opening canto. Dante's way out of the Dark Wood is blocked by three beasts: the she-wolf (incontinence), the lion (violence and bestiality) and the leopard (malice and fraud). These three represent three forms of misusing or overpowering human reason. The first, and least serious, form is incontinence, the sins of bodily appetites. These sins, which are more harmful to self than to others, relate directly to the individual's state of consciousness—or lack of it. They constitute the perversion of will. The second form, violence and bestiality or senseless aggression, are the sins of passion that can affect others as well as oneself; they are done in the moment out of a consciousness dimmed by passion. The last, and the worst sins, are those of malice and fraud. Here we see the perversion of human reason through clever premeditated calculations.

After being blocked by the three beasts, Dante meets Virgil, the ultimate archetype of human reason, and learns he must travel through hell, purgatory and paradise before he can return to his normal life. Through Virgil the meaning of the gift of human reason, with all its powers and responsibilities, is unfolded and explored. Virgil tells Dante,

> "This is the place I told you to expect.
> Here you shall pass among the fallen people,
> souls who have lost the good of intellect."

So saying, he put forth his hand to me,
and with a gentle and encouraging smile
he led me through the gate of mystery.

Virgil serves as a guide through the realms of hell and purgatory, showing first "those who had lost the good of intellect" (and the consequences of this loss) and then the realm of repentance and purification of the soul. In both realms the importance of human reason is paramount, but human reason is finite, and Virgil can go no farther than the summit of purgatory. The realm of Paradise is left to Beatrice, the embodiment of Divine Love.

According to Dante the purpose of human reason is to prepare us to receive and understand Divine Love. To do this we have to struggle for the kind of conscious choice and conscious action that can counter the nature of the three beasts with the aid of three virtues: moderation, courage and wisdom. Virgil's guidance leads to self-awareness, and with self-awareness dawns the possibility of recognizing the nature of one's deeds, for through the understanding of one's deeds come redemption and the blessing of Divine Love.

The relevance of this central theme in *The Divine Comedy* provides rich opportunities for students to become free and independent thinkers as they wrestle with the many provocative ideas set forth in the story. The problems Dante presents are as fresh today as they were in his time, and his notions of forgiveness and redemption are just as fascinating now as they were to his contemporaries. Dante dares to condemn popes and sanctify heretics— the only criterion is a clear and logical case for each choice. Dante's rebellion against the established order of the day, both temporal and spiritual, offers refreshing reassurance for the student who needs to question everything and challenge the order of life.

The nature of hell as a place representing the perversion or squandering of human reason will usually provoke irresistible and productive conversation among the students. Why is it that souls are unable to be anywhere else? What did they do, or fail to do, to earn this horrible outcome? How could they have avoided their fate?

The general pattern of the *Inferno*, as well as the *Purgatorio*, can produce some fine discussion, too. Dante categorizes in detail the levels of transgressions. There are surprises here in his judgment about certain sins. He places lying and thieving in the deepest levels of hell, while violent crimes of passion he considers to be less grievous. At first glance students may disagree with this arrangement, but on further inquiry they come to see the difference between premeditated deeds and senseless aggression. The first are performed out of a perversion of consciousness, the second out of unconsciousness.

While the *Inferno* is fascinating in its horror and grotesque pictures, the main theme of the story is forgiveness and redemption. Neither can happen without the light that self-knowledge sheds on the meaning of one's own deeds. Through this recognition, a step toward Divine Love is taken, as well as a step for the greater good of the world.

Students are well aware of the corruption, crime and disintegration in the world around them and of the many questions that challenge us today. Dante gives voice to many of these, but there is room for questions that either did not exist in his time, such as environmental issues, or were not considered then in the way they are today. Often the conversation begins by dealing with fixed situations—somewhat like the scheme of the *Inferno* itself. Capital punishment, a fixed solution to a problem, always produces energetic discussion, for example. What is its purpose? What about repentance? What about redemption? Should there be punishment once there is repentance, regardless of the crime?

A discussion about repentance and forgiveness has within it many possibilities, and students can offer insights from a contemporary vantage point. The consideration of the physical body is a good place to start, for it is the sins of the she-wolf that grip the material body. For instance, the sin of gluttony affects physical health, to be sure, but more importantly, it retards the possibility for greater consciousness. Simply put, in the perfect world of paradise there is no room for earthly appetites. There is no banquet in heaven, no ham sandwiches nor ice cream, and those who desired these things would be unhappy there and would interfere with the divine order of that realm. Disengagement from earthly appetites is necessary to enter fully into the divine realm and avoid the painful result of eternal unconsciousness. Indeed, seen in this light, the inferno is not so much a place of *punishment* as it is a place of *consequences*, for without an awakening in the inner life, redemption cannot come about.

At the deeper levels of the perversion of human reason, we come to the provocative puzzle of people who do evil deeds in full consciousness. This, more than at any other time, is a vital problem today, and teachers need look no further than the daily newspaper for examples to bring to class. In the last few years, for instance, there has been a resurgence, on the one hand, of the nazi movement. On the other hand, there has been a renewed desire to find and punish nazi war criminals who are still living. In looking objectively at what to do with these old men who perpetrated some of the greatest crimes against humanity, the reaction of students who have no real connection to that period of history can be profound. They often see what the teacher has overlooked: these men do not ask for forgiveness. After fifty years they offer the same answers as their colleagues who were brought to trial in 1945: "It was not my fault, I was just following orders." "I had no choice." The connection between repentance and forgiveness is especially poignant here. How can there be healing without forgiveness? How can there be forgiveness without the admission of responsibility?

Indeed, if there is consequence for the lack of consciousness about one's deeds, then, conversely, there is consequence when repentance is sincere and heartfelt. In the natural scheme of things, forgiveness follows repentance just as dawn ends the night.

Dante allows us to discover this natural law of the human heart: repentance and forgiveness are connected, not isolated, concepts.

In Dante's scheme, awareness of the meaning of one's deeds is accompanied by instantaneous forgiveness and the purifying process begins. With this forward-moving consciousness, from which there is no turning back, disengagement from unhealthy deeds can begin. The purgatory of life—this one or the next—is necessary to achieve the state of grace offered in Dante's paradise. But why should we strive for this, especially if paradise is not a place where all appetites are fed? What is its purpose?

Paradise is a place filled with activity—a good deal of it, in fact. It is a place very much involved in the welfare of humankind, and it is here that the perfect Divine Love, only dimly imagined on earth, is felt in its fullest measure. Yet, the paradise Dante describes has its mirror on earth in those who are striving for a better world. These struggles for the good—both personal and in the greater world—serve as representatives of paradise on earth. This is a vital point for students who, quite rightly earthbound at their age, may very naturally find paradise somewhat dull for their tastes. However, they do find the notion of heavenly beings working together in a beneficent way appealing, and many good discussions can come of the concept of divine intervention in the life of human beings.

In the great trinity of *The Divine Comedy*, Dante strives to overcome dead thinking and dead forms of the past and depict with new purpose and confidence the meaning of life; he succeeds with remarkable brilliance. What Dante puts forth with such eloquence resounds in the students' inner core. Dante's journey reflects their own struggle to bring about the birth of the ego, that central core of ourselves which gradually emerges from childhood. In this birth, like all births, there is pain and disruption as well as elation and creation. In his ego-centered and ego-bearing work, Dante delivers the hope of a better life through the exercise of conscious choice and courageous individual action.

As teachers we can open up new worlds for our students by giving them well chosen works of great literature at the right time. Just as Virgil guides Dante, we can serve as guides for our students, and we may hope that we have fostered in them the confidence and imagination to found new worlds where we ourselves cannot go.

NOTE: Any curriculum that includes Dante should be sure to take up *The Divine Comedy* as a whole. All of the *Inferno* and the *Purgatorio* can be read in a relatively short time. *Paradiso* can be studied in excerpt. The scheme of the whole as well as the main point—redemption and forgiveness—is lost when only the *Inferno* is considered.

There are several good translations for classroom use. I have found that John Ciardi's translation (Mentor Books) remains the most suitable.

CHAUCER AND THE MODERN CONSCIOUSNESS

Isabel Wyatt

"Chaucer [who died in 1400 A.D.] founded English literature," wrote Rudolf Steiner in his *Letters to the Members*. To all lovers of the pre-Chaucerian peaks in that literature, this is, at first impact, a statement hard to accept. To come to terms with it, one is faced with the task of "thinking Chaucer through" again—life, letters, era, looking before and after.

Re-studied in this light, his work shows a threefold intertwining of uniquely significant strands—of speech-development, verse-form development, and the changing soul-constitution of a whole epoch condensed into one human life-span. Re-pondered in this light, his life presents an open script of destiny which one can gratefully read. Looking before and after him in this light, one can say "Yes" to Rudolf Steiner's statement, with all the more joy since those pre-Chaucerian peaks are now bathed in a new and deeper understanding.

Speech-Development

No record has yet been found of the date of Chaucer's birth; but scholars, by a unanimous conspiracy, place it in 1340. The clearer Chaucer's part in England's evolution becomes, the happier does this appear; for it was in this year that the conception of England as a united nation was first given constitutional formulation in the Abolition of Englishry.

From the Norman Conquest onwards, the laws of England had discriminated between conquerors and conquered, even when the two races were already fast fusing. To this fusion the Abolition of Englishry now gave legal recognition and assent. From 1340 there were no longer Norman English and Saxon English; from 1340 there were only the true-born English.

But these English lacked as yet a common mother-tongue.

To a stubbornly Anglo-Saxon-speaking England, the Norman Conquest had brought Norman-French as the language of King's Court, Law Court, new aristocracy, clergy, Parliament, school and snob. In 1307, two and a half centuries later, the native chronicler is still lamenting that "children in school, against the usage and manner of all other nations, be compelled for to construe their lessons in French, and so have since Normans first came to England. Also, gentlemen's children be taught for to speak French from the time that they be rocked in their cradle; and uplandish men will fondle with great busyness for to speak French, for to be told of."

But by the thirties of that century, with the rapid fusing of Norman and English elements, and the consequent emergence of a new national consciousness, French is already beginning to be regarded as a foreign tongue, so that it is purely as the language of chivalry that it is supported by a Statute of 1334: "Ordained that all barons, knights, lords, and honorable men of good towns should be careful and diligent to teach and instruct their children in the French tongue, *whereby they might be the more skilful and practised in their wars.*"

Six years later, the Abolition of Englishry begins the chasing of the alien tongue out of office in one department after another of England's domestic life—in 1349, from the schools; in 1356, from the Law Courts; in 1362, from Parliamentary debates. So far does the pendulum swing that in 1385 Trevisa records that schoolboys now "do know no more French than their left heel," while in 1404 (Trevisa's schoolboys being now grown men), two well-born ambassadors to the French Court itself announce with complacent insularity: "We be as ignorant of French as of Hebrew."

But when English thus began to come into its own, there was really as yet no such thing as English. There were only regional dialects, descended from the four basic Anglo-Saxon variants shaped in Kent by the Jutes, in Wessex by the Saxons, in Mercia and Northumbria by the Angles. The Saxons' English of the West, now with its faint seasoning of Celtic; the Angles' English of the North, now strongly impregnated with Norse; the Jutes' English of London and the East-Midlands, now even more strongly impregnated with Danish and with stronger infiltrations of Norman-French than the rest of England—these vernaculars were scarcely intelligible to one another.

Yet each had its own literature, and each of these literatures had its own masterpieces. At the time Chaucer was writing in the London-East-Midland dialect, the Northern dialect produced the Chester, York and Townley Miracle-Plays; the North-West-Midland, *Sir Gawayne and the Green Knight,* and the exquisite *Pearl;* the South-West-Midland, *Winner and Wastour,* and, most famous of all, *Piers Plowman.*

All these have a high seriousness far beyond Chaucer's reach. But (as we shall see) they are written out of the declining splendors of the past, while Chaucer writes out of the birth-pangs of the future. So, in the generations that follow, these other English dialects slowly shrivel into non-literary folk-speech; while the dialect which Chaucer shapes as the instrument of the new impulse becomes the matrix of a new literary English, no longer merely regional, but national.

In this realm of language-making, Chaucer wrought miracles. But they were miracles born of tireless and devoted labor— "the lyf so short, the craft so long to learne." And first he quickened in himself a heightened scope and sensitivity in the sphere of the word by his long, self-imposed discipline in the making of translation after translation out of Latin, French, Italian.

For with Chaucer each translation was at the same time a new creation. His way of translating was the way indicated by Rudolf Steiner—a dissolving, an assimilating, a re-creating—so that his translations frequently achieve a stature and are fired by a fervor beyond those of their originals.

By these arduous but rewarding means he grows into a skilled and conscious alchemist in speech, so mingling its subtle substances as to bring about new precipitations; in his translations out of the Romance languages, bringing over the graces of these tongues to make his own more dextrous and flexible.

He is acutely aware that

> In Loreyne their notës be
> Full sweeter than in this countree.

So into the sturdy strength of the one he infuses the sweetness of the other. Already, in his first full-length translation, *The Romaunt of the Rose*, he teaches the point and charm of Old French and the vigor and forthrightness of Middle English (London-East-Midland vintage) to look with love on one another.

As the eagle notes of him in *The Hous of Fame:*

> Thou wilt make
> A-night ful oft thy head to ache,
> In thy study so thou writest....
> ...Dumb as any stone,
> Thou sittest at another book,
> Till fully dazèd is thy look.

So, out of "my bookes and my devotioun," grows the new English language.

He takes the weighty formlessness of the English he finds ready to his hand, and he gives it form and buoyancy, bending for the first time to "worldly vanities"—sparkling cascades of balades, roundels and virelays, many of which now live only in his delighted contemporaries' praise of them—the solemn speech hitherto moulded by religious vision, heroic saga and theological debate.

As he himself, and with him his poetry, grows beyond these "worldly vanities," and deepens and matures, his new English is continuously being fashioned into an ever more lucid, shapely and obedient vehicle, till he gives to it so catholic a compass that it can unfold the coarse humor of the Miller's Tale side by side with the exquisite pathos of the Prioress's; the Wife of Bath's savoring of life well-nigh gastronomic,

> But lord Christ! When that it remembreth me
> Upon my youth, and on my jollity,
> It tickleth me about my heartë-root.
> Unto this day it doth my heartë boot [good, benefit]
> That I have had my world as in my time! —

side by side with his own delicate delight in spring,

> Upon the smallë, softë, sweetë grass,
> That was with flowrës sweet embroidered all,
> A wind so small it scarcely might be less
> Made in the leavës green a noisë soft,
> Accordant to the fowlës song aloft —

and this in turn side by side with the stark horror of the Temple of Mars in the Knight's Tale,

> The smiler with the knife under the cloke;
> The shepnë burning with the blackë smoke;
> The slayer of himself yet saw I there;
> His heartë-blood hath bathëd all his hair.
> The nail y'driven in the shode a-night;
> The coldë death, with mouth gaping upright;
> The carter over-ridden with his cart —

and the heavy doom of Saturn's pronouncement,

> My looking is the father of pestilènce —

side by side with the moving simplicity of Griselda's piety,

> But high God sometime senden can
> His grace into a little ox's stall.

Pre-Chaucerian English literature (and, indeed, the literature of the other English dialects in his own day), with all its capacity for achieving sublimity, nevertheless wielded language clumsily, ponderously, as a mighty but intractable instrument. But into his own new-forged English, Chaucer's meaning slipped and fitted and was as entirely at home as hand is in glove. He makes his new English like all that his own Clerk spoke:

> Short, and quick, and full of high sentènce [meaning].

Thus he creates something entirely new in the history of English—the succinct phrase; as when he says of his Sergeant of Law,

> Nowhere so busy a man in any case,
> And yet he seemèd busier than he was;

or of his Doctor of Physick,

> For gold in physick is a cordial;
> Therefore he lovedë gold in speci̇al;

or of his Parson,

> Christë's lore, and his apostles' twelve,
> He taught, and first he followed it himselve;

or of his Knight,

And though that he was worthy, he was wise;

or of his Clerk,

And gladly would he learn, and gladly teach.

This new terse pithiness, later to come to be regarded as typical of English, was so immense an innovation that it sent the mediaeval world wild with delight. His contemporaries continually marvel at what they so rightly describe as the "golden dewdrops" of Chaucer's speech.

This, then, was the new "Englisshe tunge" in which, in 1399, an English king (Henry IV) claimed his crown at his coronation for the first time in history. Thus Chaucer's creation in the realm of speech became, in the year before his own death, in literal fact the King's English, gradually to supersede all other English variants and become the common mother-tongue of England's now-fused races.

What does it mean when races fuse to the point of achieving a common mother-tongue?

It means nothing less than that, invisibly directing the labors of Chaucers on the Earth, a spiritual Being of the rank of Archangel has been working at the fashioning of a language to be the emerging nation's own. For it is at this point that a nation receives its own Folk-Spirit, who can be, as it were, a body for that Archangel in his spiritual guidance of the nation towards, and in, its earthly tasks.

During that first long period of rebellious subjection to their Norman conquerors, the Anglo-Saxons had looked back nostalgically to their own last, holy king, Edward the Confessor. As the Archangel Michael was patron saint to the Normans, so Edward was to them.

Meanwhile, thirty-three years (a significant rhythm) after the Norman Conquest, the First Crusaders had found in the Holy Land a heavenly helper in St. George, whom Coeur-de-Lion brought back to England a century later, as patron of his Norman-English soldiery.

A further century and a half later, the precise moment is recorded when St. Edward relinquishes to St. George his "cure" of the whole English populace. Thomas of Washingham tells us that in 1349 (when Geoffrey Chaucer and the Abolition of Englishry were nine years old), Edward IV, besieging Calais, "drew his sword, and cried with ardour, *ha, St. Edward! Ha, St. George!*, and fell with vigour on the French, and so defeated them." It is as if, in this historic exclamation, the two saints—the one whose day as Anglo-Saxon patron saint was setting, the other whose day as patron saint of the new united England was dawning—met and embraced in passing.

It was in this same year that England's "litel clergeouns" were first given leave to construe their lessons in English. So we see English language and English spiritual leader preparing together to take up their coming destiny. By the time the new epoch dawned in 1413, St. George's leadership was consciously and enthusiastically accepted by the new English people; and Chaucer had fashioned and bequeathed to that people its own new language. It is in the service of St. George, and of the new epoch in which England is to take up her earthly task, that Chaucer toils to make of himself, in Spenser's words, a "well of English undefiled."

Verse-Form Development

That Chaucer is, in Dryden's famous phrase, "the Father of English Poetry," and this at a deeper level than ever Dryden dreamed, becomes clear when we study his verse-forms.

When, at the close of the *Canterbury Tales*, the Parson is asked to tell the pilgrims a story, he begins by excusing himself,

> I am a southern man;
> I cannot geste run, ram, ruf, by letter.

It might have been Chaucer himself speaking. For while the other dialects still continued to "geste run, ram, ruf, by letter," as Anglo-Saxon before them had done (*Piers Plowman, Winner and Wastour, Pearl, Sir Gawayne and the Green Knight, Morte Arthure, Auntyrs of Arthure at the Tarn,* and all else written in the rest of England in this century, still used the verse-form of alliteration), only the London-East-Midland dialect, the dialect of the southeast, had embarked, under Chaucer's leadership, on end-rhyme.

This is a small straw that is literally an epoch-making symptom. For alliteration and end-rhyme are marks of two entirely different states of consciousness, of two entirely different cultures.

According to Rudolf Steiner,

> The time in which the Intellectual Soul arose in man in the fourth post-Atlantean period is also the time when in poetry the memory dawned of the experience of the olden times which still extended into the ancient Imaginative world. This remembrance was expressed in the end-rhyme.

> On the other hand, all wherein the culture of this fourth post-Atlantean period had absorbed Christianity and the after-effects of the Mystery of Golgotha, had undergone quite special revival; and that into which it was poured was the European Sentient Soul. In Europe the culture of the Sentient Soul had waited in a backward state for a higher culture, an Intellectual Soul culture which arose in Central and Southern Europe, in order that what was accomplished in Central and Southern Europe might enter into the ancient Sentient Soul culture and all that it contained as strength and energy of the will.

> Therefore we see that in everything that is under the influence of southern culture, the final rhyme is quite regularly

developed in poetry; while in the Will-culture that received Christianity, alliteration is the correct expression. The Sentient Soul experienced the old Imaginations in alliteration; the Intellectual Soul in the end-rhyme.

Right through and almost to the end of the fourth post-Atlantean period, the epoch of the Intellectual Soul (747 B.C. to 1413 A.D.), the culture of England had remained within the orbit of the Sentient Soul. Old and Middle English alliterative literature bears the imprint of the Sentient Soul's working-over of the after-effects of Golgotha in its innocent holiness; its atmosphere of something held back and untouched by the world; its naïve, dedicated and profoundly Christian piety; its massive pre-occupation with morality and religion.

In 1066 the Norman Conquest had brought the French Intellectual Soul across the Channel. But as long as French remained a conqueror's language, and the discrimination between conquered and conqueror continued, the held-back English Sentient Soul remained reluctant to open itself to the influx of the culture proper to the period. It was not until conqueror and conquered were formally united into a new nation, and the ascendancy of French as an arbitrarily imposed language had declined, that Chaucer was able to bring over into the fundamentally religious literature of England the courtly culture for which French provided the language-body.

It was not that the Continent did not also produce religious poetry. But while England is writing *Saint's Lives, The Moral Ode, Homilies, The Song of Genesis and Exodus, Kentish Sermons, The Harrowing of Hell, Festae Christi* (the Sunday Gospels), *Liber Festivalis* (the Sunday Gospels together with legendary poetry), *Cursor Mundi* (a blending of Scriptural history with mediaeval legends), *The Pricke of Conscience, The Ayenbite of Inwit* (The Remorse of Conscience), and the edifying stories in *Handlyng Sinne,* the Continent's religious poetry (apart from such blazing stars as *The Divine Comedy*) is couched in the idiom of the current "courtesie," as in the *Hymn to the Virgin* translated by Chaucer:

> Now, Ladye brightë, sith thou canst and wilt
> Ben to the seed of Adam merciáble,
> So bring us to that palais that is built
> To penitents that ben to mercy àble.

While, in France and Italy, the Intellectual Soul is experiencing troubadours and Courts of Love, and love of a lady and love of Our Lady are twin roses on one stem, in England the Sentient Soul is acclaiming as a classic a book of discipline for anchoresses (*The Ancrene Rewle*), and seeking for Christ in man in the person of Piers the Plowman.

Where exceptions to this verse-form of alliteration occur before Chaucer, or outside his region in his own day, they prove on examination to be non-indigenous. The Metrical Chronicles, for example, were a fashion imported from France; and their native end-rhyme was imported as part and parcel of the fashion. The Rhyming Romances, such as *Havelok the Dane, Sir Tristrem,* and *King Horn,* were transcriptions from the French, and as such kept their native verse-form. There were translated lyrics that retained the stanza-forms of their Old French and Provençal originals. But always these verse-forms were imitated, not absorbed—a breath blown from a rose-tree growing across the sea, its scent no sooner savored than spent. But Chaucer's spade-work bodily transplants the rose-tree, to mingle its roots with those of England's oaks.

For with the new English tongue's assimilation of end-rhyme, alliteration did not die. It still blows through English poetry. It still points the pith of our proverbs. Something still flashes up in the soul-depths of the English when alliteration strikes their ears.

But alliteration as we use it today is only the pale and leaf-light ghost of the Thor's-hammer-beat in the pounding of the blood of Sentient Soul poetry, with its four strong stresses in each long line,

the first three at least of the stresses rigidly alliterative, as thus, in
Piers Plowman:

> Charity is a child-like thing, as holy Church
> witnesseth,
> As proud of a penny as of a pound of gold,
> And all so glad of a gown of grey russet
> As of a coat of damask or of clean scarlet.
> He is glad with all glad, as girls that
> laughen all,
> And sorry when he seeth men sorry, as
> thou seest children
> Laugh when men laughen and lower when
> men lowren.

Langland, here, writing in the fourteenth century, could still be
contemporary with Cynewulf, writing in the eighth. In Langland's

> Till I waxed weary of this world and willed
> oft to sleep

pulses the same weighty heart as in Cynewulf's

> Friendship' twixt friends forever without feud,

or

> I am redder on Rood than rose in the rain.

But the amazing thing is that while Langland's alliteration, and
indeed that of all the rest of England, is looking six centuries back-
ward, that of Chaucer is leaping six centuries forward. Already he
is using alliteration in a completely modern way, lightly, freely,
sparsely, no longer with its Will-culture clang as of a marching
army, but with the charm of a grace-note. His description of the
young wife Alisoun:

Her mouth was sweet as bragor or the meeth,
Or hoard of apples laid in hay or heath,

is as twentieth-century in its alliteration as, for example, Wilfred Owen's

Red lips are not so red
As the stained stones kissed by the English dead.
Kindness of wooed and wooer
Seems shame to their love pure.
O Love, your eyes lose lure
When I behold eyes blinded in my stead.

Chaucer can even use alliteration with modern levity. His description of Sir Mirth:

With meetly mouth and eyen grey,
His nose by measure wrought full right, —

or of Simkin's wife:

She was as digne as water in a ditch —

or his roguish

Nat wot I well wher [whether] that I wink or wake

breathes the same bland air as Masefield's

We're neither saint nor Philip Sidneys,

or

I look on martyrs as mistakes,

or T. S. Eliot's

> Violet hour, the evening hour that strives
> Homeward, and brings the sailor home from sea,
> The typist home at tea-time.

Where humor is the hand-maid of religion, a Sentient Soul writer will occasionally use an alliterative phrase with a twinkle, as when the shepherd in the Wakefield Plays says of his wife that she is "browed like a bristle." But to use it so at his own whimsy, as Chaucer does, would savor to him of sacrilege. For alliteration as a verse-form still carried reverberations of its origin in a stormy Nature-speech that brought the Northern forefathers of the Anglo-Saxons into connection with the divine, so that in the wind-storm they saw Wotan whirl, in the thunderstorm heard Thor's hammer thrown, and in the storm of battle felt their war-god Zui come to their aid, when, in Rudolf Steiner's words, "they stormed forward in closed ranks, yelling with a thousand throats into their shields, *Zui zwingt Zwist* -[Zui wages war]."

Seen against this cosmic background, Chaucer's overnight gift of leavening alliteration with fun takes on the air of an archetypal gesture, epitomizing all the earthward-leading aspects of his task.

So into this segregated, strongly pious, strongly alliterative island-culture, Chaucer brings the Continental culture of the end-rhyme, making the breach through which Intellectual Soul can pour into Sentient Soul. And in his own progressive use of various rhyming verse-forms can be traced the path both of his own development and of his preparation of English poetry to reach through the Intellectual Soul to the Consciousness Soul beyond.

His first experiments, those slight and charming love-lilts with which he lightens and brightens Middle English sobriety, are a prelude to the dancing measure of the octo-syllabic couplets of *The Romaunt of the Rose:*

Then mightest thou carolës seen,
And folk there dance and merry been.
And makë many a fair turnìng,
Upon the greenë grassë spring.
Then mightest thou see there flutours,
Minstrels and eke jongëlours,
That well to singës did them pain.
Some sang songë of Loreyne;
For in Loreyne their notës be
Full sweeter than in this countree.

These "sweeter notes" of this "carolling" meter, which here so
gaily sing themselves, sing again, but more poignantly, in the *Book
of the Duchess,* and yet again, now a little staider with ironic
thought, in the *Hous of Fame.* Then, in the *Parliament of Fowls* and
in *Troilus and Criseyde,* the lighthearted dancing measure, with its
simple end-rhyme, is discarded for the longer, graver measure and
dextrous interlacing of the seven-line stanza of rhyme royal.
Rhyme royal was a stock stanza-form of the "minstrels and eke
jongelours" of the Continent; but into Chaucer's manipulation of
it the usage of the future is already projected, so that it plays on the
strings of the soul in a new way. The inscription on the enchanted
gate in the *Parliament of Fowls:*

Through me men go into that blissful place
Of heartës heal and deadly woundës cure;
Through me men go unto the well of Grace,
Where green and lusty May shall ever endure.
This is the way to all good aventùre.
Be glad, thou reader, and thy sorrow off-cast.
All open am I; pass in, and hie thee fast!

belongs, in this respect of poetic impact, less to the mediaeval climate than to Masefield's

Then in the sunset's flush they went aloft,
And unbent sails in that most lovely hour
When the light gentles, and the wind is soft,
And beauty in the heart breaks like a flower.
Working aloft, they saw the mountain tower,
Snow to the peak; they heard the launchmen
 shout;
And bright along the bay the lights came out.

And now, in the *Legend of Good Women*, Chaucer passes on to a measure which, largely restricted in mediaeval times to the Rhyming Chronicles and Metrical Romances, came into its own with the eighteenth century's Age of Reason, to whose precise and lucid gifts it was so admirably adapted—the heroic couplet. In this, his first essay in it, it still has dew on it, as in its description of the birds pairing in spring:

Upon the branches, full of blossoms soft,
In their delight they turnèd them full oft,
And sangen, "Blessèd be Saint Valentine!
For on his day I choose you to be mine,
Withoutë repentìng, mine heartë sweet!"
And therewithal their beakës 'gonnen meet.

But when he uses it again, in the framework of his last, greatest and most famous work, the *Canterbury Tales*, the dew is gone from it, and it is like the miller in the nursery-rhyme—"Dusty was his coat, dusty was his colour, dusty was the kiss I got from the miller"—

Befell that, in that season on a day,
In Southwerk at the Tabard as I lay,
Ready to wenden on my pilgrimàge
To Canterbury with full devout couràge,

201

> At night was come into that hostelry
> Well nine and twenty in a company,
> Of sundry folk, by aventùre y-fall
> In fellowship; and pilgrims were they all.

To move from Sentient Soul into Intellectual Soul is to come a stage more deeply into incarnation. Middle English alliterative literature has a richer, deeper spirituality than has Chaucer; but it does not permeate outer life and the earth itself as he begins to do. It was Chaucer's task to lead that literature earthwards.

In his progress from rhyme-scheme to rhyme-scheme, we can see this earthward direction operating in the realm of verse-form—from the delicate wing-flutterings and bird-trills of the balades and roundels, quite off the earth; through the carolling of *The Romaunt of the Rose,* dancing on the earth, and the gradual sobering of this lilting measure in the *Book of the Duchess* and the *Hous of Fame;* again through the still sedater but more subtly interwoven rhyme royal in the *Legend of Good Women,* growing weightier with thought and losing a little of its music in *Troilus and Criseyde;* and so to the heroic couplet, poetic still in the *Parliament of Fowls,* but in the Prologue and the end-links of the *Canterbury Tales* coming within hailing distance of the qualities of prose.

Chaucer's poetry begins where poetry used to dwell—in the realm of song, even of dancing song. It ends where poetry dwells today—in the realm of prose, even of conversational prose. He sets out on his poet's pilgrimage as full of courtly springtime graces as his own young Squire:

> Embroidered was he as it were a mead
> All full of freshë flowrës white and red.
> Singing he was, or fluting, all the day.
> He was as fresh as is the month of May.

He ends it imbued with such modern down-to-earth naturalness that the oaths and curses of the Miller and Harry Bayley in the *Canterbury Tales* are as authentically grist to his poetic mill as in our own day oaths and curses are to Masefield in *The Everlasting Mercy* or to T. S. Eliot in *Sweeney Agonistes*.

Changing Soul-Constitution

The content of Chaucer's poetry goes hand-in-hand with his verse-forms in this earthward development. For in mood of soul, also, he sets out in the Middle Ages and ends as our contemporary.

In his first charming lyrics, so true a devoté is he to the courtly conventions of mediaeval *amour courtois* that he wins in France the title of "King of Worldly Love in Albion." It is, indeed, this "Courtesy" that beckons him into the poetic dance:

> A lady 'gan me for to espy:
> And she was clepèd Courtesy,
> The worshipful, the debonair.
> I pray God ever fall her fair!
> Full courteously she callèd me.
> "What do ye there, beau sire?" quoth she
> "Come near; and if it likë you
> To dancen, danceth with us now."
> And I, withoutë tarrying,
> Went into the carolling!

So *The Romaunt of the Rose* begins in this same courtly tradition—a dream-vision of a soul-quest dried into an allegory of "worldly love," all the characters' personifications—Friend, Youth, Sir Mirth, Amour, Idleness, False-Semblant, Pope-Holy, Reason. And significantly, Reason it is who breaks away from the true soul-quest ending, querying, already in this first courtly poem of any length, whether the original quest,

> For to get and have the Rose,

is really worth the striving.

The *Book of the Duchess* is still mediaeval, in that it is still an allegory, still a dream-vision, still peopled with personifications. Yet its tenderness and poignancy are such that already a breath—the first in Chaucer; possibly the first in all mediaeval literature—of real life blows through it. It is an elegy on the death of Blanche, John of Gaunt's young first wife, who died in the great pestilence in September 1369; so that already, before he is thirty, in this, his first original poem of any stature, Chaucer has sounded a new personal note of reality and glimpsed a new sincerity. The powers of evocation of the lover, recalling the dead girl's loveliness —

> I saw her dance so comelily,
> Carol and sing so sweetëly,
> Laugh and play so womanly,
> And look so debonaïrly —

are so strong that it is as if she had never died—

> For be it never so dark,
> Me think'th I see her evermore.

The large humanity of the Chaucer of a later stage is already here in its first germ.

In the *Hous of Fame*, a further attribute of the maturer Chaucer makes its first sustained appearance; the whole poem is conceived in a mood of indulgent irony. It is still a dream. It is still in a sense an allegory. Yet it is already distant by half an epoch from the rose-gardens of courtly romance. Chaucer is haled to the House of Fame in the talons of a learned eagle, "hent up between his toes."

> The hallë was all full, y-wis,
> Of them that writen oldë gestes
> As be on treës rookës nests.

And here he contemplates with humor the follies perpetrated by those who "would fain han had a fame," relating the whole dream in a vein of pseudo-serious burlesque already more modern than mediaeval, and leaving us free to

Take it in earnest or in game.

The charming St. Valentine's Day poem, *The Parliament of Fowls*, is a wedding song (written to celebrate the marriage of Richard II); and as such recaptures something of Chaucer's earlier freshness, music and young delight in spring:

Now welcome, summer, with thy sunnë soft,
That hast this winter's weathers over-shake,
And driven away the longë nightës black!
Saint Valentine, that art full high aloft,
Thus singen smallë fowlës for thy sake:

Now welcome, summer, with thy sunë soft,
That hast this winter's weathers over-shake.

Well han they causë for to gladden oft,
Sith each of them recovered hath his make [mate].
Full blissful may they singen when they wake:
Now welcome, summer, with thy sunë soft,
That hast this winter's weather over-shake,
And driven away the longë nightës black.

Fantasia though it is, with every sort of folk-fable about bird and beast woven into its bright fabric, it is also already like a slender forecast, transposed into the world of birds, of the pageant and clash of human personalities yet to come in the *Canterbury Tales*, already as shrewdly and indulgently observed, already as faithfully and buxomly reported.

The framework of *Troilus and Criseyde* is still that of a courtly romance, in the manner of the current popular mediaevalizations of classical stories. But dream-vision, allegory, personification have disappeared; and the stiff lay figures derived from them begin to stir and come to life. Criseyde ceases to be a charming idealization, and takes on human flesh; while Pandarus leaps to life in a burst of vigorous realism that is an unprecedented miracle. The still daintily embroidered tale is riven here and there by a common light of day utterly new in mediaeval literature, as when Criseyde calls Pandarus in to dinner:

> Wherewith she laughed, and saidë, "Go we dine."
> And he 'gan at himself to japë fast.
> And saidë, "Niece, I have so great a pine
> For love that every other day I fast" —
> And 'gan his bestë japës forth to cast.
> And made her so to laugh at his folly
> That she for laughter wendë for to die.

The *Legend of Good Women's* prologue, in which the god of love arraigns him for making Criseyde unfaithful, and in which Alceste intercedes for him, is the last of Chaucer's dream-visions. The legends themselves, which Chaucer undertakes to tell in recompense for his discourtesy to love and Criseyde, are about famous women.

> And true to love these women were each one.

As he tells them, Chaucer grows under one's very eyes in humor, realism, dramatic power and human feeling. Eventually he breaks off in the middle of a story, as if impatient to have done with legendary women, and to set to work at painting real people in real life.

And so, at last, comes the crown of all this development—the *Canterbury Tales*, no longer a dream-vision, but an acutely observed contemporary scene; no longer an allegory, but a drawing from life; its *dramatis personae* no longer personifications, but real, ordinary flesh-and-blood people of his day, who yet, in their diversity, are universal. The other end—our end—of Chaucer's progress from the stylized conventions of "courtesy" has been reached. He has stepped right out of the enclosed lovers' gardens of mediaeval romance into the actual world; and with his pilgrims he travels into that future which is our present along the high-road of a realism completely modern.

Something of the incredible innovation here achieved emerges if we compare the *Canterbury Tales* with a similar mediaeval collection of stories, some of which, indeed, Chaucer annexed—Boccaccio's *Decameron.* Boccaccio died when Chaucer was thirty-five. Yet the two collections give the impression of being the fruits of different epochs.

Boccaccio's framework is a group of young lords and ladies, very faintly characterized, who have fled from the city to avoid the plague, and who spend their time in graceful idleness within their walled garden, telling Boccaccio's stories to enliven their *ennui.* But Chaucer has set a great company, all real people, and of all classes, knowledgeably observed and vividly reported, riding with a certain saucy cheerfulness through the actual English landscape.

Here we have the beginning of that verbal portrait-painting in which, in drama, character-novel and *vers nouvelle,* later English literature was to excel. We see that Dryden tells us only a fraction of the truth when he calls Chaucer the Father of English *poetry*— that, as Rudolf Steiner says, it is English *literature*, in all its various later aspects, that Chaucer founded.

What, in actual fact, has Chaucer done? He has himself passed, taking English literature with him, out of the mediaeval world and into the modern world. We can see in Chaucer the birth of our modern language and our modern poetry, as well as our modern soul-constitution. He has overleapt the generations between, and already attained a robust handling of the robust human plane belonging to a state of consciousness for the preparation of which England had scarcely yet been separated out from France at the time of his birth.

For when Chaucer was born, the leopards were still quartered with the lilies. From the Norman period onwards, by marriage, inheritance, conquest, great possessions in France had come to England, and the beings of France and England had become strongly interwoven. One could even say that England, while holding at arm's length the cultural dower which France could offer her, tried in its place to wrest from her a territorial one.

It was a necessity of evolution that they should be disentangled, and go their separate ways. Within their entanglement, by fits and starts, a kind of internecine warfare had long been raging; and in 1339 (the year before Chaucer's birth), there had begun in earnest that Hundred Year's War which was to end in Joan of Arc's releasing them from each other's bonds, that each might turn to the differentiated tasks of a new era.

While France turned to the working-over, with a more modern consciousness and in further evolved conditions, of the fruits of the epoch of the Intellectual Soul, then just ended, England turned to the integrating into the human soul-constitution of an impulse quite new in history—that of the Consciousness Soul.

What does it mean to achieve the Consciousness Soul? To incarnate for the first time so fully into the mineral body as to become an island, withdrawn in isolation; through that island-quality to approach human beings from the outside, experiencing other souls as severed entities, respecting their personalities, and thus acquiring the spectator qualities of tolerance, moderation, balance; to develop, together with a certain staidness and reserve, a faculty of objective observation, and sharpened sense-perceptions; to gather practical expertise in the handling of the things of the earth—this is to live within the Consciousness Soul as we know it in our day.

This, also—and it bursts upon the mind with the force of a revelation—is to be Chaucer. This is to live within the Consciousness

Soul when its own recapitulations of Sentient Soul (the Elizabethans) and Intellectual Soul (the Age of Reason) are over. This is to be Chaucer when French period and Italian period are behind him, and his third and greatest English period begins.

Those twelve years in the prime of his maturity, when he lived in one of London's gatehouses, and there wrote the larger part of his more native works, are themselves like a little picture of this third state of the Consciousness Soul. He could at will become an island, for he lived in the tower over Aldgate, whose very position imaged forth a state of balance, windows on one side looking inwards into the city, windows opposite looking out upon the countryside. Here he could retire into himself to study and write in quietude when, as Jove's eagle comments,

> thy labour done all is,
> And hast y-made thy reckonings —

in other words, when his day's work at the counting-house was over.

For Chaucer, in his English period, was a modern man even to the point of being a businessman, going daily to his office in the City. His post of Comptroller of Customs and Subsidies (what a contemporary sound that has!) carried with it the condition of regular attendance at his office in the Port of London, and of writing the rolls with his own hand. The fact that on occasion he called out the Revenue "cutter" and himself chased and captured a wool-smuggling ship suggests that he was capable of carrying his controlling of customs to very active and effective lengths.

Further, he busied himself with public affairs in a thoroughly modern way, as Justice of the Peace playing his part in what was to become that typically English local dispensing of the law by amateur magistrates, and as Member of Parliament in the typically English system of government based on the ideal of reciprocal understanding among individual human beings.

We see him in the isolation of the island-tower personality in
the eagle's indictment of him in the *Hous of Fame*:

> But of thy very neighëbors,
> That dwellen almost at thy doors.
> Thou hearest neither that nor this,

and in the Host's in the *Canterbury Tales*:

> And unto no wight doth he dalliance.

But though he screens it by his modest mien and downcast
glance, out from that island-tower the shrewdest eye in the whole
of English literature is turned upon the world.

Sharpened sense-perception is already stirring in him that
delight in Nature's minuter miracles which was to distinguish the
English poetry of the Consciousness Soul. Chaucer's daisy, for
example, is the first flower in English literature to be not merely
used symbolically or decoratively or to play some formal, graceful
part in dream or allegory, but to be lovingly contemplated for its
own sweet sake:

> Of all the flowrës in the mead,
> Then love I most these flowrës white and red
> Such as men callen daisies in our town.
> To them I have so great affectïoun,
> As I said erst, when comen is the May,
> That in my bed there dawneth me no day
> But I am up, and walking in the mead,
> To see this flower against the sunnë spread.

Nor are his sharpened sense-perception and objective observation turned only upon Nature. They register human nature with the
same fidelity. This, his sense of other human beings as personalities

and an absorbing interest in them, combines with his gift of phrase-making to produce an endless gallery of delectable vignettes of real people—the ponderous Merchant, with his forkèd beard and his mind set, even on pilgrimage, upon his "winnings;" the lean Clerk, with threadbare cloak and horse like a rake, to whom scholarship was his whole life, who

> busily 'gan for the soulës pray
> Of those that gave him money to scolay;

the Franklin, florid of face and white of beard, so great a gourmand that

> It snowèd in his house of meat and drink;

Perkin Revelour, the London apprentice in the Cook's fragmentary Tale —

> Gaillard he was as goldfinch in the shaw,
> Brown as a berry, a proper short felaw;

Absolon, the Miller's Parish Clerk —

> Curled was his hair, and as the gold it shone.
> In twenty manners could he trip and dance
> (After the School of Oxenfordë, though),
> And with his leggës casten to and fro.

The foibles of one and all lie uncovered before him. He paints them all with the same faithful impartiality, even the villainous black-browed Summoner, with a garland on his head above "the knobbës sitting on his cheeks;" the worldly, self-indulgent Monk:

> He was a lord full fat and in good point;

211

the crafty Pardoner, extorting money from the pious for "reliques" which were merely "piggës bones;" the ribald, thieving, quarrelling Miller, with his squealing bagpipe and his songs "of sin and harlotries."

These true-to-life thumb-nail sketches are a far, far cry from the stiff and artificial personifications of *The Romaunt of the Rose*. And from the moral judgments implicit in personification it is an equally far cry to this large, calm, genial, unexasperated and uncensuring humanity. For never is there any chastising word, but only a wise, shrewd, judgment-withholding characterization. This ability to portray individual personalities is itself startlingly new; but the onlooker objectivity of the accompanying absence of moral stricture is epoch-making. It is already Shakespeare five generations beforehand.

Because of this quite un-mediaeval objectivity, Chaucer can do something quite new in English literature—he can look at himself from outside; he can even laugh at himself, as when the eagle, toiling skyward with Chaucer's round frame between his toes, exclaims

Saint Marie!
Thou are noyous [troublesome] for to carry!

or when the Host of the Tabard Inn rallies him on his self-effacing reserve and his portly figure:

And then at erst he lookëd upon me,
And saidë thus: "What man art thou?" quoth he.
"Thou lookest as thou wouldest find a hare,
For ever upon the ground I see thee stare.
Approachë near, and look up merrily.
Now ware you, sirs, and let this man have place.
He in the waist is shape as well as I;
This were a poppet, in an arm to embrace,
For any woman, small and fair of face!"

212

or when the man of Law, finding himself "right now of talës desolate" when his turn comes round to entertain the pilgrims, expostulates:

> But Chaucer, though he can but lewëdly
> On metres and on rhyming craftily,
> Hath said them in such English as he can
> Of oldë time, as knoweth many a man.
> And if he have not said them, levë [dear] brother,
> In one book, he hath said them in another.
> Why should I tellen them, since they ben told?

So much indeed of our own kind is Chaucer's mature soul-constitution that when we regard him attentively he has the appearance of someone belonging to the England of the present who has been set down in its past. We feel that not only did he shape the language of the Consciousness Soul; that not only did he found its literature; but that this soul itself is already working in him. In the words of Rudolf Steiner:

> There were persons [in the Middle Ages] in whom the very essence of the Consciousness Soul shot forth its brightest rays; who, by the constitution of their souls, were united to the Michael-Forces with a strength which for others would only come centuries later—individualities such as Huss, Wyclif and others came on the scene.

Among these "others" we may surely number Chaucer.

Life

Jove's golden eagle, flying to the House of Fame, philosophizes to the portly poet hanging from his claws:

Geoffrey, thou wottest right well this,
That every kindly [natural] thing that is
Hath a kindly stead where he
May best in it conservèd be:
Unto which placë every thing,
Through his kindly ènclining,
Moveth for to comë to.

When we review Chaucer's life in the light of the tasks he came to earth to perform, we receive the most powerful impression of everything in it, with the most natural inevitability, "moving for to comë to" its appointed place. We become aware of a higher wisdom shaping his ends, and bringing him just those life-experiences needed to educate and equip him for his great destiny.

In these days of universal literacy and of a plethora of reading-matter pouring daily from the printing presses, it is easy for us to overlook the fact that for a fourteenth-century layman Chaucer was a quite exceptionally learned man, with a love of books and a hunger to "scolay" equal to his own poor Clerk of Oxenford's. When one reflects that his task was the blending of the culture of the developed Intellectual Soul of the Continent with the culture of the cloistered Sentient Soul of England, that out of this union the Consciousness Soul might arise, one realizes how essential a qualification for this task such learning was.

And one marvels as one traces out how from the first this essential qualification was prepared for. In this context, his very birthplace becomes the happiest of inspirations. For he was born in London, in the quarter of the Merchant Vintners of Gascoyne. Within the Merchant Vintry, Gascon and Genoese colonies lived side by side with the English master-vintners. So Chaucer grew up naturally tri-lingual, speaking French of the first, the Italian of the second, and the London-East-Midland English of the third. Thus already in childhood he had received the languages which were to be the speech-instruments of his task. Moreover, his acquisition of Latin, the mediaeval key to classical scholarship, was thus enabled to proceed unimpeded by the vicissitudes of French and English in the schools, since he could "construe his lessons" with equal ease in either.

In this period before the invention of printing, poets of the courtly convention had still this in common with the minstrels and harpers who were their predecessors, that their poetry was written to be sung or spoken before leisured and cultivated audiences in courts and castles. Again, we find Destiny pre-arranging, through his father's Court connections, a familiarity with such society for the adolescent Chaucer.

His introduction to the princes who will one day foster his art as patrons is as a page at the court of the Countess of Ulster, in the train of whose husband, Prince Lionel (the third son of Edward III), his father had formerly traveled abroad. A pleasant entry in her Household Accounts for 1357 records an Eastertide gift to Geoffrey Chaucer of "short cloak, shoes, and red-and-black tight hosen." At the age of seventeen he is transferred to the Court of Edward III, where his duties as a Yeoman of the King's Chamber include making the royal bed and carrying and holding torches. Two years later he goes with the king to fight in the French wars, and is promptly taken prisoner in battle.

Rarely can this particular personal misadventure have been so fruitful for posterity. For it took a considerable time to raise his ransom, even with the king's contribution of £16; and the long interim gave him leisure and opportunity, in honorable captivity, to drink deep of French culture at its fountain-head.

He was brought to this fountain-head at a moment of deep significance. He was nineteen years old, and so at that "moon-node" peak which can be marked by a flaring-up of creative activity. At this peak, for example, Schubert wrote as many as seven and eight of his exquisite songs a day; Joan of Arc parted lilies from leopards; Byron burst as a poet in full panoply upon a dazzled world; at the moon-node of his departure Odysseus came home from Troy.

The young French court-poets took the young Chaucer into their fellowship; he won especially the friendship of Eustache Deschamps, later, like himself, to become internationally famous. He heard them declaim their poems; he heard them dissect niceties of prosody, meter, cadence; and his own poetic gifts, asleep till now, were kindled.

And they gave him leave to write down their gay love-songs, to take home with him on his recall to England. So began that first stage of translation, which he carried out with such brilliance and devotion, and yet of which he confesses, half a lifetime later,

> to me it is a great penaùnce,
> Since rhyme in English hath such scarcity.

Again we must dissociate our minds from modern conditions if we are to understand the fertilizing of Sentient Soul by Intellectual Soul which followed Chaucer's return to England. It was an age when books were most rare and most precious. They were all in manuscript; and any copies made had also to be written by hand. Indeed, in order to get a glimpse of a manuscript, it was often necessary to make a hazardous journey into a foreign land.

This very fact had helped English vernacular literature to retain its Sentient Soul characteristics in singular purity, separating it from the main stream of Continental culture, and keeping it in a kind of holy and enchanted sleep. And now home came this glowing young squire, flushed with the upsurge of new powers, bringing with him the precious parchments which later, in his death-bed *Retractions*, he was to deplore as "worldly vanities and lecherous lays," but which by then had started a new ferment working in the English soul-constitution.

Though Chaucer's French period lasted for the next twelve years, during this glittering apprenticeship Fate was already bringing to him such life-experiences as would nourish his last, native flowering.

By now he had been promoted to Squire of the King's Household, and as such he accompanied the king on his royal progresses through provincial England, for his duties now were to taste the king's food, carve for him, and serve his wine on bended knee. "The king journeyed," says the old record, "not passing ten or twelve miles a day." Thus impression after slow impression of English countryside and English country folk passed from Chaucer's eye to Chaucer's mind, the deeper for their slowness, leading him forth from the rose gardens of courtly allegory, and laying broad and firm foundations for his later drawing from life.

So it was that when, on the death of Prince Lionel, the king's next son, John of Gaunt, became his patron, the elegy Chaucer wrote for the young Duchess Blanche contained the first delicate indication of the robust portraiture of his maturer years.

Following his marriage to Phillippa Roet, one of the countess of Ulster's ladies, and sister to John of Gaunt's third wife, Chaucer was sent, first to France, on a secret diplomatic mission, then for a year to Florence and Genoa as the king's ambassador, "to treat with the Duke, citizens and merchants, to choose some port in England where the Genoese might settle." So began a second period of continental contacts, quickening and deepening the inflow of European culture through himself to England.

And what riches Italian culture had to offer him! They far transcended even the generous gifts of France. Noble sculpture, paintings, architecture, classical remains; and, ruling all, three living writers of a stature almost legendary—Petrarch, Dante and Boccaccio. To meet Petrarch in the flesh; to handle and pore over and copy manuscripts written by Dante's and Boccaccio's own hands— small wonder that the artist in the maturing islander was stirred and quickened by Italy as no English poet till then had ever been, so that right up to the time, a whole century and a half later, when the Renaissance brought in a new Italian ferment, it was through Chaucer's paraphrases that this greatest literature of the whole Middle Ages continued to flow in to fertilize insular England.

During the twelve years of Chaucer's Italian period, the cultural sluices were kept open by his frequent diplomatic missions to France and Italy. Edward III died; Richard II came to the throne, but still Chaucer remained the trusted intermediary between island and continent.

For his last, his native period, he put down roots at home, entering deeply into England's leisurely life, serving her by day in prosaic, practical, administrative ways, wholly in keeping with the coming epoch—as J.P., M.P., Forester, Knight of the Shire for Kent, Member of the Thames Conservancy, Clerk of the Works at Westminster, Clerk of the Works at Windsor, Comptroller of Wool and Skins and Leather, Comptroller of Petty Customs; serving her by candlelight in more far-reaching ways, as he shaped the Prologue and endlinks of his greatest, most English work, growing gradually into new manner and new matter of the coming Consciousness Soul.

Destiny, having found so suitable a place for Chaucer to be born in, found one equally suitable for him to die in. On Christmas eve of 1399, two months after his patron John of Gaunt's son became King Henry IV, Chaucer took a long lease of a house in the Chapel garden at Westminster. Here, ten months later, he died. But for his dying where he did, his tomb would not now be, as it so appropriately is, the first literary monument in the national shrine of Westminster Abbey. For it was not as Father of English poetry that he was buried there, but as a tenant of the Abbey monks!

As the golden eagle in the *Hous of Fame* bears him upward, Chaucer whimsically wonders "wher [whether] Jove will me stellify." He asks in "game," but we can reply in "earnest." For we know that he is "stellified" in the language-body he wrought in the service of Michael for Michael's aide-de-camp, St. George; in the poetry by which he led England into her appointed path; in the modern soul-constitution which was already his nearly six centuries before our time. Wherever there is

any man
That English understonden can,

there Chaucer's work works on. We, in our soberer enthusiasm, cannot go all the way with Caxton when he says that Chaucer's English will endure forever, but we know that it will at least endure as long as St. George has need of it.

REFERENCES

Boccaccio, *Decameron*
Geoffrey Chaucer, *Book of the Duchess*
—— *Canterbury Tales*
—— *The Hous of Fame*
—— *Hymn to the Virgin*
—— *Legend of Good Women*
—— *Parliament of Fowls*
—— *Retractions*
—— *The Romaunt of the Rose*
—— *Troilus and Criseyde*
Cynewulf
T.S. Eliot, *Sweeney Agonistes*
John Masefield, *The Everlasting Mercy*
Wilfred Owen
Piers Plowman
Rudolf Steiner, *Letters to the Members*
—— *The Spread of Christianity in Europe*
—— *Symbolism and Fantasy*

FAIR MOUNTAIN AND FINE CITY

A Study of the Images in The Merchant of Venice

A. C. Harwood

All the evidence of mythology, fairy tale, and tradition points to the fact that humanity had a pictorial consciousness before developing an intellectual one. Pallas Athene was earlier than philosophy, and the wrong-doer saw the Erinnyes pursuing him centuries before the word conscience was conceived or used. Our concepts were indeed born by a process of abstraction from concrete picture and experience. People knew that wine was good and giants were big, long before they could speak of quality and quantity. The dwellers on islands saw and felt their remoteness from the world long before anyone thought of the idea of isolation.

Our modern abstract and colorless words are the whitened bones of a once living and heartfelt vocabulary. But this ossifying of speech represents only one half of that great change in consciousness which has precipitated our technical civilization. The other half, its corollary, is less well recognized and less easy to describe. It is a question of human vision, and may perhaps best be illustrated by reference to the starry constellations. A single star considered alone in the heavens is as much an abstraction as the idea of position or duration.

The two kinds of mentality, the modern mind making a fanciful picture based on sense experience, and the mind which sees a spiritual vision beyond the boundary of sense experience, have been illustrated by William Blake in a well-known saying:

What, it will be questioned, when the sun rises, do you not see a round disk of fire somewhat like a guinea? O no, no, I see an innumerable company of the heavenly host crying, Holy, Holy, Holy is the Lord God Almighty. I question not my Corporeal or Vegetative Eye any more than I question a window concerning sight. I look through it and not with it.

The difference is whether you look with the eye or through the eye. Today we look with the eye and see the disc of fire "somewhat like a guinea."

This may, perhaps, seem remote from the time of Shakespeare, but in fact the modern abstract consciousness is very modern indeed, and the remnants at least of the older pictorial consciousness survived well into the Renaissance. There was still at least an instinctive feeling for the "correspondences," and the knowledge of them was based on the old pictorial vision, not on sense perception.

Sometimes, indeed, sense perception will help us to understand some of these old connections between diverse phenomena. The sight of gold may at once suggest that this metal is an expression on earth of the power of the sun, and the pleasure in seeing it, which most people instinctively feel, may help us to imagine that it is also connected with the heart, the "bosom's Lord," which is to the rest of the body what the sun is to the lesser lights of heaven. But we should hardly go so far as to give gold as a heart medicine (as Chaucer's Doctor did), merely because of what we would describe as a fanciful feeling based on a similarity of color. Color might also associate silver with the moon, or iron with Mars. But nothing in our senses (I use the phrase equivocally) would make us attribute lead to Saturn, or tin to Jupiter. Such connections were established in ancient times when one saw a picture of correspondent character shining through planet and metal; and not only through planet and metal, but also through herb and tree, and the parts of the body and fishes and animals,

221

and the days of the week and the hours of the day, until every-thing became a mirror reflecting the qualities of other things, and every organism—the human being above all—was a picture in miniature of the whole great universe.

You may not believe in these "correspondences," but most people in Shakespeare's time still did, and you will miss a great deal in the plays unless you understand them. They are particularly important in *The Merchant of Venice*, where they play as necessary and pervasive a part in the plot as the ghost does in *Hamlet* or magic in *The Tempest.* For the play (as C.S. Lewis has pointed out in an admirable essay on *Hamlet*) is really about metals. But I think it is about metals which are not merely metals, but which evoke corresponding human and cosmic qualities; about gold, which is also the sun in the heavens, and kings who are the sun in their kingdoms, and the heart which is sun and king of the body, and the blood which carries the light into all parts of the human body, and love and mercy and generosity which are the virtues of the heart and the glory of kings and the likeness of the sun in human life. For all these things lived as neighbors in the mind of Shakespeare and his audience. Each evoked the other; none could be thought of except as endowed with the qualities of the rest.

Gold, therefore, is to be sought for in many places and diverse spheres. If there were no such metal on the earth, we would still know its essential quality in the light of the sun, in the attributes of kings, in the human heart and its virtues. From these we could invent or imagine the metal, even if God had not chosen to place a physical representative of it into the earth itself. But the actual metal is the lowest form of gold. It is to be loved, not for itself, but for the qualities which it represents. The metal fulfills its real mis-sion when it is the servant of kingly generosity and mercy. *The Mer-chant of Venice* is a play of contrasts in the uses of the power of gold.

The more obvious contrast is, of course, between the Jew Shy-lock and the Christian Antonio. The Jew makes the metal his god, and confounds dead substance with living flesh. His justification for the increase of the metal by interest is taken from the breeding of the parti-colored lambs by Jacob, and to Antonio's objection that gold and silver are not ewes and rams, he replies, "I make it breed as fast." We have here the instinctive mediaeval feeling against usury. Cows produce calves, and sheep produce lambs, but metal does not beget metal. Shylock repeats the confusion between the living and the dead in his cry for "my daughter and my ducats." He has begotten the one no less than the other, and they are equally tangled in his heart. Antonio, by contrast, lends money freely without the "breed of barren material." He puts the price of usury down, and, were Antonio out of Venice, Shylock says he would make "what merchandise I will." The Christian is a pattern of friendship. He loves the world only for his friend, and at Bassanio's need he pledges the pound of flesh *nearest his heart.* The heart is pledged for love against gold.

This is the obvious and exoteric contrast, pleasing no doubt to Shakespeare's Christian audience, only too ready to believe that a Jewish physician had plotted to poison their queen. But there is a more subtle though hardly less well marked contrast between the two places in which the action takes place, Belmont and Venice. In the fine city, the shining of the metal is all attractive and casts a dullness over the light of day; in the fair mountain lives and rules a kingly lady who is all light and sun and heavenly gold. In Venice everyone is something of a Jew; in Belmont everyone is, or turns, Christian. Even the wit in the city is somewhat forced, as though designed to cover up uneasiness or melancholy; on the mountain, gaiety and high spirits are at home with wisdom and modesty.

In Venice, Antonio is especially the representative of the Christian principle. But even he has no Christianity towards the Jew. He spits upon him and foots him like a cur, and is like to do so again. The sign of a gentile spirit in Jessica (for which the Christians praise her) is to steal her father's jewels and money. Nor did she spare the ring he had from Leah when he was a bachelor. Shylock describes the barbarous way the Venetians treat their purchased slaves—and no Venetian present denies the charge. The reason why the Duke does not interfere to save the life of Antonio is that such an action would lessen the confidence of foreign traders in Venetian law and so jeopardize the wealth of the State. In Venice, Bassanio is, or is content to be known as, a mere fortune hunter; it is Portia's wealth that draws him to Belmont, and the journey is not the first of its kind; in Belmont he becomes the lover, willing to renounce love altogether if he may not have the lady of his heart. That is, indeed, the condition of love at Belmont.

A moralist or a sentimentalist might perhaps have wished to see Portia beautiful but poor, to contrast her with the riches (and ugliness) of Venice. This, however, would obliterate the metal theme from Belmont. The point about Portia is not that she should have no gold, but that she should use gold in the right way. She is indeed all gold. We first hear in Venice that her hair "hangs on her temples like a golden fleece." It is for this reason, not for her metal gold, that "many Jasons come to woo her." She is the sun as well as the queen of the fair mountain, and even says of herself, "Let me give light but let me not be light." To win her (being first prepared to renounce all other love if you fail of this), you must make the choice between the caskets of gold, silver, and lead. But in Belmont you do not win the golden fleece by fixing your attention on what "many men desire," or on what you conceive you deserve. The true gold can be won only by the man who can "give and hazard all he has."

Bassanio rejects the "gaudy gold, hard food for Midas," and the silver, "pale and common drudge 'tween man and man." As his friend Antonio has done on his behalf, he chooses to "give and hazard all he has." He is true to that noble generosity which is the very air of Belmont. With what gracious freedom Portia bestows herself and all she has on Bassanio, and when the paper comes announcing Antonio's danger (which is a gaping wound issuing life-blood), how promptly she offers her gold to save that blood, and nobly she urges Bassanio to set out even before their wedding night, with no thought for her own disappointment, but only for the safety of her lover's friend whom she has never seen!

It is because Antonio in Venice has also "given and hazarded all he has" that Belmont must come to his aid. In the court Shylock is sharpening his knife to cut the pound of flesh nearest the heart, when the learned young Doctor arrives. And what is her first plea? In substance, merely the plea for mercy which the Duke has made at the opening of the trial. But the language and images are different. The mercy of which Portia speaks drops like the gentle rain from heaven; it becomes the throned monarch better than his crown; it is enthroned in the hearts of kings; it is an attribute of God, and in deeds of mercy earthly power "shows likest God's!" It is only when Shylock has rejected the vision of the heavenly mercy, and has indeed retorted that he has carried vengeance to the place whence Portia would draw mercy, and has an "oath in heaven," that the law is turned against him.

We may, perhaps, suspect that the plea for mercy comes from Portia, and the knowledge of the subtleties of Venetian law from the learned doctor Bellario. And what is the point that turns the law against him? Shylock has forgotten the living element—the blood—in the pound of flesh for which he has contracted. His mind is so fixed on the metal gold that not merely the qualities of the heart elude him, but even the element of life. He is crucified on the cross of his own gold, because he knows it only as dead earthly metal, and not as the representative of heavenly powers and living forces.

When we return to Belmont, our mind is at once led to the idea of correspondences by the comparisons of famous nights. We look up and find that Belmont, the home of the lady of the golden fleece, is covered with a mantle of heavenly gold:

> Sit, Jessica. Look how the floor of heaven
> Is thick inlaid with patines of bright gold.

Lorenzo tells Jessica of the Harmony of the Spheres to which earthly music is correspondent. The immortal soul incarnate can no longer hear the music of the macrocosm which fills it, but the man who is not sensitive to its correspondent earthly music is "fit for treasons, stratagems and spoils."

This is the state of Shylock, not only in that he hates music, but in that he sees nothing of the heavenly correspondence to his gold. Portia next enters and speaks at once of the candle in her window shining "like a good deed in a naughty world." But when the moon shines, the greater glory dims the less, and so

> A substitute shines brightly as a king,
> Until a king be by.

Bassanio arrives and greets Portia as the sun:

> We should hold day with the Antipodes
> If you would walk in absence of the sun.

And Portia replies:

> Let me give light, but let me not be light.

Heavenly Gold, Sun, Light, Kings—these are the images through which we enter the house of love on the fair mountain. Even the last spirited joke is concerned with the rings—the gold which is not coveted for its own sake, but as a pledge of the love of the heart. Such is the contrast in the play between the Mountain and the City. I think it is a more important contrast than the obvious one between Jew and Christian because it is both deeper and more hidden. You may not believe in the correspondences on which the contrast is based, but you will hardly be able to appreciate an important aspect of the play unless you take them into account. And for those to whom these things have again become real, this play and many others of the Shakespeare canon begin to have a new life and significance.

It was the nineteenth century (as C.S. Lewis has pointed out in the paper already quoted) that discovered the development of personality and character in the plays—perhaps sometimes even where it was not discoverable. To the twentieth century the plays are beginning to reveal themselves as something more like Mysteries, speaking to a picture-consciousness which has long been overlaid, but is again breaking through to the surface in our changing human consciousness. It is a test of inspiration in a work of art that it reveals new things to succeeding generations; custom cannot stale its infinite variety.

REFERENCES

William Blake, "A Vision of the Last Judgment"
C.S. Lewis, "Hamlet: The Prince or The Poem?"
William Shakespeare, *The Merchant of Venice*

SHAKESPEARE'S TROUBLED KINGS

Adam Bittleston

Few people knew better than John Heminge and Henry Condell, the editors of the First Folio, that Shakespeare was a practical writer for the theatre. His plays are written to be acted, and to be seen. And yet they said:

> Reade him, therefore; and againe, and againe: And if then you do not like him, surely you are in some manifest danger, not to understand him. And so we leave you to other of his Friends, whom if you neede, can bee your guides: and if you neede them not, you can leade your selves, and others. And such Readers we wish him.

Their advice has been followed. In countless editions, and by people of many tongues and faiths, the plays are read. What do we find by reading, that would be less evident on the stage?

Reading, we can stop to think, and look back. We can try to follow the development of a particular person or theme through a play. And we can compare plays more closely with one another. There are indeed dangers in such attempts. A living thing may always be destroyed or damaged by our attempts to study it; and Shakespeare's plays are in the most far-reaching sense alive.

Nineteenth-century critics, and many people since, feeling the vivid reality of Shakespeare's characters, have been tempted to pass on them moral judgments, or express their liking or disliking of

228

them. Considering Henry V's rejection of Falstaff, for example, they take sides; either they regard Henry as an ungrateful prig, or they point out that Falstaff is a disgusting scoundrel, after all, and thoroughly deserves to be treated in this way.

But the reading of Shakespeare can lead to a strong impression that such comments are not relevant to his fundamental purpose. For him, each being is a world, containing opposites. The stars and the abyss, the lion and the lamb and the wolf, all are present even in the soul of a Second Murderer, as in everyone else, although the world and the abyss may seem to have their way. There is a Falstaff in the king, a king in Falstaff.

It is when we compare one play with another that it becomes increasingly plain how Shakespeare intended such things. Again and again outer conflicts and inner conflicts are compared; and this is not just an external similarity. The storm in the world and the storm in the human soul are one. Who then can be at peace?

From very early, right into the last plays, Shakespeare puts before the audience characters who have a responsibility for order in the outer world, as kings or leaders, and who suffer, and cause suffering, because of an inner failure. This is for Shakespeare no theoretical problem; it is a mystery, which leads through terror and despair into the greatest discoveries. It is an evident theme in Histories and Tragedies; but it can be matter for comedy, too, in any of the three moods which are found in the plays grouped as comedies in the Folio. The fall of a king is terrible and ridiculous, and his recovery the greatest happiness.

*   *   *

A country needs a king as the outer world needs a sun, or the body a heart. But kings who fulfill this need are hard to find. In the Histories there is only one who comes near to it, Henry V, who says indeed in the course of his wooing of Katherine:

A good Heart, Kate, is the Sunne and the Moone, or rather
the Sunne, and not the Moone; for it shines bright, and never
changes, but keeps his course truly. If thou would have such
a one, take me? and take me; take a Souldier: take a Souldier;
take a King.

Prince Arthur, in *King John*, has the promise of being such a
king. When he is dead, having thrown himself down from a wall
when attempting to escape from imprisonment, and Hubert lifts
his small body in his arms, Faulconbridge says:

> How easie dost thou take all England up,
> From forth this morcell of dead Royaltie?
> The life, the right, and truth of all this Realme
> Is fled to heaven:

A king should be guardian of his country's life, right, and
truth—of what we can describe today as its economics, its justice,
and its spiritual activities. In Shakespeare's picture he is indeed to
be the representative on earth of the heavenly streams of life, right
and truth. And as an ordinary sinful man, this is obviously very
difficult. Henry V can come so near to doing it through a kind of
miracle:

> The breath no sooner left his Father's body,
> But that his wildness, mortify'd in him,
> Seem'd to dye too: yea, at that very moment,
> Consideration like an Angell came,
> And whipt the offending *Adam* out of him;
> Leaving his body as a Paradise,
> T'invelop and containe Celestiall Spirits.

But a man with kingly responsibilities dare not give himself too
much to Consideration—to study, meditation and prayer. If he
does, the results will be terrible, as for Henry VI, or for Prospero

when driven from his dukedom—or ludicrous, as for Navarre in *Love's Labours Lost*. The ruler must stand firmly in both worlds, not losing either for the sake of the other, if he is to bring strength from the spiritual world into the life of his country, and to approach the spiritual himself with a peaceful heart.

And yet—were he able to do this, would he now be much more than an ordinary man?

In the Histories Shakespeare enters the hearts of seven or eight men, all of whom experience their task as King of England as one that brings, at least at times, an appalling inner tension. They are real, individual men, not examples of the perils of bearing a crown—though they may not resemble the historical personages who bore those names. They are men with whom the individuality of Shakespeare, in the course of world history, has some connection of destiny, which enables him to describe them. They have in common that they have to face the discrepancy between what they are and what they need to be, in a particularly terrible form.

Men without such responsibilities find it easier to sleep. Shakespeare returns in remarkable ways to this theme, for example in *Henry IV, Henry V,* and the famous passage in *Macbeth,* until we come to Prospero who can *give* sleep. The 'ordinary man' can indeed bring from sleep impulses which have their origin in the spiritual world. The kings bar their own way into sleep through great guilt, or perhaps sometimes by over-absorption in externalities. When Henry IV describes with such power the sailor-boy who can sleep in a storm, it is not just a contrast with his own situation—it is a picture of the storm which goes on continually within him, and which must one day burst out over his whole kingdom, as a consequence of his overthrow of Richard II. This storm rages now between him and the spiritual world, from which he longs to draw. Healing might come—if he could go to Jerusalem.

For the king with his troubled soul, abdication is no remedy. To give up his crown by his own act is to deny his own "I." This is demonstrated with fearful clarity in *Richard II*, and then in a more complex way in *King Lear*. Richard, after his abdication under Bolingbroke's pressure, is imprisoned at Pontefract. In his loneliness, he feels his own being as a world—but there is no master, no spirit to reconcile and unite the struggling thoughts and feelings there. Even the words of the Gospel do battle with each other in him. And then we meet themes, with which Shakespeare is to be concerned to the last. Richard alternates between thinking of himself as a king, and as a beggar.

> Then am I king'd againe: and by and by,
> Think that I am un-king'd by *Bullingbrooke*,
> And straight am nothing. But what ere I am, [*Musick*]
> Nor I, nor any man, that but man is,
> With nothing shall be pleas'd, till he be eas'd
> With being nothing. Musicke do I heare?
> Ha, ha? Keep time: How sowre sweet Musicke is,
> When Time is broke, and no Proportion kept?
> So is it in the Musicke of mens lives:
> And heere have I the daintinesse of eare,
> To heare time broke in a disorder'd string:
> But for the Concord of my State and Time,
> Had not an eare to heare my true Time broke.
> I wasted Time, and now doth Time waste me:

Time, and Nothing, and Musicke: when a man comes through guilt or grief to a place where the world and his own soul seem to have reached an ending, Shakespeare calls upon these. For one part of the soul Time is the senseless destroyer; for the other it is the redeemer, and itself to be redeemed. All things are plunging into Nothing; sights, thoughts and desires. But out of Nothing there sounds a music; and though it, too, is itself apparently Nothing, one may find in it the greatest power of all.

Where did Richard II fail? He is accused of many things by others in the play, by himself, and by the critics. And yet he is remembered after his death with increasing affection. The play itself does not particularly show him doing the things he is accused of—listening to flatterers, wasting time and wealth, or causing Gloucester's death. What it does show very powerfully is his refusal to listen to the advice of John of Gaunt, his dying uncle. John of Gaunt himself compares what he has to say, his words of earnest counsel and rebuke, with music, when he is warned that Richard will not listen to him:

Oh but (they say) the tongues of dying men
Inforce attention like deepe harmony;
Where words are scarce, they are seldome spent in vaine,
For they breath truth, that breath their words in paine.

His hope is not fulfilled; Richard has no ear for this music, and suggests indeed that the sooner he is dead the better. This is a decisive failure in kingliness, according to the Shakespearean ethic. The king has a special duty to listen to the truth, however unpleasant; above all, when it comes from one who has deserved well of his country.

On the path of Initiation, as Rudolf Steiner has described it, there is a great parallel to this. The seeker for Initiation must be ready to sacrifice much in the abundant and joyful realm of Imagination, in order that into one's emptied consciousness there may sound Inspirations, which will lead one to participate in the suffering which underlies true creative processes in the world. In ordinary life the power to listen quietly and receptively to others is analogous to, and a necessary preparation for, the capacity of Inspiration in Rudolf Steiner's sense.

Richard II has human qualities which are a preparation for Imaginative powers of a noble kind—but little of those which lead towards Inspiration. Even John of Gaunt's references to the meaning of his own name —

For sleeping England long time have I watcht,
Watching breeds leannesse, leannesse is all gaunt

—are relevant. The abundance of Imagination can be pictured as
fatness; willingness to sacrifice in order to receive Inspiration as
the acceptance of a beggar's leanness. Richard does not love his
lean uncle, and himself comes at last to grieve over the rarity of
love "in this all-hating world."

There is a similar failure to listen among those kingly figures
who fall into groundless jealousy. Leontes, before he has learned
to hear Paulina's harsh truth, failed to hear his wife. Imaginations
that are not noble, but which spring from dark powers in the
blood, obsess him; the dead man's nose, the spider in the cup.
Leontes is "in rebellion with himself." Rejecting Hermione, he
rejects part of his own being, his vision of eternal beauty. In one
way or another, the violence in the king's soul leads to the death of
others, and then their death too will haunt him. His victims may
appear and curse him in his sleep, as happens to Richard III before
his last battle; or they may work upon his conscience in waking
life. It is the most thorough denial of kingliness, a quality which
should be as life-giving as the sun, to have caused death out of
hatred, or in order to gain the crown. And with *this* situation
Shakespeare is constantly concerned.

*   *   *

It is indeed a theme which can be followed back to the great
Greek tragedians, and to ancient myths; to Typhon's murder of
his brother Osiris. In ancient times, it is mainly a struggle among
the spiritual beings themselves, in which man may come to be
involved. In the *Bhagavad Gita* in the East, and in Greek tragedy
in the West, the conflict begins to be felt as an interior one,
though the counsel from the divine realm may still be decisive. In
the *Elektra* of Sophocles, Orestes can kill his mother with hardly

a shadow of uncertainty, if this is Apollo's will. But, as Rudolf Steiner pointed out, the Greeks are beginning at this time to discover conscience as an inner experience. In Christian times, the kingly man feels his own absolute responsibility as a more and more terrible, inescapable fact.

Shakespeare's kings face their responsibility for causing death very differently. At one extreme, Richard III and Macbeth do not seem, on the surface, to be troubled by conscience at all; for them it works outwardly, in the ancient way, as warning figures in dream and vision. At the other extreme, Prospero succeeds in not causing death at all, by Ariel's help; and Hamlet—

It was probably felt at the time of Shakespeare, and generally since, that Claudius has to be killed, and Hamlet should get on with the job. But was this Shakespeare's own belief? As so often, he gives us the full, stubborn facts; there may not be an easy answer. John Vyvyan, comparing *Hamlet* with other plays, describes it very effectively as a spiritual Fall, not after all so unlike that of Macbeth. Hamlet learns to accept killing, but thereby denies his own true being. He rejects Ophelia because he is rejecting the best in himself, the pilgrimage to eternal realities.

Thus, if we take *Hamlet* in the whole context of troubled kingship, we can see that this problem is represented in the play not once, but three times over; in Hamlet's father, in Claudius, and in Hamlet himself. The poisoning of the father, like the poisoning of King John (which is similarly described), is not simply a crime done against him; it expresses the tragic fact that he has already poisoned his realm, by what as Ghost he acknowledges, "the foul crimes done in my days of nature." He is both hero, as Hamlet sees him, and wrong-doer; he meets after death the significance of what he has done, but is not yet purged. So he is still possessed by an anger that is unkingly, since every kind of personal resentment, or indeed personal affection, disturbs the function of a king. He cannot therefore give Hamlet counsel that would help Denmark; he does not come as near as John of Gaunt does to the utterance of "deep harmonies," in which a human voice becomes the instrument of the spiritual world. But into his angry and anguished words there enters compassion for the Queen.

Claudius knows himself a wrongdoer—but a king as well. And even if nothing is known about his crime, it will infect all Denmark; it is in his heart, and he is the heart of the country. Hamlet has the potentiality, as Prince Arthur had, of becoming Denmark's true king, of defending life and right and truth. But his kingship will be vitiated from the start, like that of Bolingbroke-Henry IV, if it is won by violence and falsehood.

That is not just a terrible human dilemma. Shakespeare treats it, as Rudolf Steiner shows in his lectures on St. Mark's Gospel, with a deep and accurate feeling for the whole course of human history, and for the metamorphoses that come about in the passage of an individuality from one incarnation to another, before and after the Deed of Christ. Hamlet stands before the mystery of the abyss in his own soul; no counselor, no beloved, no friend can interpret it to him.

* * *

If Shakespeare had stopped writing plays after *Hamlet*, it would have seemed that he saw little hope for the sick king. Had there come into existence, during the centuries preceding his time, any representation of the problem of similar grandeur, which offered more hope?

About four hundred years before Shakespeare began to write, the greatest versions of the Parzival story were becoming known. The Grail Castle is the home of a sick king, Amfortas. Wolfram von Eschenbach says of him:

The king cannot ride or walk; he cannot lie or stand. He leans but cannot sit, and he sighs, well knowing why. At the change of the moon he suffers much.

The wound which cannot be healed he received in a tourney, in which he fought because of a personal love, not allowed him by "the writing on the Grail."

Neither the Grail itself, nor the compassion of those who care for him, nor the wisdom of his brother Trevrizent, can heal him. He waits in grief for Parzival. Why can Parzival help? Wolfram gives no explicit, direct answer. His name is to be read in the writing of the Grail. He is the chosen successor to Amfortas.

He has, however, one quite evident quality, which is in this connection of far-reaching significance. He is young; as the nephew of Amfortas, he belongs to the next generation, as do Sigune and Schionatulander. The meeting of human beings of different ages is as familiar in ordinary life as eating and sleeping; and it is equally mysterious. Parzival's father and mother have died. One uncle, Trevrizent, has been able to give himself entirely to the task of Consideration, as a hermit; and to the "deep harmony" of his counsel Parzival is able to listen, though much of it is bitter for him. Another uncle has the inescapable task of kingship, until Parzival comes, in the way that only he can do, with his compassionate and understanding question.

Much has happened within his own generation before he does this. He has seen Schionatulander dead, and the mourning Sigune; he has found his own wife again, and found his black and white half-brother Fierifis. Inwardly he has gone through something like a death of faith, and the loss and recovery of a sense for the meaning of Time.

All this, of course, is told, by Chrétien and Wolfram and others, in a mood and with methods utterly different from those of Shakespeare. And yet far-reaching comparisons can be made—fundamentally for the reason that the greatest works of art are in some way always rooted in the Mysteries.

At an unknown date, though it is thought probable that this was two or three years after writing *Hamlet*, Shakespeare wrote *All's Well that Ends Well*. This is regarded as one of the "problem comedies" between the earlier straightforward comedies and the late "romances" (this classification is something of an oversimplification). In this play, the King of France has a physical sickness of which he is dying. No one can help him, until the daughter of a wise physician who has died comes to Paris. She is Helena, who hopes to marry a man of much nobler birth than herself. Shakespeare has taken the plot fairly closely from an English version of a story told by Boccaccio, but he has added an extraordinary consciousness in his heroine of what she is doing. Helena feels that she has a mission given to her by the spiritual world; when she is persuading the hesitant king to try her remedy, she says:

Of heaven, not me, make an experiment.

And when the king has been convinced by her, he says:

Methinks in thee some blessed spirit doth speak
His powerfull sounde, within an organ weake:

Here quite explicitly a sick king is healed by a younger human being, through whom the spiritual world works. In seven out of the twelve plays Shakespeare probably wrote, or shared in writing, after this time, something similar happens; a younger human being, by a sacrifice or simply by existing, helps decisively towards the healing of a sick king—taking sickness in the wide sense in which Shakespeare himself uses it. Those who are young have indeed often to go through an apparent death—as Helena herself does, and Marina, and Perdita, and Imogen, and Ferdinand in *The Tempest.*

Pericles is indeed not included in the First Folio, and there is a reason for this. But the scene of Marina's birth is strongly Shakespearean; and her meeting with her sick father, who believes her dead, is among the most magical in all the plays.

Why does it so often happen in the later plays that someone is believed to be dead, and then found to be alive? This is not, of course, peculiar to Shakespeare. In the *Elektra* of Sophocles, the death of Orestes is described with great effect; the urn which is said to contain his ashes is brought on, and Elektra mourns her brother in one of the most moving of all elegies—and yet he is alive, before her. These are not just theatrical tricks; something happens in the people concerned, and in the onlookers. In deep secrecy, the ancient Mysteries had led to the enactment of a death and resurrection, in which the candidate for initiation was laid in a grave, and called back into life by the Hierophant after three days. When Lazarus was raised by Christ, a great transition began from the old forms of initiation to the new, in which the candidate for initiation has to remain active in the everyday world, without anything of the transformation through which he is passing being evident to those around him.

Dramatically, Shakespeare could indicate a path towards initiation through the apparent death of a man or woman. The connection with the ancient mysteries is just touched upon, for example by letting the events in *The Winter's Tale*, where both Hermione and Perdita are believed to be dead, be guided from Delphi, or by showing Thaisa in *Pericles* brought to life again at Ephesus. Not that they are represented as having become initiates; but something of initiate strength is imparted to them, through which they are capable of exceptional courage, and of making new beginnings. They have become servants of the spiritual Sun.

Sometimes indeed a member of the new generation, and one who is potentially a bringer of healing, suffers actual death. He may have fallen too far into the temptations with which the older generation is sick, as do Romeo and Hamlet; or death may come upon him or her in innocence, as it does for Mamillius in the *Winter's Tale*, for Desdemona, and above all for Cordelia. *The* extraordinary difference in atmosphere between *Hamlet* and *King Lear* is very much due to this; Cordelia comes so near to healing Lear, to bringing him music and teaching him to listen, and to making him at peace with Time. When she dies, Lear believes to the very last that she will overcome this death, and sees her lips move as if in speech.

Parzival does not die in his youth; but he sees Schionatulander dead, who has been killed in his place. Just as the mother whose heart was broken by his departure continually watches over him, Schionatulander, too, will be his invisible companion, inspiring him in the fulfillment of his tasks.

That the dead can shelter and sustain those still on earth, as the Grail story indicates, is in Shakespeare much more than a belief; it permeates his whole relationship to life. In his plays it is perhaps most important not where it is explicit, as in the protection of Posthumus by his dead parents and brothers in *Cymbeline* (though this passage is remarkable enough), but where it is implicit in the pattern of events.

* * *

At the end of Shakespeare's work, there stand two great descriptions of kings: *The Tempest* and *Henry VIII*. Since the nineteenth century, many have doubted whether Shakespeare himself wrote much of *Henry VIII*. This was entirely for internal reasons; it was not thought worthy of him, by Tennyson and many eminent judges. But there is no external evidence to support this; and there is the single, powerful fact that it was included in the First Folio. Heminge and Condell might perhaps be a little vague about the authorship of something written thirty years before, as were the three parts of *Henry VI*. But *Henry VIII* was written only ten or eleven years before the First Folio was published and was staged with the utmost splendor by them (and others) at the Globe Theatre, which was burned down while it was being performed. If it was largely written by Fletcher, there was no reason why they should not say so; and every reason, including their explicit and genuine concern for accuracy, why they should. (Of course, the spelling and punctuation of the First Folio, of which examples are given in this article, are remarkable to our eyes. But they are not simply odd, or utterly careless; they often help us towards recognizing the way in which the lines were originally spoken.) In recent years many critics have returned to the view that it is entirely Shakespeare's. The same sources are used throughout, in ways very characteristic of Shakespeare; and it has held the stage through the centuries as nothing by any other dramatist of the time has done.

Shakespeare knew well that reality is full of contradictions. The philosopher nearest to him in spirit (and perhaps in style) is Heraclitus. Both are continually concerned with the great polarities in the world—light and dark, hot and cold—and the unities hidden behind their differences. *Henry VIII* is based on a paradox of this kind. Just as the great rule of Henry V was derived from a wrong— his father's overthrow of Richard II—so the great reign of Elizabeth springs from a cruel injustice, the divorce of Katharine. From an action tainted by passion came the long years of government by a Virgin Queen (of whom, at the time, Shakespeare had been by no means uncritical). Conscience is the best in us, and yet one can have a genuine belief that conscience is counseling an action which has in reality quite different motives.

Prospero knows what he is doing; Henry does not. Both have servants of very different kinds; Prospero knows already the inner qualities of each, Henry learns by fits and starts. Prospero was cured before his play begins, Henry is sick almost to the end. But for both it is a daughter who brings healing. And both are complex, mysterious personalities, difficult for those around them to understand.

The sickness of Henry VIII shows itself not only in his confused conscience, but in his general inability, at first, to distinguish truth from falsehood. He lets Buckingham be condemned on perjured evidence; he does not see through Wolsey's double games, with their consequences in the economy. Such failures could be disastrous to a king. In putting away Katharine, he is rejecting a part of his own soul, the part open to the spiritual world. It has indeed been complained that similar consequences should follow, as for Leontes. But even apart from the fact that he has promised to show history as it happened, Shakespeare knows that in human life similar causes produce different results.

The king is sustained by qualities in those around him, with which the whole play is deeply concerned—humility and compassion. Even Wolsey, the proudest, learns to say at his fall:

> I know my selfe now, and I feele within me
> A peace above all earthly Dignities,
> A still, and quiet Conscience. The King has cur'd me,
> I humbly thanke his Grace:

It is no accident that the play seems often to be more concerned with the King's servants than with himself. For he is studied through them, and develops through them. For a very long time Shakespeare has been concerned with the problem of the loyal servant, who recognizes the mistakes or even the crimes of the master, and nevertheless goes on serving: Kent in *King Lear* and Gonzalo in *The Tempest* are examples from the mature plays. But *Henry VIII* is quite particularly concerned with the relation of master and servant; it is his own servants who betray Buckingham, while Katharine has servants who accompany her into poverty. Henry is led towards insight by the loyalty of two people who have such genuine humility that the spiritual world can reveal itself to them: Katharine and Cranmer. (It is characteristic that one is Catholic and the other Protestant.)

In contrast with the great outer ceremonies that are shown and the dance at Wolsey's house, Katharine in her seclusion shares in a ceremony performed by heavenly visitants, who dance about her and hold a garland over her head. Afterwards she asks her servant Griffith:

Saw you not even now a blessed Troope
Invite me to a Banquet, whose bright faces
Caste thousand beames upon me, like the Sun?

She is privileged to see already beyond the time of purification after death, to the spiritual communion of heaven and earth in which the dead can share. While Catholicism brought a dogmatic element into the faithful's relationship to the mystery of Transubstantiation, and Protestantism often attacked this mystery intellectually, it was the task of esoteric Christianity to guard it in its holiness; but often it was rather the dead than those on earth—and rather the spiritual beings, than human souls—who could preserve the continuity of understanding from the time of Golgotha.

By his office a king or an archbishop should be a protector of this Mystery; but lack of self-knowledge and of humility could make him a wounded Fisher-King indeed. Macbeth is driven away from his own table—and every table spread for a meal is an image of the greatest—by the warning figure of his victim; and the spiritual banquet revealed by Ariel cannot be approached by the guilty rulers.

Henry, like other rulers of his time, was faced with terrible responsibilities; like others, he was a sick king. Shakespeare shows him led by his physician to see through a window a definite picture; a man standing at a door, humbly and patiently waiting, with the other servants. This is the man from whom he can hear about the future, who receives the Inspiration of which Henry can say:

Thou hast made me now a man.

Macbeth, too, was granted a vision of his successors, but it brought him nothing but bitterness. Henry is sheltered by the soul of a Queen who died at peace; and he can rise to the selflessness of rejoicing at the coming wonders in his country, on which he will be able to look down after his own death.

*   *   *

Now we are all kings. Even in Shakespeare's time, there will have been many who identified themselves deeply with his troubled and heroic, his lamentable and ridiculous figures, whatever outward differences there were between character and onlooker. The Globe knew itself and its audience as little worlds. Today, direct and effective responsibility for the spiritual life, the political life, and the economic life is very much more widely shared than under the Tudors; in particular those who have practical leadership in any of the three spheres have to find resources of initiative within themselves, which were much more rarely demanded in earlier times even of responsible leaders. Traditions and conventions help much less.

Wherever there is a responsibility to lead, there is the searing necessity of trying to distinguish between ideas that can be genuinely constructive and those too much influenced by personal emotion. The good spirits of a community, whether one as small as a family or one wider than a nation, need to be heard. They may speak through any soul, responsible head or servant or child; most of all, indeed, where the generations meet.

REFERENCES

William Shakespeare, *All's Well That Ends Well*
—— *Hamlet*
—— *Henry V*
—— *Henry VIII*
—— *King John*
—— *Love's Labour's Lost*
—— *Richard II*
Wolfram von Eschenbach, *Parzival*

IN QUEST OF THE HOLY GRAIL

Ursula Grahl

When first we become interested in the subject of the Holy Grail and begin to go in search of information, we make an interesting discovery: almost everyone whom we approach with our questions has heard of the story but nobody can tell us very much about it.

We have similar experiences when we consult the many books that have been written on the subject: they offer us a tremendous wealth of detailed and obviously significant knowledge, and yet, the more we absorb of this knowledge, the more we come to realize that we know nothing at all.

We begin to see that at one and the same time the theme of the Holy Grail seems to be close at hand and infinitely far removed. We feel quite clearly that it concerns us deeply, but whenever we reach out for it we find that it withdraws and becomes inaccessible.

These strange experiences—so we are told—have come to everyone who has set out on the Quest of the Holy Grail. Every available account of the story says that the seekers for the Holy Grail pursue their goal for many, many years. Often they are so close that they can almost touch it, but the very next moment they may find themselves further away from it than ever.

At the present time most people have gained whatever knowledge they may have of the subject from the well-known legends of King Arthur, from Richard Wagner's two operas, *Parsifal* and *Lohengrin,* and from the romances of the Middle Ages. From all these sources we certainly learn a very great deal, and yet the core of the subject tends to remain a deeply veiled mystery.

We encounter very interesting and moving accounts of many different versions of the story, but these versions not only complement one another—they contradict one another very considerably, too. While we receive innumerable fragments of the truth we are seeking, riddle is heaped upon riddle and the central question remains unanswered. Although some of the stories appear to be telling us quite clearly and openly what the Holy Grail is, we still cannot fathom it because one story tells us that it is a precious stone, another that it is a platter, and yet another that it is a chalice. From further versions we learn that it is a flower-cup, an organ in the human body, a beam of light, a healing remedy, a draught of the water of life, a bestower of every kind of required nourishment, a constellation in the starry sky, a subconscious experience in the depths of sleep.... Moreover it has never yet been possible to determine the site of the original Castle or Temple of the Holy Grail. Many places in turn have been named as being the one and only location on earth where the lofty secret has been guarded.

If, then, we set out to trace the story historically and ethnologically, we make another interesting discovery: the theme is found to be spread out all over the earth. While at some point of our investigations we had begun to understand that the story of the Holy Grail tells us of the sublime essence of Christianity, we now learn that very similar stories have appeared in pre-Christian times in connection with the innumerable pagan sanctuaries all over the earth. The theme of the Holy Grail, in many different versions, appears to have a place in most of the great religions of the world.

Wherever we turn in our search, with every step we take, we encounter some of these greater and smaller riddles. How can we hope to solve them? How can we solve, above all, the riddle that the unique sacred vessel of the Holy Grail appears at the center of so many heathen mystery-cults, and yet represents the deepest and highest mystery of Christianity?

Here and there from time to time we find a few steps of a stairway that appears to be ascending to our goal, but it breaks off in mid-air; or we find traces on the ground that seem to indicate a path, but after a while the traces become indistinct or end in a thicket, even as the traces of Kundry and of the Grail Knights disappeared when Parzival tried to follow them.

Undoubtedly all along in our research we receive the greatest help and guidance from Rudolf Steiner, but in the study of his work, too, we make similar interesting discoveries. In his books and lectures there are many passages in which he deals clearly and comprehensively with certain aspects of the subject; moreover some of his pupils have worked hard at compiling all these relevant passages, and their work is of great help to us; but still, we do not find it easy to approach the mystery.

Slowly then it begins to dawn on us that the obstacles to our progress are not inherent in the subject but arise from our own immaturity. Increasingly now we feel called upon not only to expand the quantity of our knowledge but to alter the quality of our knowing.

A strange experience, repeated ever and again, brings this home to us: we happen to be re-reading a passage in Rudolf Steiner's works, a passage we had often read before and thought we had understood. All of a sudden now, we recognize it for what it is. It is the answer to one of our burning questions. Desperately we may have needed this particular answer. Now we see that Steiner had formulated precisely and unmistakably what we needed to know. It was an open secret and we could have seen it, but obviously we were not ready to receive it.

We are made to feel very humble—but at the same time we are comforted and reassured—when one day we discover that Rudolf Steiner himself patiently pursued his search for many years before he found the answers to some of his questions. We are then faced with the difficult task of curbing our impatience without losing the urgency of our quest.

Continuing on our path, we are led eventually to find the answer to another question that may have puzzled us for a long time. In Wagner's *Parsifal*, the young boy asks, "Who is the Grail?" Gurnemanz answers: "That cannot be said; but if you yourself are chosen by Him, the knowledge will surely come to you." In the ninth book of Wolfram von Eschenbach's *Parzival*, we read that Parzival, the lonely seeker for the Holy Grail, has experienced such despair that he has almost yielded to the temptation of abandoning his quest. Then the grace of destiny leads him to the hermitage of Trevrizent, and the meeting with this hermit becomes the turning-point in his life. Trevrizent goes even further than Gurnemanz in that he says: "No-one can ever conquer or even approach the Holy Grail except those who have been elected and named by Him."

The words "elected" and "named" may at times have tempted us to think that the fulfillment of the quest was a matter of predestination. If it were true that we were subject to an unalterable fate—so we were tempted to think—we might as well give up the quest. But now we remember another passage that helps us further, a passage of fundamental importance in Rudolf Steiner's book, *How to Know Higher Worlds: A Modern Path of Initiation*. Here Rudolf Steiner states that no occult knowledge may ever be given to anyone before he has made himself worthy to be entrusted with it, but that no such knowledge will ever be withheld from anyone who has prepared himself to receive it in the right way.

From these passages we now learn to understand the secret that, however hard one may strive, no one can come to the Holy Grail who remains the same. All efforts will be in vain when they are directed towards a "conquest of the mystery." The seeker's efforts must be directed above all towards the conquest, the transformation and perfecting of one's own self. One must first of all try one's very best to make oneself ever more capable in dealing with the tasks of life and in serving one's community.

Whenever one has reached the degree of maturity that renders one worthy of being chosen by the Holy Grail, one's name will appear on the sacred vessel, and the call will then find one wherever one may be. Kundry, the messenger of the Holy Grail, will come to meet one, summoning and guiding one to the sacred place that through no effort of one's own one could ever have reached.

The word "Grail" is connected with the Latin word "gradalis," from which again is derived the English word "gradual." Only "gradually," through strictly determined stages of inner development can we hope to come nearer to the mystery. The whole of the sublime truth is available indeed—everywhere and at all times— but our own nature obscures it and breaks it into fragments. Answers to our questions will often be given to us, but our own immaturity may prevent us from recognizing them. Now we can even begin to be grateful for the fact that the truth is so difficult to assess. The very efforts we have to make towards finding it help us to transform ourselves and to acquire the necessary degree of inner maturity. The moment we have—through our own efforts— achieved the inner victory, the outer realities of life tune in on it and, as if by magic, the truth reveals itself.

Gradually, then, with the help of Rudolf Steiner, we become able to piece together the components of the story that we find scattered through the literature of all times and all peoples. Some legends place the origin of the story far back into mythological ages, long before the dates of recorded history. This is true indeed, because the story of the Holy Grail is the oldest and most important of all earthly stories. Like a golden thread, it runs through all the epochs of earthly history and tells us of the innermost secret of human evolution. This is inseparably bound up with the Coming of Christ, Who represents the Divine Egohood of humanity. The story of the Holy Grail is the story of Christ or, more precisely, the story of Christophorus, the bearer of Christ.

For the first time the full strength of the Divine Egohood was received into a human being when, at the Baptism by John in the

Jordan, Christ entered into the body of Jesus of Nazareth. Three years later, for the salvation of the whole of humanity, Christ performed His Deed on Golgotha. The Mystery of Golgotha is the central point, the core and essence of the earthly cycle of human evolution. This greatest event of earthly history had been carefully prepared through all the earthly ages preceding it. Moreover it had been cosmically prepared even in pre-earthly cycles of evolution. Through the Mystery of Golgotha, human beings were to be imbued with the Being of Christ, with their own Divine Egohood. However, they were not intended to receive a higher ego through a divinely ordained act of necessity. The way had been cleared for them to reach out for the fulfillment of their being through the freedom of their own Good Will.

For the sake of making this possible, Lucifer had been called upon to lead humanity into the "Fall."

We must not regard Lucifer as only an adversary power. He is indeed a mighty adversary power, but at the same time he is one of our great benefactors. To the glorious gifts of Lucifer we owe the splendors and achievements of all the great pre-Christian cultures and, above all, the possibility of attaining freedom.

In ancient legends the name of the Holy Grail appears for the first time in connection with a "Precious Stone" that fell from the crown of Lucifer, or, according to other versions of the legend, was struck from the crown of Lucifer by the Archangel Michael. From this "Precious Stone"—so we are told—the Cup of the Holy Grail was fashioned, the Cup that was used by Jesus Christ at the Last Supper.

This jewel from the crown of Lucifer was no stone in the ordinary sense of the word. The "Crown" of Lucifer was the great circle of his hosts who served him as their master. Each "Jewel" in this "Crown" was a being, a servant, a follower of Lucifer. But one being, the most precious jewel in the crown, was different from all the other Luciferic beings. They were all imbued with great cosmic wisdom. This one being, the most precious jewel in the crown, had formed his wisdom into a vessel for the Love of Christ. He had made himself the servant of Christ and his wisdom was to embrace and contain the power of love. He was a being of high divine origin, both human and superhuman at the same time. We may regard him as the bearer of the full strength of the divine human egohood received in freedom.

On earth, humanity was to be exposed to the further influence of the Luciferic hosts. The high being, who bears the name of the Holy Grail, accompanied the fall of the Luciferic spirits and of humanity. With them he descended into the earthly realm in order to protect, strengthen and sustain us in the struggles that were to follow. This high spiritual being united himself with the earthly destinies of humanity to help human beings guard their freedom, the most precious gift from Lucifer, while endeavoring to save them from falling prey to Lucifer's further temptations.

Through many cycles of pre-earthly and earthly evolution, this high divine being prepared the way for the Coming of Christ. Three times before the Mystery of Golgotha, he made himself the vessel in which Christ could dwell for a time so that impending dangers could be averted and the path be cleared for further human development.

Throughout the pre-Christian epochs of earthly history, Christ was coming ever nearer to the earth, approaching His Incarnation in a human body. This Descent of Christ was known and witnessed by all the priests and kings of old who served in the ancient Mystery Centers and were the initiated leaders of humanity. Under many different names in all the great pre-Christian religions all over the earth, people were worshiping Christ, as he slowly descended from the spiritual realms of the starry regions. There were Christians on the earth long before Christ Himself incarnated into a human body, long before He Himself established the name of Christianity on earth through His Deed on Golgotha.

This is why, in the histories of the peoples in pre-Christian times, we find many stories of sacred vessels containing the healing essence, the life-giving forces that were needed to maintain the progress of evolution. Wherever we hear of such a sacred vessel being treasured in a sanctuary—be it in oriental shrines or in some Celtic centers of worship; be it in the temples of Syria, in the heart of Asia or Africa, in the South or in the North—we are hearing of pre-Christian Temples of the Grail, where the mystery of Christ's approach to the earth was known and guarded.

In studying all these many different stories we must, however, be very careful and use our discrimination. Between the golden streams of the genuine mysteries of the Holy Grail we come across many degenerate streams which fail to guard the lofty secret in its purity. Moreover we discover some dark places of worship where at the heart of the rituals we find vessels that are filled with adversary powers. One of the most powerful anti-Imaginations of the Holy Grail is the theme of the head in the dish. We find it in a number of stories from many parts of the earth. The most famous story on this theme takes us close to the Mystery of Golgotha. It is the story of the events that took place in Machaerus, the center of darkest black magical powers, where John the Baptist was beheaded by order of Herod and Herodias. The head of John the Baptist, placed in a dish, was carried into the banqueting hall by Salome and set before the king. From all the stories of the Holy Grail we learn that good and evil are always to be found close to each other. We cannot learn about the mysteries of Monsalvat without also learning about the secrets of Klingsor's castle.

Let us now follow the path of the most important of the pre-Christian streams of the Grail Mystery, the stream that leads straight to the Incarnation of Christ. We are told that the sacred vessel of the Holy Grail was kept at a temple in Tyre in Syria. King Hiram of Tyre gave it into the keeping of the Queen of Sheba, and she in turn took it to King Solomon. Henceforth it was guarded in the Temple of Jerusalem. Furthermore the legend tells us that Jesus Christ used this vessel at the Last Supper; that a Jew took it to Pontius Pilate and that Pilate gave it to Joseph of Arimathea, who is said to have brought it to Glastonbury in England in the year 63 A.D.

When the time of the Mystery of Golgotha was approaching, the high divine being who had served the Christ for so long once again made himself the vessel for Christ. This time he helped to fashion the human body that was to be capable of containing the Being of Christ for the duration of the Three Years. Among the Hebrew people forty-two generations of the tribe of David had prepared for the coming of this child. They had been guided in their preparations by the sacred knowledge of the Holy Grail that had been guarded in the Temple of Jerusalem since the time of King Solomon.

This child, whose birth-story is told in the Gospel according to St. Luke, brought with him the purity that existed prior to the Fall. When he was twelve years old, he received into himself the ego of Zarathustra, who represented all human earthly achievements and earthly wisdom since the Fall. In his lectures on the Fifth Gospel, Rudolf Steiner tells us of the further path of Jesus of Nazareth up to the time of the Baptism by John in the Jordan, when he became the vessel for Christ. As already mentioned, people have often wondered where to look for the site of the original Castle of the Holy Grail. Many different places have been named. Now we can begin to understand that there is no single Center of this Mystery on the earth. Christ says: "Wherever two or three are gathered in My Name, there am I in the midst of them." Thus, sanctuaries of the Holy Grail are to be found in all the places on the earth and in the spiritual worlds where true servants of the Christ Mystery are actively gathered in His Name. Over thousands of years the destinies of the Grail stream are manifold. They are inseparably bound up with the destinies of all the groups of beings and of all the single individualities who have been able to join this stream.

Since Christ has made Himself one with the earth, it is no wonder that the healing powers of His Resurrection have begun to radiate into many aspects of life on earth. One day the whole of the earth will be redeemed. All its Kingdoms will be permeated with the Healing Power of Christ. Every single part will then have become a vessel wherein the Christ may dwell. Thus, the Holy Grail is the most precious of earthly stones; it is the Chalice of the Sacrament that, at the same time, we behold in the purity of each flower cup; it is a healing remedy, for Christ is the Healer of the whole world; it is a beam of light, for Christ says of Himself: "I am the Light of the world." It is a draught of the Water of Life that is bestowed on us every night in the depths of sleep; it is an organ in the human body, the organ where this mystery of renewal takes place every night in sleep; it is a constellation in the starry sky, where the name of the Holy Grail and the name of Parzival may be read in the occult script of the stars. The Holy Grail is all these wondrous things and many more.

Slowly the Mystery of Christ is permeating the whole of the earth, bestowing Life and Light upon all who dwell thereon. The goal will be reached when every single human being is able to say with St. Paul: "Not I, but Christ in me." When these prophetic words have come true, the Holy Grail will appear to the whole of humanity, and everyone will see the other's countenance in a new light. The whole development is of such gigantic proportions that we begin to understand why so many riddles and problems have beset us for so long. We begin to expect, too, that many more riddles and problems will surely beset us in the future. Long and steep is the path that still lies ahead of us, but infinitely glorious is the distant goal to which it will lead us, the goal at the completion of the earthly cycle of evolution.

Since the story of the Holy Grail is the story of the most sublime secret of the whole of human evolution, it is, at the same time, the individual story of the innermost secret of each single human being. This throws new light on the questions we asked at the beginning. It is no longer surprising that everyone has heard of the story, but that no one is far enough evolved, as yet, to grasp the whole of the lofty truth. The theme is always close at hand because we live by the grace of it, but for our limited understanding it is still far removed.

Every night, while we are asleep, Grail processes take place in our organism to heal the tiredness of the previous day and to bestow on us the new life-forces needed for the following day. When we wake up in the morning, our consciousness is not yet strong enough to remember our experiences during sleep, but they sustain us in all our activities during the day. The reality of our existence is so far greater than our present capacity for understanding, which is as yet neither strong nor large enough to match the full truth of our own being. From this point of view it becomes clear, too, why again and again we encounter the answers to our questions without realizing that we have met them. Our task is then to develop and strengthen that part of our being which Rudolf Steiner calls the "Consciousness Soul." Now we experience the Mysteries of the Holy Grail in deep sleep. One day, when we shall have fully developed the strength and capacity of our Consciousness Soul, we shall awaken to behold the Holy Grail.

The epoch for the development of the Consciousness Soul began with the fifteenth century. Whether we are aware of it or not, we of the twentieth century are all engaged in the task of developing the faculties of our Consciousness Soul.

The forerunner of our epoch, who prepared the way for us all, lived in the ninth century. He is known to us by the name of *Parzival.* So, many centuries ahead of the rest of humanity, he achieved what for most of us is still a task for the present and future. The name of this historical personality, who became Grail King in the ninth century, signifies a degree. Every human being will sooner or later reach this degree and rise to become a Parzival. The archetypal stages of the path towards this goal are inscribed in the life story of the individuality who bore the name of *Parzival* in the ninth century. These archetypal stages of the path are the same for everybody, and yet they are always individually different, even as the archetypal form of the human countenance appears in innumerable individual variations. Hence, all the life-stories of different historical personalities who achieved the Quest of the Holy Grail are fundamentally the same and yet individually different. Therefore, it is important to occupy ourselves with the archetypal images of the experiences they had to meet, the battles they had to fight, the trials they had to endure and the many victories they had to gain. Above all, we receive the greatest encouragement and the safest guidance in our own quest when we live with the story of Parzival and ponder deeply again and again the archetypal stages of the path he had to travel, the path that leads to Mont Salvat.

REFERENCES

Margarethe Kirchner-Bockholt, "A Grail Castle in the Brain"
  (*Golden Blade* 1975)
Wolfram von Eschenbach, *Parzival*
Rudolf Steiner, "Christ and the Spiritual World and the Search
  for the Holy Grail"
—— *The Fifth Gospel*
—— *How to Know Higher Worlds: A Modern Path of Initiation*
—— *Pre-Earthly Deeds of Christ*
Richard Wagner, *Parsifal*

THE TRIALS OF PARSIFAL

L. Francis Edmunds

A saga is a universal tale centered about a particular hero. Since it is universal, it holds a place in us all. It is not merely for the reading—it has to be lived. We are with Sigurd, the Sun-hero, in his grim battle with Fafnir, the loathly worm. We pass between Scylla and Charybdis with Ulysses, we have heard the enticing call of the sirens, have fallen to the witchery of Circe and rejoiced to regain our human shape. We may even have crossed the Styx, and met the three-headed Cerberus, and reached the borders of the dead to bring back renewing forces for the living. All this is deeply inscribed in us, as are also the accompanying triumphs and despair that make true history, for the saga reaches us from a higher source and is history in the making.

Parsifal is a saga of post-Christian times. The heroes of old were as though god-born. Often their divine origin is stated. They come already equipped for their due tasks. They are richly endowed. Not so with a Christian saga that begins with "Blessed are the Poor"—begins with nothing. Parsifal stands midway between old and new. Thus his life also divides in two—a before and an after.

Parsifal begins poor, even less than poor, for his father dies before he is born. It is the will of his mother that he remain poor and as little known in the world as is possible. Yet he is richly endowed as all must see who meet him. He is ever described as "fair," as though a light shines through him. But in his early

257

unpreparedness he commits great follies. He abandons his mother in a heartless manner. He brings untold suffering into the innocent life of beautiful Jeschutte. He slays the Red Knight for wanting his armor, invests himself in that armor and rides forth in it still wrapped as a child in the garments his mother placed round him. And so he comes to his first teacher, Gurnemanz, who nevertheless recognizes his worth and trains him in the shortest possible time in the needs and disciplines of knighthood, clearly born for the part, as were all the heroes of old. Parsifal takes easily all that comes his way, is greatly successful, wins the love of Condwiramur, noblest and loveliest of women, becomes ruler of three kingdoms, and is acknowledged as the Perfect Knight, the flower of all Knighthood. Then, and only then, does the actual Saga begin. Possessing all, he is to find that he holds nothing. Henceforth every step he is to take is through pain and sacrifice. He stands between two worlds, an old and a new; between two loves, the one born of the senses, and the other born of Christ. It happens in this way.

At the peak of his achievement a very simple wish enters into him. His wish is to see his mother once again, not knowing she died when he left her. He finds himself on unfamiliar ground, sees a water, comes upon the Fisher King, and through him finds his entry to the castle of the Grail, where he is to meet him again as Amfortas. What world is he in? He must learn to live in the world and yet move in it as from an inner world. He has to awaken to the kingdom that is not of this world, yet to live in this world. And to begin with he is utterly lost. In this world he is the poorest of poor. He does not meet his mother but he finds himself as a young child again.

Has destiny abandoned him? Destiny never does, but how is one to know one's destiny? Before, it was through the adventures met on the way, but what shape are the adventures to take now? He does not know that the dead are with him in that they follow him step by step: his grandfather King Gandin, his father Gahmuret, whose life, cut short, was a preparation for him, his mother

Herzeloyde, who lived and died for him, and many others whom he may come to know later; but for now he knows nothing.

Yes, there has been some preparation to meet what has to come, but does he recognize it? Shortly after leaving his mother he meets the maiden Sigune, torn with grief, carrying in her arms the form of Schionatulander, her dead lover. He can not know that Schionatulander has died in defense of what is his. Schionatulander in death has become the guiding star of Sigune's being and, through her, of Parsifal too. From Sigune he learns for the first time that his name is Parsifal. In those days one's name was an indication of one's spiritual path. For Parsifal it is a moment of awakening but he scarcely knows it. Yet it brings an element of purpose into his life.

So Parsifal is now within the Castle of the Grail at Munsalvaesche. He meets the Fisher King in the figure of Amfortas, he sees the agony of his suffering, hears the whole company lamenting at the sight of the bleeding lance, witnesses a great sacramental procession at the coming of the Grail, and then the nourishing through the Grail, even receives the Sword of the Grail from the hands of Amfortas, yet his soul remains dumb and silent and he lets it all go by. The world is waiting for one little question but it does not come. Parsifal cannot grasp the moment, he cannot awaken to it, but nor can the moment be waiting for him—it melts away.

That night he sleeps surrounded by "tapers bright." Once before we have seen him sleep amid light all round him—a waking sleep. Condwiramur had sought him out in the night to ask his help. We have heard how Nicodemus came to Christ in the night. Where do we meet in the night if not in Heaven? That is the waking dream. But in this night Parsifal is beset by a swarm of swords; he is in the midst attacked by them all and experiences a suffering as of multiple death. It is as though the sorrows of the world were thrust at him from every side. "Thus fear and unrest awoke him, and the sweat streamed from his every limb."

He wakes to find himself deserted by everyone, yet not entirely alone, for the Sword of the Grail is still there to companion him— so it was not just a dream. He dressed, donned his armor, and mounted his horse. He called but there was no answering call. And then, as he crossed the courtyard and was about to issue from it, the drawbridge was suddenly lifted, flinging him forward with his horse. And now a voice cried out, the voice of the squire who had welcomed him so graciously. "Goose that thou art, ride onward, to the sun's hate hast thou been born."

The words rang through his soul as though resounding from within him, "Goose that thou art." Was it he himself calling, beholding the goose in himself?

Stunned and bewildered, he saw a path and followed it, and there once again he came upon the figure of Sigune, with the dead Schionatulander, now embalmed at her side, as though further removed in death. It took some time before they knew each other. Recognition in the spirit has to be reborn each time. She asked where he had slept. "In a castle a mile away." "Impossible," she cried, "there is no dwelling of any kind for thirty miles around." Then she told him of Monsalvaesche and of Amfortas, bringing the whole vision of his experience vividly before him. Now came the question, "Did you ask?" Yes, he had seen and heard it all as she described, but no, he did not ask.

Then her voice, which had been tender with her own sorrow, and that of Amfortas, and with memories of Herzeloyde his mother, changed abruptly and she said,

> Dishonoured, curst art thou,
> Who bearest wolf's fangs empoisoned.

So she roughly dismissed him, and he heard, as though resounding from his own soul from a greater depth than before, as though he himself were uttering it, "Wolf that thou art."

All trace of the castle had vanished. "Great sweat drops stood on his forehead as he rode on his lonely way." Twice had he been thrust down, but, as though by grace, a special adventure awaited him a little further on his way, maybe to restore his courage.

He met the figure Jeschutte in rags and in fearful distress, hunted and humiliated by her outraged husband Orilus, because of the ring of their plighted troth which he, Parsifal, had wrenched from her finger, totally misreading the counsel his mother had given him at parting. The battle was fierce until Parsifal overcame Orilus, and in a chapel nearby swore to the innocence of Jeschutte and restored her wedding ring. Orilus had been an enemy of Arthur, an enemy of the Grail, an enemy of Parsifal in particular, for it was he who had killed Schionatulander, thinking it was Parsifal he was encountering. Now Parsifal sent Orilus and Jeschutte to the court of King Arthur, thus bringing about a double victory over Orilus, the second being his reconciliation and redemption.

But now whither further must Parsifal go? He has seen the reunion and the renewal of love, and set a goal to others, but he himself has to continue in loneliness along a road that seems to offer nothing and revealed no ending. He is caught in a midworld between the call of the senses and the call of the spirit; between the grace and beauty of Condwiramur, for whom his love had never diminished, and the vision of the suffering Amfortas which now never leaves him. There is no going back and there seems no way forward.

There was snow on the ground in the month of May, winter at Whitsuntide, when the love of heaven descended in tongues of flame upon humanity on earth. Of this Parsifal knew nothing. He had spent the night in a woodland, his sole companion a solitary falcon, lost to its flock as he was. As morning dawned a company of wild geese rose into the air. The falcon sped after them and struck one of them, and three drops of red blood fell upon the snow. Parsifal gazed at the three drops as though in a trance. They stirred in him the greatest longing for Condwiramur and the love he had left behind. He did not know that Arthur and his court were nearby. First a young knight Segramors, seeing him standing there, challenged him, and receiving no reply charged at him. He neither saw nor heard until his horse swerved and then with a single blow he felled Segramors to the ground and became once more absorbed in contemplation of the blood. Then Keie the Seneschal attacked him with even more dire results: for again, the spell broken for a moment, Parsifal cast him heavily to earth, and returned entranced as before. Then came Gawan, a master in the affairs of the heart. He quietly covered the blood by laying his mantle across it. Only then did Parsifal come back to himself. Gawan greeted him and led him to the great company, Arthur and Ginevra and a host of knights and ladies. He was welcomed with great rejoicing, for long had he been sought and now was come. Thus did he sit greatly honored, a wonder to all, but in himself lonely as ever and lost in inner musing.

Then arrived Cundrie, messenger of the Grail, and the host grew silent. Gay were her garments and cultured her manners, but her frame was composed of a disharmony of beasts: long black tresses, bristles of swine, the nose of a dog, tusks of a boar, ears of a bear, hands sharply clawed like a lion's paws, and skin of an ape.

She recounted at great length all the intimacies of Parsifal's background with many details—the nobility of his father Gahmuret, the sorrowing heart of his mother Herzeloyde who had lived and died for him, his splendid half-brother Feirefiz in the far East—and then she spoke so movingly of Amfortas that every heart was melted, and much more she told and finally turned fiercely upon Parsifal whom she reduced to contemptibility, that he had been with Amfortas and had not asked the question of healing that would have brought blessing to all. What was it Parsifal was seeing now and what was he hearing, and what was Cundrie that she could humiliate him so?

He heard the words:

And I deem thou art but a monster, and myself shall fairer be.

All his own unworthiness rose up before him. And she said further:

Thou hawk in fair feathers hidden, bright serpent and poisoned fang.

And there resounded in him from deepest depths:

"Serpent that thou art."

He knew himself now as Goose and Wolf and Serpent, three monsters to be overcome before he could reveal himself in the true likeness of a man. Whatever the others might have seen and heard, the revelation was for him. Early he rose and left the company, bitter at heart, for he saw no way ahead.

We must imagine now that Parsifal was moving through many adventures, meeting with many encounters, and that always his battles led to healing and redemption, as in the case of Orilus. All this was revealed much later, but there were times when rancor assailed him, times when he would revile a merciless God who mocked him whilst concealing from him every way forward. Yet, unbeknown to him, many unseen eyes in heaven were watching with infinite care.

And so it was that on a Good Friday, with snow again on the ground, quite lost to time and his whereabouts, he found himself beside a small hermitage. He called and the figure of a woman came towards him. Again they had to learn to recognize each other. Schionatulander lay in a tomb newly prepared. Faithful Sigune, this last time she and Parsifal were to meet on earth, pointed out a path he was to take. They parted in tenderness. He left it to his horse to find the way and it led him to the threshold of his second and spiritual teacher, Trevrizent. And now it was through Trevrizent that a new stream of life was to flow into his soul, as though the time of probation was over and the time for enlightenment had come.

Three stages of conquest lay ahead of him, three battles with himself. First with the goose.

Trevrizent taught him much: about the fall in Eden; the casting down of Lucifer, prince of pride; the descent of the Grail with the transmuted blood of Christ that flowed from His wounds at Golgotha for the healing and redemption of all humanity. Much more he learned about the Grail and its guardian Templar Knights and the heavy destiny of Amfortas and how he, as King of the Grail, had beclouded his clear vision through earthly desire for a maiden who betrayed him against her own will. Through Trevrizent, Parsifal was able to bring the light and the deed of Christ into his thinking. By degrees the Goose began to transform into the Dove, symbol and bearer of the Holy Spirit, sign and symbol also of the Templar Knights, guardians of the Grail. Parsifal now knew in Christ the meaning of sacrifice and the will to sacrifice.

He left Trevrizent with journeys still to go and tasks still to be met, but he left him filled with a new understanding, with a new resolve, and with a newborn patience to bide his time.

The middle adventure of the heart is left ostensibly to Gawan. He has to pierce the delusive enchantment of the senses to the roots of innocence within. It is he who has to win Orgeluse from her bondage to Clinschor, though for long she treats him as her enemy—taunting, reviling, scorning him, all of which he carries with unflinching faithfulness for the sake of the love he bears her. Only when he has conquered the Chateau Merveille, set up by the evil magic of Clinschor for the imprisoning and transfixing of all that flows as generous love from the human heart, and when he has mastered the dangers of the Perilous Ford, now freed from Clinschor through Gawan's deed, does she reveal her true being to him. We do not meet the image of the wolf directly but we meet its ravages in the human soul. Gawan has to meet the raging lion and bring that rage to stillness and to death. In the end we see how the final stage of this adventure passes to Parsifal, in whose service Gawan labors as his brother and second nature.

And now we come to the third and last adventure in the meeting of Parsifal with Feirifiz, who has come from the East seeking for his father Gahmuret, not knowing that he is dead.

What does Feirifiz represent in this threefold drama, presented in the version of Eschenbach in the guise of three heroes who really are as three-in-one, Parsifal, Gawan and Feirifiz?

Feirifiz appears as a hero of old. His queen Secundille, of whom we only hear, is wondrous wise. She must know of the mysteries of the West. It is she who sent Cundrie as a gift to Amfortas, of whose kingship of the Grail she must have heard, and with Cundrie her brother Malcreatiure, whom Amfortas donated as servant to Orgeluse.

In that love for Orgeluse is his downfall and his grief. He, the King of the Grail, appears on the jousting green like any other knight and there it is an Eastern knight who hurls a poisoned spear at him which pierces him in the groin, inflicting the wound which no outer measure can heal. Feirifiz has a great army and navy at his beck and call, but he sallies forth alone to seek adventure. He has never known defeat. His strength streams to him from the heavenly spheres whose help he calls upon. His virtues he owes to them. He carries as his badge "That wondrous beast Ecidemon," gift of his beloved and loving Secundille.

> . . . on his helmet he bare,
> Ecidemon, all poisonous serpents they must of
> its power beware.

It is therefore not Feirifiz alone but Ecidemon, too, that Parsifal must now confront.

There is a yearning in Feirifiz to know what lives behind the visor of his opponent, but that is denied and they must fight and test the worth of their wills.

There is a moment when a mighty stroke of Feirifiz brings Parsifal down on his knee. The combat grows fiercer and fiercer and now it is Parsifal who with as mighty a blow brings Feirifiz down—but with that blow the sword of Parsifal breaks. With what sword has he been fighting? With the sword of Ither, the Red Knight, whom he brought to his death. The sword of Ither has failed him, a sword that was not his own, and now he is at the mercy of Feirifiz. What is it that moves Feirifiz so deeply that he flings his own sword far from him saying, "Now we are equal, let us rest." Parsifal mentions he is an Anschewin, but Feirifiz, too, is an Anschewin, though he is both black and white. And so the world of East and the world of West meet in these two half-brothers. Parsifal leads Feirifiz to the court of Arthur where they meet Gawan, too.

As they sit, all rejoicing, Cundrie appears again to declare that by heaven's decree Parsifal is now King of the Grail. His dominion holds sway through all the seven heavenly spheres, whose influence is now born anew.

Cundrie leads the two brothers to Monsalvaesche, where Feirifiz hears the question Parsifal puts to Amfortas and sees the miracle of healing take place. Feirifiz sees the queen of the Grail, Repanse de Schoye, and he is caught in a joy and a love he has never known before, great as was his love for Secundille, the wondrous queen of the East. But the Grail he cannot see. Only after the baptism does he behold the Grail and the source of the love that has enraptured him. Rudolf Steiner describes how at the baptism by John the Baptist, the imagination living in the soul is changed, the Serpent of Lucifer is transformed into the Lamb of God. So it is now at the baptism of Feirifiz. Now Secundille has fulfilled her task, and, dying, frees the further way for Feirifiz. He is then able to lead Repanse de Schoye back with him to the East, where she becomes the mother of Prester John. Of him the prophecies tell that he will bring the Christianity of the Grail into Eastern lands, Asia and Africa included.

Parsifal is a saga born of the western world. It is a saga of inner battles that the light and the love and the will of heaven may, through uniting with Christ, grow manifest in us on earth. This is the tale of Parsifal who confronts and overcomes in himself the goose in his thinking, the wolf in his feeling, the serpent in his willing so that the noblest of knights may be raised to become a Son of God.

Rudolf Steiner said that in the countenance of Amfortas we behold the suffering of all humanity. We all have our share in Amfortas. The question put by Parsifal is in the simplest of words. In Eschenbach it is written as "What ails thee, uncle?" The answer is not in words. It is a question born of the deepest compassion of the heart from one human being to another. The answer is not in words but in healing. The world is waiting for Parsifal to be born from within the soul of each one of us.

GRAIL MOUNTAIN AND GARDEN OF MARVELS

Hugh Hetherington

In the last few decades the general respect for mythology and the great legendary images of our ancestors has greatly increased. Indeed the image, whether mythological or not, has come to be regarded by many as a powerful means of communication with our fellows, as well as an indispensable instrument in self-understanding. Copywriters and artists working in advertising make very conscious use of the image as a means of conveying shortly and cogently a particular message, while transpersonal psychology, a development along Jungian lines, uses the symbol as a potent means of discovering the self. It is small wonder that this is so, as the mind moves easily among images and through them reaches out into spheres unvisited by rationalism, unrepresented by the wooden contrivances of mere allegory.

One of the most powerful images in the Western world is that of the Holy Grail, and nowhere more compellingly and richly presented than by Wolfram von Eschenbach, who brought out his version of the story in German in 1200 A.D. It is the purpose of this short study to look at some of the images Eschenbach uses and to attempt to assess their relevance to our spiritual life today.

Those reading Eschenbach's *Parzival* for the first time will be puzzled by the fact that a large part of the poem is not concerned primarily with Parzival's adventures at all, but with those of another hero altogether: Gawain. Further reading will soon reveal that the poem is carefully constructed to reveal the polar difference between

Parzival and Gawain and between their respective adventures. Eschenbach is here concerned with one of the most fundamental polarities of our earthly existence, perhaps most thoroughly worked out by the ancient Chinese in their descriptions of *yin* and *yang*. It appears in European literature as the opposition between emotion and reason, Romantic and Classic schools, in philosophy as the division between subject and object, in biology as the differentiation into female and male, in physiology as the opposite functions of blood and nerve, in psychology as introversion and extroversion, and in mythology it is fully reflected in the great images of moon and sun, of Lower and Upper Gods. But, as the Chinese well knew, *yin* and *yang* are never fully expressed in any identifiable pair of opposites. Each new, freshly worked out polarity throws additional light on the essential nature of *yin* and *yang*, and Eschenbach's contribution is as valuable as any. Its very unexpectedness quickens the imagination to new understanding.

Besides presenting us with a subtle and revealing study of *yin* and *yang*, Eschenbach weaves in two more themes, also of very ancient origin: first, that the human spirit struggles from imperfection to perfection, and secondly, that because of some catastrophe in the remote past the world and humanity stand in need of redemption and this can be carried out only by the perfected human being. So we find both Parzival and Gawain are at the outset, for very different reasons and in very different ways, very far from perfect. Their weaknesses lead them into sore trials from which they learn much. They finally succeed in their quests by reason of their steadfastness and refusal to give in. We also find that the two castles which the two heroes win are each vitiated, lessened in power and enthralled by sickness and enchantment, awaiting the hero who will deliver them. In all other ways they are very different.

Munsalvaesche, the Castle of the Grail, is built upon a high eminence in the middle of an untouched primeval forest, a true wilderness, pathless and waste. In the environs of the hill, the Knights Templar, servants of the Grail in white armor, ride through the glades and rough ways of the forest, guarding the approaches and challenging all strangers. When he first comes to the castle as a young knight, newly wed, Parzival meets no Templar Knight, but unhindered and unchallenged draws rein by a lonely lake at the foot of the Grail Mountain. He sees a boat being rowed on the waters and reclining in it a nobleman in rich clothing. Parzival calls across the waters to this man, enquiring, as night is drawing in, whether there be any lodging in the neighborhood. The King of the Grail, King Fisherman, as he is mysteriously called, is that nobleman and so Parzival is invited to stay the night with his royal host.

This scene calls for imaginative attention: the young man in red armor sitting on his horse by the lakeside, the quiet of the evening and the lonely boat on the water, cutting the still surface and making little eddies in the wreaths of mist rising from the surface at sundown; the still air disturbed by the raised voices of the stranger knight and the nobleman in the boat: all this scene breathes the authentic atmosphere of the Grail. The sense of solitariness, of quiet reflection, of the silence of twilight, of the urgency of the encounter expressed by the ringing call across the water, echoed back by the cliff face of the rocky eminence, the mystery of the boatman on the water and the invitation to visit the Grail Castle, all these build up the sense of a personal quest, undertaken in the inevitable loneliness of spiritual endeavour. What follows is the natural development of this extraordinary beginning. Our eager expectation is aroused and, blessedly, the poet is able to satisfy it to the full. The great images which unfold during Parzival's first visit to the Grail Castle are worthy successors to this deeply poetic overture.

How different is the starting point of Gawain's conquest of his castle. He finds himself in a fair, cultivated and prosperous country, well populated and busy, where the poor work and the rich play: a kind of medieval tapestry, full of incident and adventure. While in some ways it is debatable at what point we can say Gawain begins his quest to redeem *Schastel Marveil*, the Castle of

Marvels, for he is led into it unwittingly and without conscious intent, it is perhaps his meeting with Orgeluse which spurs him on, fiercely and passionately, in the direction he has to go. The scene of this meeting is as carefully composed as the one just described of Parzival by the lake, although it is as different as it could be in atmosphere and coloring.

Gawain sees a castle on a hill and a road that winds round the eminence leading up to the castle gates. This track makes its way through trees, many of them bearing fruit; it is a place of great profusion and vigorous life, no wilderness like the environs of *Munsalvaesche*. Riding up this track, Gawain comes upon a fountain beside the road and, sitting by it in a flowery meadow, a lady so beautiful that he falls in love with her utterly and finally. We soon hear how dangerous it is to love her and that she has lured many a knight to his destruction. Her beauty holds Gawain despite all warnings, despite all her scornful and derisive treatment of him, despite the many trials she bids him undergo. It is during the course of winning this lady's hand that Gawain comes to *Schastel Marveil* and undertakes the perilous adventure which is able to redeem it from the power of the baleful magician, Klingsor. As did Parzival, so does Gawain come upon his castle unawares. How often in life are our major spiritual adventures undertaken without conscious decision on our part.

Moving among the contrasts of this extraordinary story we naturally begin to ask questions. Where in ourselves do we find the wilderness of *Soltane* in which the Grail Mountain is situated, and where *Terre Marveil*, the land on which Klingsor built his castle.

We know both domains well. The one is that land which we must inevitably tread on the path of inner development, where no fellow human being can accompany us or be our proxy. There we have simply to journey, facing whatever comes our way with stoic calm and patience, expecting nothing, but receiving with gratitude what grace may grant us as a gift. The Grail, Parzival is told, cannot be won by feat of arms, or stormed like any common citadel. He who aspires to be called thither must live the good life of a knight and wait for his summons. Gawain's land of marvels is a very different place, but we all know it much better than the lonely forest of *Soltane*. At once the source of the greatest delight and the most acute pain, it is known by every married couple, every lover, every artist and poet, all of whom recognize the need to enter and master it for the sake of his or her own humanity, as Gawain did.

The Grail story makes it quite plain that this mastery of *Terre Marveil* by Gawain is a necessary antecedent to the final consummation of Parzival's quest. Until Gawain is master of his land, Parzival cannot be master of his. In the story there are several veiled hints of the mysterious fact that in essence Gawain and Parzival are one and the same. Both heroes reside in each one of us. The success of the one is entirely dependent on the success of the other. Only when we have achieved true humanity in our relations with others will we be fitted to go that final way to spiritual enlightenment and the beginnings of wisdom on the spiritual path.

It is interesting and indeed somewhat puzzling to find that whereas Gawain's adventures are described in all their colorful detail, Parzival, once he has failed his first test at *Munsalvaesche*, retires into the background. While we hear of him from time to time and know him to be ceaselessly active, and ever more purposefully so as he matures, we know very little of his adventures. We are given towards the end of the poem a list of champions he has overcome in battle, but no details of the combats or history of his opponents. This tantalizing state of affairs suggests that the full adventures of Parzival have still to be written. Maybe it is not fanciful to wonder whether it may be possible to do this in the twentieth century, for Parzival belongs to the future and his achievements are to come. We have to admit with a heavy heart that Amfortas, the wounded Grail King, still suffers and the Castle with him.

For most of us the final achievements of the Grail must wait our further experiences in *Terre Marveil*. There most of us still have to undergo the agonies and tests of Gawain in that enchanted land

and to learn to hear behind the strident tones of some silly quarrel the mocking laughter of Klingsor as he watches his enchantment exert its disrupting and divisive influence on foolish men and women. If this is an admissible interpretation of the images in question, then the seemingly unbalanced composition of Eschenbach's poem is explained. Most of us are more deeply involved, at least consciously, with Gawain and his troubles, and the adventures of Parzival await their final conclusion in the future!

The characters of Parzival and Gawain repay careful study. Of course, they are not rounded individuals as are, for instance, the great Shakespearean characters; rather are they archetypes moving like radiant foci of spiritual forces through the evolving story. They represent, among many other things, of course, the opposites of innocence and experience. The strength of Parzival's growing understanding is precisely that it is fresh, wondering and untainted by past memories which could have dulled and habituated the intensity of immediate, novel experience. It can be compared to the simple wonder of the shepherds in the Christmas story, whose untutored minds alone were worthy to receive the glad tidings of the Angels. Gawain, by contrast, is an experienced man of the world, possessing many of those princely attributes we associate with the Three Kings from the East. What he finds as problems and difficulties, troubles Parzival not at all, and what perplexes Parzival is clear to Gawain. The two characters sound two different notes which together form a wonderful harmony.

Let no one think that any one interpretation or illumination of a symbol explains it finally or completely; rather is it just one tentative and momentary questioning of the life and power of the image. It is touched momentarily by the intellect, yielding perhaps one answer, but many other possible readings exist and will present themselves. If this little study has suggested that the Grail story is incapable of being pinned down to any one rational explanation and remains an endless source of new insights, then the tentative indications of possible approaches will have done no harm.

WOLFRAM AND WAGNER

Eileen Hutchins

Even in his early operas Wagner expressed two of his most dominant themes. In *The Flying Dutchman* (1839) and *Tannhäuser* (1845) appeared the motif of the power of love and sacrifice to redeem one who labored under a curse. In *Lohengrin* (1848) he first revealed his connection with the Grail mystery. He had been very much moved by Wolfram von Eschenbach's *Parzival*, but it was not until 1857 that he had the experience which gave him the impulse for his final work.

In *My Life* he wrote of a bright spring morning following a period of damp cold weather and many personal difficulties and discomforts:

Beautiful spring weather now set in; on Good Friday I awoke to find the sun shining brightly for the first time in this house: the little garden was radiant with green, the birds sang, and at last I could sit on the roof and enjoy the long-yearned-for peace with its message of promise. Full of this sentiment, I suddenly remembered that this day was Good Friday, and I called to mind the significance this omen had already once assumed for me when I was reading Wolfram's *Parzival*. Since the sojourn in Marienbad where I had conceived *The Mastersingers* and *Lohengrin* I had never occupied myself again with that poem; now its noble possibilities struck me with overwhelming force, and out of my thoughts about Good Friday I rapidly conceived a whole drama of which I made a rough sketch with a few dashes of the pen, dividing the whole into three acts.

But it was not until 1882 that this great work was matured and perfected to become Wagner's outstanding final achievement.

To concentrate a long mediaeval romance into an opera of three acts was no mean feat; but Wagner had a wonderful power of distilling the essence of a rich and varied substance. It was not possible to follow Parzival's gradual development through his attainment of judgment, of inspiration and of intuition; but he was able to illuminate certain transcendent moments.

In the first act of the opera we are in the realm of the Grail Castle where the old knight Gurnemanz relates the story of its founding by Titurel and of the opposition of the black magician Klingsor. Titurel's heir, Amfortas, on inheriting the kingship, has proved false to his calling. Through yielding to sensual love he had fallen into Klingsor's power, and not only lost to him the Holy Spear which was able to protect the Grail Community but also received an incurable wound. However the Grail has foretold that redemption will finally be brought by a blameless fool.

Kundry now enters in the form of a wild, frenzied creature whom the esquires regard as a witch or the devil's mare. She has little in common with Wolfram's Kundrie, the Messenger of the Grail, except in the rather menacing impression of her first appearance. The Grail Messenger seems ugly and apparently cruel, because the blows of fate which direct our lives into their rightful channels appear at first incomprehensible and hard to bear. Wagner's Kundry is a complex character. On the one hand, when she is under the spell of Klingsor, she comes in the guise of a beautiful enchantress to seduce the Grail Community and brings soothing balsam for Amfortas. When the esquires discuss her strange behavior, Gurnemanz reminds them that she serves them as a faithful messenger and that perhaps she is laboring under a curse, atoning the guilt of an earlier life.

In Wolfram's poem, Parzival, before approaching the Grail Castle, has already attained the power of judgment and won himself a position in the world; but with Wagner he still appears as an untaught boy. In a few strokes Wagner gives the impression of his hero's ignorance and the pain he causes the Grail Knights. He takes up an episode from Wolfram's story and transmutes it. Wolfram relates how, as a child in the forest, Parzival took joy in the singing of the birds. But when, after having learned to make a bow and arrow, he shot and killed some of them, he was filled with distress and wept bitterly.

In the opera Parsifal's approach is made known by the sight of a swan which sinks wounded to the ground, pierced by an arrow. Parsifal is dragged in and accused of the outrage. But Gurnemanz's expostulation wakens in him a knowledge of what it is to take life. In grief he breaks his bow and arrow. His description of his adventures in pursuit of the Arthurian Knights and his response to Kundry's report of his mother's death show that he has not learned to control his acts and feelings, but the death of the swan is his first awakening.

Gurnemanz, aware of the prophecy, and wondering if this foolish youth may be the promised redeemer, invites him to be present at the Grail Ritual. Here Wagner departs from Wolfram's account and follows other mediaeval traditions. The squire with the bleeding lance, a picture of Amfortas's misdirected will life, does not appear. The Grail ceremony is not represented as a procession of maidens, followed by their queen, bearing "that thing which is called the Grail." The stone which fell from Lucifer's crown has become the Sacred Chalice of the Last Supper; and the Ritual is akin to the celebration of the Mass for which Amfortas is required to fulfill the priestly role. We realize here that spiritual truths can be represented by differing imaginations.

The drama is heightened by the King's frenzied attempt to evade his task until summoned by his father, Titurel. The different musical themes of the Grail, of the love feast and of the declaration of faith, all add up to the solemn mood of the ceremony. Parsifal does not in the least understand what he has seen but his gestures show that he has been deeply moved. Gurnemanz, bitterly disappointed, declares, "Thou art then nothing but a fool." And he pushes the lad impatiently away. But the stirring of compassion is the sign of Parsifal's awakening consciousness, and this is confirmed by the Voice from above, "By pity awakened, the blameless fool."

From a dramatic point of view, Wagner's merging of the two characters of Gurnemanz and Trevrizent is most effective. It is fitting that the one who drives Parsifal from the Grail Castle should also be the one to welcome him back. Although there seems little connection between Wolfram's and Wagner's Gurnemanz, they have an attitude in common. The former, while teaching Parzival the knightly skills, attempts to bind him to the past, both by offering him his daughter Liasse and by teaching him that it is improper to ask questions. Wagner's Gurnemanz, after the Grail Ritual, fails to recognize Parsifal's true destiny and angrily rejects him.

In the second act we are in Klingsor's domain. Wolfram gives the task of overthrowing Klingsor to Gawain, but Wagner assigns it to Parsifal. This is both poetically and dramatically justified. In Wolfram's poem the destinies of Parzival and Gawain are closely related and each from time to time helps the other. When, without recognizing each other, they engage in combat and Parzival discovers he has overthrown his friend, he cries, "Alas that I should have fought with the noble Gawain! It is I myself I have vanquished." Within the scope of Wagner's opera, it is essential to keep Parsifal as the central figure so that the conflict between Klingsor and the Grail Knights may become a leading dramatic theme.

In this act we become more fully acquainted with Kundry, who is one of Wagner's most powerful creations. While she has little relationship with the Messenger of the Grail, she can be compared with Wolfram's Orgeluse, who lures Amfortas into Klingsor's power and wins the ardent admiration of Gawain. When, however, Gawain fulfills the task by which she hopes to destroy him, he has the strength to reject her. This redeems her so that she becomes free from Klingsor's spell.

But while Kundry can be compared to Orgeluse, she is by no means a shadowy reflection; she is a character in her own right. Through her, Wagner affirms the law of reincarnation. Klingsor addresses her as Herodias who brought about the death of John the Baptist; and Kundry herself tells Parsifal that she laughed when she saw Christ carrying the Cross. She is unable to escape the burden of her destiny and so she is under Klingsor's power, although she longs to free herself.

With great skill she tries to entangle Parsifal by telling him of his mother and, having won his attention, to convince him that Mother-love has to be transformed into sensual satisfaction. But, when she bestows upon him a passionate kiss, he is suddenly made aware of her wiles. He feels the pain of Amfortas's wound and rejects her with violence. She then tries another approach. She strives to stir his pity. She confides in him her tragic destiny and pleads that if he will yield to her for but one hour, she will be saved. But Parsifal experiences only horror at her approach.

In fury Kundry summons Klingsor to her aid. He appears with the Holy Spear; but the power to use it fails him. It hovers over Parsifal's head and, as he makes with it the sign of the cross, Klingsor's castle of evil enchantment falls into ruin.

Before leaving, Parsifal gives Kundry a note of hope. He says, "Thou knowest where thou canst find me once again."

Her further progress now depends on her own effort.

A brief comment needs to be made here on the part played by the Flower Maidens. In Wolfram's poem we are told that Klingsor held captive in the Chateau Merveil four hundred ladies, including the mother of King Arthur and Gawain's sister. Whereas the Grail Castle reveals itself only to those regarded as worthy to approach it, the way into Klingsor's realm is easy to find, but no escape is possible. It is implied that those who are unable to transform their feeling life are likely to be his prey. The Flower Maidens are only shadowy reflections of these dignified ladies, but their seductive music and song provide a welcome interlude between the stormy conflict of Klingsor with Kundry and the dramatic awakening of Parsifal.

In Wolfram's poem the deed that can heal Amfortas is the question, "Uncle, what is it that ails you?" For the initiate, his words have attained the power of an act. In Rudolf Steiner's words, "the knight of the sword" has become "the knight of the word." With Wagner the Holy Spear is the symbol of the purified will which is no longer directed to self-interest but has become an instrument to serve world karma.

In the third act we are once more in the neighborhood of the Grail Castle. Gurnemanz, like Trevrizent, has now retired as a hermit. The Grail Knights have fallen on evil days, for Amfortas has ceased to perform the ritual and has thus brought about the death of the aged Titurel.

It is Good Friday and a beautiful spring morning. Gurnemanz is disturbed to hear the sound of groaning. In a nearby thicket he discovers Kundry, chilled and apparently lifeless. When he has restored her to consciousness, she humbly begs to offer her services; he is surprised at the change in her behavior, as she now appears humbled and softened.

At this moment they notice the approach of a knight, clothed in black armor. Gurnemanz reproves him for entering this holy realm in war apparel on the morning of Good Friday. When the knight removes his armor and kneels in silent prayer before his spear, Gurnemanz and Kundry suddenly realize that he is the Fool, and in astonishment they recognize the Holy Spear.

Parsifal now describes to Gurnemanz the paths of error and suffering through which he has passed. He has had to face many dangers and fight many battles since overcoming Klingsor; but he has kept the Holy Spear unprofaned by these conflicts. We are here given an impression of the gradual process of development before initiation can be attained.

Gurnemanz is now able to greet Parsifal as the deliverer who will bring Amfortas's agony to an end; but Parsifal himself is overcome with sorrow to think of the long delay caused by his own failure. He is led to the spring where Kundry bathes his feet and Gurnemanz anoints his head with the pure water as token of his atonement. He addresses him with the words:

Thrice blessed be, thus purified, thou pure one.

Meanwhile Kundry has drawn a golden vial from her breast and, pouring the oil over Parsifal's feet, dries them with her hair in the gesture of the repentant Mary Magdalene. Parsifal takes the vial from her and passes it to Gurnemanz, who now anoints him as King, with the words:

Thou blameless! Patient in suffering, by pity wakened!
As the Redeemed One's sufferings thou hast suffered.

As his first kingly act, Parsifal bends down and, gathering water from the spring, baptizes Kundry who sinks weeping at his feet.

We now come to one of the most beautiful moments in the opera, when Wagner is drawing on his own spiritual experience of the joyous mood breathed out by the world of nature on Good Friday.

In Wolfram's poem, when his hero comes to Trevrizent, he has already attained mastery over his own soul powers, but he has not fully realized his guilt or united himself with the Christ. In the opera, Parsifal has already accepted his failure and has achieved the strength to heal Amfortas, but his experience of the Christ Being has still to be deepened. In both the poem and the opera the meeting with the hermit is a central moment in the development of the story. When Christ's blood flowed from the Cross, the world of nature rejoiced, for He had now united Himself with the Earth and His Deed had redeemed the sin of Adam. The mood of joy and peace is all pervading.

Now all Creation doth rejoice
In this the Saviour's love to trace—
On the Cross uplifted Him no more it seeth,
It therefore looketh up to man redeemed.

Through the power of the music Gurnemanz's words are raised into a higher realm.

The bell now tolls for the funeral of Titurel, and Gurnemanz guides Parsifal and Kundry to the Grail Castle which appears before us. There is a dramatic contrast with the Good Friday scene when Amfortas cries to his Knights to slay him, as he can no longer bear the anguish of his pain and guilt.

At this moment Parsifal enters and, laying the point of the Holy Spear upon Amfortas' wound, declares:

One only weapon serves:
The Spear that smote must heal thee of thy wound.

A wonderful transformation takes place. Amfortas's expression of agony gives way to holy rapture. Parsifal ascends the steps of the altar and unveils the Grail, which glows with light while a dove descends over Parsifal's head. As the newly appointed King waves the Grail in blessing over the assembled Knighthood, Kundry sinks lifeless to the ground, her curse at last removed; and a Voice from above proclaims:

Wondrous high salvation! Redeemèd the Redeemer!

Wagner reveals the knowledge that without human recognition, Christ's deed would have been ineffectual, but, through this recognition, the Divine and the human are reconciled.

In his lecture, "Richard Wagner and Mysticism," given in Berlin on December 2, 1907, Rudolf Steiner said, "An impulse akin to that of Spiritual Science lived in one of the greatest artists of our time." However, he went on to point out that Wagner was not fully conscious of his inspiration, for he considered himself a pupil of Schopenhauer, and nothing could be further from this pessimistic philosopher's outlook than that which is expressed in Wagner's art. It is as though the legends which provided the content of his operas spoke to him and revealed their secrets. Whatever myths he accepted, whether from early Germanic times as with *The Ring*, or from mediaeval sources such as *Tannhäuser* or *Lohengrin*, Wagner was able to express their deepest meaning. *Parsifal* itself wonderfully conveys the mediaeval wisdom of esoteric Christianity.

At a time when Science, Art and Religion had become separated and dramatists turned more and more to realistic interpretations of life, Wagner strove to unite these different realms and, like the Greeks, to seek inspiration from Mystery Wisdom. He considered that all works of art should express truth and be acts of religious worship. Wagner considered that the two geniuses able to give revelations from a spiritual realm were Beethoven and Shakespeare, the one creating out of an inner world of inspiration, the other through a waking clairvoyance which enabled him to penetrate the inmost hearts of his characters.

In an article on Beethoven Wagner describes how the Overture to *Coriolanus* illuminates the leading theme of Shakespeare's play. Through the union between the inner realm of music and the outer world represented by Shakespeare, one is able to understand more deeply the leading theme of the drama: namely, the conflict between the characters of Volumnia and Coriolanus. Music and drama should enhance each other. Wagner set out to achieve this enhancement in his own operas, in which the poetry plays as important a part as the music.

We owe a great debt to Wagner, not only for his vision of Art as Mystery Wisdom, but also for his bringing to recognition the Parsifal theme. It was the performance of the opera that inspired Jessie Weston to translate Wolfram's poem and thus introduce it to the English-speaking world. At a time when materialism was gaining its greatest power, this representation of the true human being in relationship to the life of our times appeared as a shining light and, for those who were able to understand, prepared the way for the present age.

REFERENCES

Wolfram von Eschenbach, *Parzival*
Rudolf Steiner, "Richard Wagner and Mysticism"
  (lecture in Berlin, 2 December 1907)
Richard Wagner, "Beethoven" (in *Prose Works*, vol. 5)
—— *My Life*
—— *Parsifal*

CHRISTOPHER FRY AND THE RIDDLE OF EVIL

Adam Bittleston

Meadows, the oldest of the four soldiers in Christopher Fry's *A Sleep of Prisoners*, says towards the end of the play:

> Thank God our time is now when wrong
> Comes up to face us everywhere,
> Never to leave us till we take
> The longest stride of soul men ever took.

The wrongs done in the twentieth century have been of a kind, and on a scale, baffling all ordinary comprehension. If we take a most terrible example—the murder of six million Jews in Europe—we can see how minds everywhere, not only in Germany, can hardly begin to face or understand this fact; there is a strong temptation to push it out of consciousness. And yet we may feel that unless we achieve more genuine knowledge of how evil can take hold of us—creatures, as we are accustomed to see ourselves, on the whole well-meaning, but weak—our time will hold further horrors against which we have no adequate defense. "The longest stride of soul men ever took" must include the determination to find out the source of evil, and the reasons for its power.

Rudolf Steiner had much to say about this. He recognized that the great traditional Christian teachings could not by themselves satisfy our needs; for many people these have become remote, and themselves in need of explanation. From his own spiritual research, he could often describe how and why evil has been at work in human history. Such descriptions are not easy to assimilate. While external, visible evil seems to present us with an unknown, with something at least more extreme than what we meet in our own character, the initiate appears to be describing beings and events still more difficult to grasp, utterly beyond our experience.

Neither realm is as distant as we suppose. But to discover this we need courage and imaginative self-knowledge. In his lecture, "Evil and the Future of Man," Rudolf Steiner points out that in every modern human being the inclination to all possible evil exists. Even if we are willing to see this, it may evade our recognition unless we can trace quickly the connection between great things and small ones, and can form pictures sufficiently vivid and mobile to illuminate them both.

Here the true artist and poet can help us greatly. They give us pictures that are both near our particular experience, and transparent for universal realities. Where they represent evil, it will not have the nightmare bleakness of a newspaper report, because their accounts are more complete. And in a description, however terrible, which contains imaginative sympathy, we shall be helped to recognize ourselves. It may even be comedy that does us some of the best service in this way.

In the dedication of *A Sleep of Prisoners* to Robert Gittings, Christopher Fry writes:

We were talking even then [about 1932] as we are talking, with greater instancy, now [1951], of the likelihood of war. And I think we realized then, as we certainly now believe, that progress is the growth of vision: the increased perception of what makes for life and what makes for death. I have tried, as you know, not altogether successfully, to find a way for comedy to say something of this, since comedy is an essential part of men's understanding. In *A Sleep of Prisoners* I have tried to make a more simple statement, though in a complicated design....

Do the pictures given in Christopher Fry's plays—which have this intention of describing "what makes for life and what makes for death"—accord with the vision of the nature of evil to be found in Rudolf Steiner's work? Quite apart from any question of a poet's own personal opinions, we may expect to find harmony between what is born of genuine artistic imagination and what comes from true spiritual knowledge. Such things test and illuminate each other mutually. We can be confident, too, that nothing which is widely loved and enjoyed is without relation to the deep needs of its time.

To grasp Rudolf Steiner's descriptions of history, and in particular the above-mentioned lecture, we have to understand his account of three elements in the human soul, distinguished (by terms not altogether satisfactory in English) as the Sentient Soul, the Intellectual Soul, and the Spiritual or Consciousness Soul. Through the element of the Sentient Soul we make immediate responses—of joy and grief, for example—to the impressions of the external world. Through the Intellectual Soul we form a coherent inner life, interpreting experience, guiding action by thought. In the Spiritual Soul an objective comprehension of the world is achieved, a vision detached, above the personal, even towards one's own self, one's own thinking, feeling, and willing. In everyday experience these elements are intricately mixed. The distinction between them is not meant just as an intellectual analysis, but as a guide to basic facts of human origin and development. Thus any description of these elements is not intended as a definition, but as a signpost pointing in the direction of a reality.

It is most striking that Christopher Fry seems to observe vividly and accurately the clash and contrast of these elements of the soul. In *The Lady's Not for Burning*, two people find themselves out of place in the late mediaeval society around them. One, a young soldier, having looked at the vastness of the world and what seems the unending pattern of hopes and disappointments in human life, comes to the Mayor of the little town and asks to be hanged. The other, the Lady, an alchemist's daughter, has looked at the small things of Nature with wonder and has been led on to experiment so that she has come under active suspicion as a witch, and should be burned. But when they meet, both come to think better of the future, and during the Mayor's birthday party, they slip away.

In these two persons, human beings are described who already in youth feel the urgent pressure of the Spiritual Soul, in the midst of an environment complacently mediaeval, dominated by the achievements of the Intellectual Soul—orthodoxy, law, convention. Figures of a comedy, they have their affinity with two tragic figures of the age in which the Spiritual Soul began to have pervasive influence. The young soldier is a Hamlet driven, until he meets a rescuer, to despair—not over the complexities of his personal situation but over life generally. The girl is a relation of Faust's—but young, fresh, and a woman. Through mutual support they can hope to protect the dangerous birth and childhood of the new age.

In *The Dark is Light Enough*, set in Austria in 1848-49, the Countess Rosmarin Ostenburg has three friends, who are usually present, but take no direct part in the actions involving her destiny. They make their comments, give their advice, but cannot intervene; their own lives are somewhere else. These three can be seen as precise representatives—as well as being personalities in themselves—of Sentient Soul, Intellectual Soul, Spiritual Soul. Once more it must be emphasized that these are not abstractions, but real powers in the soul, of which one or other will be prevailing in any human being. In Jacob there is towards the gracious, witty Countess a resolutely uncritical loyalty that springs from the Sentient Soul. Belmann is a fascinating study of the Intellectual Soul, worrying about approval and disapproval. Dr. Kassel has the patient objectivity of the Spiritual Soul.

From the account of the Spiritual Soul given up to this point, it might well seem that this element in our being has least of all to do with evil. And yet Rudolf Steiner describes that the very influences that can spiritualize the Spiritual Soul—can develop, in fact, its full potentialities—are also at work in every kind of evil impulse.

The Spiritual Soul is concerned with *facts*. In its historical development, the facts to which it at first has access are those of the physical world. It sees this, to begin with, bare of purpose and meaning—which it must allot to the sphere of human opinions, not to the realm of facts. But from this bare vision no satisfactory guidance for conduct can be obtained, in spite of all the efforts of utilitarians and ethical societies—as the twentieth century has amply demonstrated in its use of the inheritance of the nineteenth. The Spiritual Soul needs to make the transition from an objectivity only capable of grasping physical (or mathematical) facts to a much more comprehensive objectivity.

In *The Dark is Light Enough* there is a figure, Richard Gettner, who brings about the situation on which the play turns. Earlier he had been married to the Countess's daughter, Gelda; but the marriage had been dissolved. Now he has come to the middle years of life. In the revolution of the Hungarians against the government at Vienna, he has allowed himself to be swept into the Hungarian service. But then he deserts from the revolutionary army and appeals to the Countess for protection.

Everything seems to have gone wrong: his political relationships, his marriage, and also his work as a poet and writer. But he says:

No one has ever failed to fail in the end:
And for the very evident reason
That we're made in no fit proportion
To the universal occasion; which as all
Children, poets and myth-makers know

Was made to be inhabited
By giants, fiends, and angels of such size
The whole volume of human generations
Could be cupped in their hands;
And very ludicrous it is to see us,
With no more than enough spirit to pray with,
If as much, swarming under gigantic
Stars and spaces.

In Gettner's way of thinking we find the impulses of the Spiritual Soul powerfully at work. For him the traditions about man's place in the universe, developed through the other forces of the soul in earlier times, have withered away. Thus the Countess can describe him (in one of what a dramatic critic called her "impenetrably Sibylline utterances"):

Richard sometimes reminds me of an unhappy
Gentleman, who comes to the shore
Of a January sea, heroically
Strips to swim, and then seems powerless
To advance or retire, either to take the shock
Of the water or to immerse himself again
In his warm clothes, and so stands cursing
The sea, the air, the season, anything
Except himself, as blue as a plucked goose.
It would be very well if he would one day
Plunge, or dress himself again.

He has taken off all those clothes from the past that hold him, like stiff, yet comfortable uniforms, within a particular status and the kind of conduct that belongs to it. He feels himself and others in their bare weakness and failure. Only self-preservation, and at times one other principle, guide him. This occasional light comes from the recognition that a spirit shapes the actions of the Countess which is quite different from the traditional rules and loyalties of the rest. What it can be, he does not yet know, and wandering in the gap between past and future, he comes near to breaking Gelda's second, happy marriage and to killing the Countess's son.

In the realm of bare facts, human beings appear separate from one another. This can lead to unbearable loneliness. But if the Spiritual Soul is to find a way out of isolation, without violence to others, it must do so through the power of imagination. Directly we reject imaginative understanding, we begin in some way to impose ourselves upon another. Gettner has fought against this danger. During the time of their marriage, he explains to Gelda:

> There you were,
> Rambling your way out of childhood,
> Not knowing what innocence was, being innocent,
> And, in a way, perfect in your imperfection.
> I don't know how I was expected
> To pair with that, unless I was willing
> To be the misfortune around the house,
> The disappointer of expectations,
> Affecting virtue so that I should not see
> The shadow go across you.
> I preferred to remain unracked, as I preferred
> To stay silent....

Then he succeeded not to be her disaster. But unless he can understand more about her, can reach beyond saying to her, "I begin to wonder who you are," the danger is there again.

* * *

How exactly Fry shows the entry of evil at the point where imaginative understanding is refused can be shown from the earlier play, *Venus Observed*. The Duke of Altair, many years a widower, asks his

290

twenty-year-old son Edgar to chose a stepmother for himself from among three women, to whom the Duke has been at various times attached. It is the morning of an eclipse of the sun. To this the Duke gives the enthusiastic attention of a devoted amateur astronomer. Almost immediately afterwards, he starts to make havoc of the situation, already uncomfortable for most of those concerned, by falling in love with his agent's young daughter, Perpetua.

The theme of *Venus Observed* is the need for maturity. In his astronomy the Duke can practice the clear impersonal awe, the exact observation, which belong to the Spiritual Soul. In his dealings with people, and his judgments about himself, such qualities are present very fitfully.

It is one of the original, unconscious candidates for stepmotherhood who brings him to reality. Rosabel has least of all acquired any of the qualities of maturity, and is a good deal younger in her reactions than those young in years. Everything, including the eclipse of the sun, is regarded by her as it affects her own emotions, and in no other way. And what seems to her the Duke's remoteness from human feeling infuriates her, to the point of her setting fire at night to the observatory, and nearly causing the death—though this was not her intention—of the Duke and Perpetua.

Early in the play, Rosabel expresses her rejection of the task that would lead her to maturity:

> It's a thing I have no love for,
> To have to go groping along the corridors
> Of someone else's mind, so that I shan't
> Be hurt. No one has any right to ask it.

The need to make an impression on the Duke, whom she refuses to understand, becomes in her an obsession, which she vaguely recognizes as akin to the great impulses of evil at work in history:

One thought in my head,
Persevering like someone running on a race-track;
When it seems to be going it's coming again.
I wrestle with it, and hold it close,
I can't let it go, nor laugh it away. Is this
How men get driven to send history lurching on
To God knows where? Nothing matters
Except that he should be made to feel.

Rosabel wishes herself to remain at the stage of the Sentient
Soul—in the mood characteristic of the age between twenty-one
and twenty-eight. But what drives her to violence is a frustrated
impulse of the Spiritual Soul, a fire that seeks to become comprehension. And the external fire she lets loose does in fact enkindle
compassion and humble self-knowledge in the Duke.

There is no escape from the forces of evil by staying behind, or
by turning back. We have to try to cross the gap, to plunge into
the deep waters. What happens then?

In *Venus Observed*, no one altogether expresses maturity. To
hear mature voices, we have to listen to the Countess herself, or to
Tim Meadows. These are shown as happy and wise in age,
through the power of their inner being, achieving, as Gettner says,

a stability
Beside which any despair was compelled to hesitate.

As we have seen, the Countess can form pictures of other human
beings' inner conditions, instead of judging their actions. Gettner
cannot at once interpret her picture; he knows only that she is in
some way at home by the "still waters" where others, and he himself,
fear storm, and peril of drowning. The Countess has followed a
path described in certain respects by Rudolf Steiner in his lecture;
through imaginative perception of others, to compassion, and on to
a still deeper union with the needs and destinies of humanity.

292

The first two steps given by Rudolf Steiner here are a vision that can feel and interpret the significance of another's bodily form and movements, growing warm and cold as it does so; and then the recognition of another's thought, in its light and color. Gettner supposes that the concern of the Countess for his life, the intimate warmth of understanding which he feels in her presence, must come from the Sentient Soul, from "loving" according to Eros or at least "liking." And it seems at first a contemptuous answer, when the Countess says he means to her

Simply what any life may mean.

She (whose own writing is so inscrutable) can read in the outward form the signature of the eternal being. She knows, too, the dark and the gleaming light of his thought. Her whole practice of the "Thursday evenings" is indeed a school for the second faculty Rudolf Steiner describes. A group of people meet for discussion, on widely varied subjects, not in order to convince one another, but to hear and experience one another's thought. She is continually at hand to divert them from collisions, to lift the discussion into freedom. There has always to be, at such meetings, a shaking loose of meanings from the dried shells of words, and a discovering, *behind* what is said, of one another's deepest spiritual loyalties. There comes to light how a man is connected with the spirit of his country, the Archangel (as Rudolf Steiner speaks of him), or with the spirits of other nations; and with the spirit of his time, and other times.

The next, exceedingly difficult step is into one another's life of feeling. Rudolf Steiner relates this to the process of breathing, which is normally related intimately to our *own* feelings, but can become the bearer of compassion in quite concrete ways. We receive three streams of the world's being into ourselves: through the senses, through breathing, and through food and drink. Of breathing, as something continuing uninterruptedly, we are least aware. There is always (since we were weaned) something in some way foreign to us, one-sided, too little or too much, about our food, and also in what we receive through the senses; our eyes and our stomachs have always some tendency to make us ill. But our breathing mediates and pacifies. Often Rudolf Steiner showed how in its rhythm it reflects in miniature the great rhythms of sun and stars, and the lesser rhythm of sleeping and waking continued through life.

And yet the point of balance, the way in which mediation is achieved, is individual in each one of us. Ultimately, it is conditioned by the kind of balance that we have in the soul, between knowledge of the world and action. To have compassion is to enter another soul's struggle for the achievement of this balance. All the complicated efforts of another's heart can become reflected, one day in the future, in our own breathing—just as we know at present, on the simplest level, the infectiousness of laughter or yawning.

But sympathy may be refused. The friends of the Countess are not willing to feel with Gettner; Belmann sees him not as a man, but as an animal or less: "I should more likely weep for stags or partridges." Yet *something* we have to do with one another. If we will not breathe *with* a man, we may find ourselves trying to knock the breath out of him. There is a vivid example at the beginning of *A Sleep of Prisoners*. Of the four soldiers locked up in a church, Peter Able and David King are young and friends. But Peter does not take the war, or their imprisonment, or the enemy, very seriously. He laughs at his friend's anger. And in fury at last David springs at him:

> You laugh: I'll see you never laugh again.
> Go on: laugh at this.

He is pulled away before he has strangled Peter; and in a moment he is filled with concern and shame. But the murderer who is hidden in us all has stirred. He lives in our minds, willing to silence the other's thought; but still more deeply in our lungs, willing to stop the other's breath. We can form some inkling of how it is that the *same* force which enables us to leap out of ourselves, as it were, in sympathy with another, can lead, if it is distorted and frustrated, to the violent imposition of our own feelings outside ourselves, which is the mark of many kinds of evil.

* * *

Finally, Rudolf Steiner speaks of human beings in the future, who have a common task, learning to digest one another's will. At the critical moment, when a Hungarian officer demands from the Countess that she deliver up Gettner, she says:

> You put me very near the hard heart of the world,
> Colonel, where bad and good eat at the same table.
> No man is mine to give you.

At the table of Earth, as at the Last Supper, there is a place for each, even for the betrayer. It is hard indeed to digest the equal right of each to live and be accepted and understood. It is a very great temptation to claim the right to *make* the other conform to one's own pattern, if we have to live at close quarters.

A Sleep of Prisoners may be understood as the achievement by the four soldiers of thorough mutual acceptance. It is shown in dreams, containing in a single night what in waking life might take months or years of effort. Each man dreams events of the past, brought near by the church in which they sleep; the murder of Abel, the death of Absalom, the offering of Isaac, the men in the fiery furnace. In each dream the dreamer pictures himself and the others in characteristic forms.

At first, the impulse behind the attempted murder, just before they slept, shows itself in all the tragedy and terror of Cain. But then, through the experience of David and Absalom, the soldier David knows how within his very anger there is something of loving, grieving concern for the other. And when the night is still deep, but turned towards morning, Peter, the victim, feels himself in Isaac. (The name means "Laughter"; "And Sarah said 'God hath made me to laugh, so that all that hear will laugh with me.'") Now his friend is Abraham, who is indeed prepared to kill, but in obedience, as an offering, without any whisper of hate.

Last, Corporal Adams dreams, who bears responsibility for the rest; and his dream they all come to share. Through the pictures in which their souls have lived, compassion for one another is strong in them. They see a spirit of evil, not an earthly person, as the common enemy; a power that poisons human language, and claims complete ownership over human beings. But to understand this power thoroughly, the spirit that obsesses great and small dictators, brings liberations from it. They feel themselves within a great fire, that does not kill:

> Look, how intense
> The place is now, with swaying and troubled figures.
> The flames are men: all human. There's no fire!
> Breath and blood chokes and burns us. This
> Surely is unquenchable? It can only transform.
> There's no way out. We can only stay and alter.

The wrong kinds of human society try to impose their standards, to make us something less than human creatures serving some one-sided purpose. A Christian society calls us to alter particularly by making the genuine sacrifice of accepting us as we are. The Countess Rosmarin influences people far-reachingly, as Belmann truly sees, by complete respect for their freedom. The four soldiers form a miniature society based on this principle—though it is not a "principle" in the ordinary sense, but Christian magic.

It has been objected that Fry is preaching a quite unpractical pacifism. But this misses the point; the activity of the Spiritual Soul, the inward "digesting" of the other as Rudolf Steiner describes it, is equally possible for combatant as for Quaker; and either can equally neglect to make any step towards it.

The Spiritual Soul lives in a far-reaching tension. It experiences consciousness as bound to the momentary conditions of a particular body; and yet its own nature is without frontier, drawn by kinship to the universal and eternal. This tension is summed up in the fact of death.

> Protect me
> From a body without death. Such indignity
> Would be outcast, like a rock in the sea.
> But with death, it can hold
> More than time gives it, or the Earth shows it.

The Hungarians have been defeated, and the government is executing their leaders. The Hungarian officer, who came at the head of his troops searching for Gettner, now comes as a fugitive in his turn. The Countess is warned that to protect him will bring further disaster on the household. And though she is calmly determined to do so, she acknowledges the truth of this advice almost with bitterness:

> There is nothing
> They may not do; there's no foolishness
> They may not think; souls who will not budge
> Out of their barren islands.

As the Spiritual Soul works with increasing power in coming centuries, it cannot be avoided that the forces of death encroach further and further into human lives. We shall be more and more aware, unless in some way we drug ourselves, of carrying death about with us. But at once, when we acknowledge the barrenness of our islands, we open ourselves to the power of the Resurrection.

The death of the Countess, in the course of her final conversation with Gettner, can be included in a comedy because we know that she has long carried in her the victory over death. She is only turning a further corner in the devious and yet direct journey on which she has set out to help him.

From the first, the Spiritual Soul is at home with the earth-element in us, represented above all by the skeleton. But unless it is to remain a prisoner, it has to find confident relationships with those elements among which it can learn about the living unity of the world, and not only about dry fragments: with water, air and fire. Water teaches the mutual dependence of living things. Air awakens to the power of the soul. Fire leads life from the spirit, and back into the spirit. Each asks of us an understanding far more active and flexible than we are accustomed to give. And this is the understanding needed for the transmutation of evil.

St. John relates that on Easter Sunday evening the Risen Christ breathed upon the disciples and said: "Receive ye the Holy Spirit: whosoever sins ye remit, they are remitted unto them; and whosoever sins ye retain, they are retained."

The awakening of the disciples to the soul-element in the breath of Christ brings the power to distinguish among earthly sins. From a part, they should be released. There is much, belonging to the general blindness and stupidity, best altogether forgotten; or, if remembered, not laid to the account of any particular person. At the same time, there are responsibilities that should be completely accepted, and turned into strength; Paul, for instance, would never forget that he had persecuted the Christians.

Deeds of the second kind, the work of individual will, have to be written into Earth, as Christ shows with the women taken in adultery. Their consequences have to be met through the earnest acceptance of the working of destiny. But we are clouded, in the perception of such things, by all the effects of blundering and triviality obscuring the essentials.

Good comedy can be part of the healing breath that laughs things clear. The great responsibilities must not be hidden; but a fresh wind blows, lifting us free of obstinate entanglements of will and feeling, or stiff habits of thought. Thus Hroswitha sought to transplant comedy into the Christian tradition; thus Shakespeare turned back to comedy, without in any way forgetting what he had learned about evil, after the great tragedies; thus Molière held up a mirror before the absurdities into which the Intellectual Soul can fall, unless it learns about the time into which we have come.

And now, in the twentieth century, we certainly need a mood in comedy that is not trivial, and that can lift us out of some muddy obsessions and despairs. For, as Meadows says, in words that follow those quoted at the beginning:

> Affairs are now soul size.
> The enterprise
> Is exploration into God.
> Where are you making for?
> It takes
> So many thousand years to wake,
> But will you wake for pity's sake?

NOTE: Teachers especially will find treasures in two of Christopher Fry's plays which Bittleston does not mention here. *Thor with Angels* has often been acted by 11th and 12th graders in Waldorf schools. It is intensely dramatic and furnishes them with a vivid backdrop for their studies in the history of literature. Taking place just as St. Augustine is approaching England, it foreshadows the great changes that follow upon the coming of Christianity. Best of all, it is couched in magnificently vital Anglo-Saxon language: "I'll carve your dropsical torso to a tassel." Eighth and ninth graders also enjoy the charm of *Boy with a Cart*. [CB]

REFERENCES

Christopher Fry, *The Dark is Light Enough*
—— *The Lady's Not For Burning*
—— *A Sleep of Prisoners*
—— *Venus Observed*
Rudolf Steiner, "Evil and the Future of Man"

QUESTING TOWARD A TRUE
UNDERSTANDING OF GRAMMAR

Susan Demanett

In the 1990s, English teachers often face, from students, some-times from parents, and even from other teachers, dumbfounded incomprehension as to why grammar should form an essential part of the curriculum. At the same time, educators and parents bemoan the decadent state into which language has fallen, and wonder why students seem unable to speak with clarity or find meaningful forms of expression—a condition Jane Healy refers to as "McLanguage," with all the predictable associations to junk food, junk words, and ill health.

From the medieval tale of Parzival, an image arises as an icon of the approach one might take toward language, grammar, and its mission today. In the legend, Parzival enacts the inner human drama of 'piercing the veil.' Parzival's path takes him from dullness through doubt to blessedness (or salvation, or soul health and san-ity perhaps). Likewise, we too could seek to resurrect or heal lan-guage by pressing on from lack of awareness through resistance and denial to a true understanding of the cosmic mystery of the Word made manifest in human speech. T. S. Eliot serenely exhorts us "to arrive where we started and to know the place for the first time." Just as the esoteric mystery hidden within the songs of Eschenbach appeared to some as a mere adventure story, there were others whose wakefulness could catch the *flying metaphor,* and detect profound mysteries expressed therein. I suspect also that with language, its true redemption lies—among other things—in grammar, the power of which often goes unrecognized, or is perhaps forgotten—lost in our ignorance or denial.

What has happened to language? Can we trace its fall? In the *English Journal*, the magazine of the National Council of Teachers of English, January 1944, the president of the council, Max J. Herzberg, offered some telling comments. In his address, he referred to the horror of the world wars—"this mad age of terror... and a thunderous, bewildering world"—and considered the state of language as follows:

> Language study meanwhile is proceeding, although at a much more laggard pace, away from such narrow and usually very wasteful techniques as grammar and spelling toward a truer conception of the whole vast system of ideas that today we call *communications*.... To a broader view of language [youth's] interest might more readily be drawn.... We realize with poignant regret that a failure in human communication plunged mankind down this abyss....

These comments provide testimony that even in the eyes of linguistic scholars, by the 1940s, language had been demoted from its earlier status as a vehicle for the voice of the *Muse*—or gods, as it had been for Homer and Moses—to an instrument of mere utilitarian value, a tool for *communications*.

To arrive at a true appreciation of the potential role of grammar in the resurrection of language, it is worthwhile to retrace the origin of language and its subsequent descent.

In the beginning was the Word. We are told the cosmic Word was uttered as an unfathomably profound creative force—the Word; an act of will, the utterance of *a* Word, *the* Word, spoken by and from the gods. And what precisely was uttered? Rudolf Steiner tells us that the primal Word uttered was the sentence that is the alphabet. The whole alphabet arises out of images in the cosmos. What streams from the zodiac is the forming, sculpting force of the consonants, while from the planets arise the music of the vowels. The echoes of each work comes right into the physical body.

As we follow the descent of the Word during human evolution, we find language existing first as gesture, expressed as will but unconscious; then gesture becomes focused in the larynx and sound is born into language, with speech and song much resembling one another. We perhaps still find vestiges of this condition in Mandarin Chinese, in which intonation renders meaning, or in the eloquent cooing of babies. Steiner described it in this way:

Human feelings were guided by sound, differentiated complicated images in consonants, picturing outer processes and vocalic forms, interjections, expressions of feeling occurring within.

The Word and its manifestations were recognized as having enormous power in these primordial times, an awareness self-evident to most children in their games. *Mantras*, spells, giving one's word, saying the magic word or password all belonged to that stage of human evolution. As a child once said to her teacher regarding the word *boxing*, "I thought it was the *word* that hit."

As the long march of time and transformation continued, the word in itself *being* meaning changed to the word *expressing* meaning. The act of speaking became less conscious while the speech attempted to catch the thought. What was previously achieved by sound configurations then needed word configurations. It would seem that as soon as word configurations existed, a form of grammar would begin to become evident.

More recently, yet still in the distant past, of course, came the step from oral language to written language necessitated by the need to fix or plant an experience or an idea. People needed a record of what was formerly accessible to memory. The ancient Hawaiian culture, for example, with its totally vocal language, had priests or *Kahunas*, whose sacred task it was to remember tribal history, and to be able to retell it.

Eventually, pictures, usually related to nature, were used to record the experience of the word, and this was soon followed by a progression of various forms of ciphers, runes or letters that represented what then became the language. These were frequently held in either great esteem or great fear. The Japanese thought of them as gods; the native Americans thought of them as little black devils. We can recall Odin hanging upside down for nine days to decipher the runes. The Greeks and the Hebrews gave each of these ciphers names but no longer experienced them as beings, and by the time of the Roman culture, these expressions had become merely letters. It is interesting to note that this descending progression paralleled the descent from poetry to prose (the birth of logic), which was devoid of rhythm. By the time of the Graeco-Roman epoch, as individualized human consciousness and self-consciousness were developing, awareness of the relationship between word and the human being was dimming.

By the Middle Ages, only a faint memory remained of the relationship between the incarnating human being and the starry spheres. In various mystery centers, however, a remembrance of the true significance of language in the cosmos was preserved through study of the seven liberal arts. The sevenfoldness, first of all, bore a direct relationship to the planets, and it was thought that by undergoing a progressive course through the seven liberal arts, a person could become purified.

The first of these arts undertaken was GRAMMAR. René Querido, in his book *The Golden Age of Chartres*, shows how medieval scholars linked the study of grammar with astronomy. It dealt with every aspect of the living word: structure, laws of speech and parts of speech. An intense study of *grammatica* connected the neophyte to the moon—what is the moon, after all, but a reflector of the Sun, the living word?

The next two liberal arts were also linked with language. Dialectic was related to Mercury and had to do with the development of logical thinking, with making oneself clear in things of both heaven and Earth. Rhetoric was related to Venus and had to do with the expression of beauty in speech, as well as goodness.

One might consider these three gestures and ponder whether they reflect an image of the three pristine gestures of *uprightness*, *speech*, and *thought* that express themselves in the incarnating process of every human being, and bear witness to the logos in each one. Further, it is tempting to note a parallel to the progression of three guiding gestures that Rudolf Steiner suggested should frame children's study of their native language: correctness of expression, beauty of language, and power of linguistic command.

As we approach modern times, two parallel streams become evident: first, the progressive dimming of awareness of the cosmic origin of language and its role in allowing human beings access to the genuine mysteries, and second, the increasing emphasis upon language as a utilitarian tool of *communications*, as described by Max Herzberg. An urgent appeal lived and perhaps lives among English teachers and scholars to abandon the structural basis of language and advance full force into either free, utterly subjective expression of oneself or practical, inartistic communication.

One cannot help but ask just how much progress has been made in communications by abandoning structure. As much as a need for communication skills was recognized and valid, as noble as the mission is of the United Nations, just how much genuine improvement has been achieved? Are more conflicts resolved through conversation? Or are we, in fact, seeing just as much if not more violence in response to frustrations? We might ask ourselves in the age of *Wayne's World* and McLanguage, of driveby shootings and "wildings," of Rwanda and Bosnia, how we can best help our children to become "servants of the Word," and whether, here in the 1990s, we might all, "like, ya know, be sort of, I don't know, wow, kind of" in danger of forgetting the names of the gods, still hidden in our language. Could a better understanding of grammar and more conscientious teaching of it serve this end?

Skills, Syntax and Incarnation

Somewhere along the path of efforts to restore a greater measure of humanity to education, I suspect a phantom rises out of a swamp of ignorance and stalks English teachers and class teachers. This phantom whispers into our fatigue and feasts on our doubts, telling us that skills harm children. It speaks in extremes and unconditional phrases, avoids genuine research, postures in denial, and helps us mask the real question: do we know the skills sufficiently ourselves? Do we teach them or avoid them? Do we recognize their significance?

English skills cannot exist of themselves; they need context and application. Much like the best organically grown carrot in the world, it can, if properly prepared and ingested, provide high quality nourishment. Injected directly into the bloodstream it can kill. So, also, with academic skills, the teacher's ability to penetrate the subject with understanding, accuracy and a sense for its qualitative aspects will make the difference in the effect skill development has on the students.

Rudolf Steiner has provided us with many guiding considerations for the teaching of language and grammar as a wholesome and essential source of human growth. We might remember that just as humanity and language both descended from the starry spheres, so did each of those children sitting before us. As they passed through the zodiac and the planets in their descent to birth, the cosmic Word was incarnating into them. Our task as teachers is to help this process of incarnation, not to keep our students dreamers and visionaries, and to do it in such a way that they may excarnate again healthily. All incarnation can be seen in a certain sense as a sacrifice of the spirit, which we all make at birth in order to help realize each of our pre-earthly intentions and to become more conscious beings. Waldorf education sets as its task the goal of helping human beings move from unconscious to conscious living by a carefully conceived educational philosophy and method.

By teaching grammar, we can assist the process that the child has already begun. In a course of lectures given in Basel, Switzerland, Steiner said:

One can indeed presuppose that the whole of grammar is already inherent in the human organism; and if this presupposition is acted on in earnest, then, my dear friends, a person will learn to say: In drawing forth the conscious knowledge of grammar from the unconscious life of grammar at the right time and in a living way you are simply working at bringing forth the I-consciousness of the child. And with this knowledge in your bones, if I may use this expression, then toward the ninth year when the I-consciousness normally awakes properly, you lift the unconscious up into consciousness.

It is also useful to remember that this sounding of the starry spheres right into the organism stems from pre-birth and continues to sound further into the astral body, being released again upon death to unite with the music of the spheres.

In addition (though I cannot substantiate these assertions by quoting chapter and verse), a right study of grammar can benefit the etheric body. Avoidance of the teaching of grammar has to do with a misunderstanding of the etheric body. This is the body of formative forces, after all. We have seen the relationship of the skeleton to grammar, and it is not difficult to see it as an image of structural support. But it can also bear witness to the beauty of structure in the eloquent form of bones. For this structural basis of language to serve the etheric soundly, its practice must move in healthy ways into the life of habit, not just in free expression, but in a manner similar to the way a musical instrument is practiced— through rhythmic repetition of scales, for example. Just as one guides the imitative phase of early childhood—not by sitting on the floor continually playing, but by providing daily activities of human beings engaged in useful work worthy of imitation—so too the wholesome basis for the process of making grammar conscious can come through healthy, regular practice.

For older students, the study of grammar can help order a chaotic life of feeling, or be a comforting assurance, as of being housed in fine architecture. Frank Lloyd Wright acknowledged this parallel between grammar and architecture when writing of one of his structures:

> Each building will have a grammar of its own, true to materials, as in the new grammar of Fallingwater.

Steiner is quite clear in his indications that grammar is not only a matter of convention, nor is it placed in the curriculum so that our students can impress inspectors. It is essential for the healthy development of the human being. He tells us that between the ninth and tenth years it is necessary to acquire grammatical knowledge in order to find a proper transition to the I development of the human being, and that memorizing rules enhances the development of the I. He tells us that we as teachers need not ask how we should develop the I through the teaching of language. Grammar itself achieves this.

In the "Ilkley Course," Rudolf Steiner reminds teachers:

> If language were taught without grammar, a person could only attain consciousness, but not consciousness of self. An impossibility! We would not provide a person with the inner solidity needed for life.

We can find repeated indications of the essential role of grammar in developing the right kind of self-consciousness in children. As with any subject in a Waldorf school, one can present these lessons artistically, but nonetheless Steiner insisted on the necessity of taking up this activity at a *conscious* level continuously throughout the child's schooling.

The activity carried out in teaching grammar and syntax by means of sentences [judgments] takes place in living conclusions, and this must not sink down into habitual dreamlike states; it must take place in fully conscious life.

Or:

Beginning in the twelfth year, especially in the eighth and ninth grades, the instruction in the mother tongue must be vigorous.... They must know what a sentence is, must acquire a feeling for style. Otherwise they cannot become mature. They undergo a mutation in inner style of their sentences as well as in their voices. If this is not taken into consideration, they become inwardly defective.

While accepting the need for teaching grammar, we need to find the most healthful time and the most artistic method to bring this about. As often as Steiner has urged the teaching of grammar, he has also warned of the "monstrousness" of teaching this too soon.

By considering the teaching of grammar as a vehicle for the awakening sense of self, there seems to be a clear indication that the ninth or tenth year, when the first definite distinctions between self and the world occur, is the time to introduce this subject in a formal way. This is not to suggest that before that time children cannot experience distinctions between various parts of speech in an *unconscious* way. But if we follow the parallel course from the study of housebuilding (in third grade) to architecture, the queen of the arts (in twelfth grade), we may find corresponding indications for grammar, since both studies relate to structure and form. In both cases, the same broad subject matter comes before the student at regular, repeated intervals, but in a more highly refined, evolved, complex and mature way.

The earliest lessons in grammar have most to do with *identifying*, in a feeling way, the parts of speech and the sense for the wholeness of a sentence. The approach seems to come to its crowning in fifth grade, with contrasts built up between active and passive, direct and indirect speech, and a partial complex of the verb tenses. By the twelfth year, *syntactical elements* can be approached in such a way that the sentence can still be experienced as a melody (as Steiner suggests), perhaps with a bit of drama. Nouns no longer are simply nouns, but have a role to play within the context of a sentence—a role that needs to be deeply experienced by the pupil. Is the noun acting, for instance, as a direct object or as a predicate nominative? How differently the two kinds of *verb-kings* (transitive and linking verbs) behave—not unlike early Roman kings!

Prepositional phrases, so familiar from fourth grade, may serve now as adjectives, then as adverbs, with whole phrases behaving as if they were single words, having completely different countenances. Students learn the variety of meanings made possible through phrasing by forming conditional expressions. Through this study of language, they can gain command of, and support for their future thought life by coming to understand what is not immediately visible on the surface of their speech. Does this not seem to correspond to the mastery of the physical world that is being made simultaneously in the study of history in the sixth through eighth grades—as the world and its materials were pressed into service from the Romans, through the age of exploration, and up to our modern time? Thus, it does not seem surprising that by the end of eighth grade, most fundamental elements of grammar, both in parts of speech and in sentence structure and formation, have been touched upon.

As students enter high school, many of these same elements of grammar will again be taken up, but in a different way. Not only by identifying and determining the role they play, but now in a vigorous review of all the varieties of grammatical expression, the students can also begin to *see the effect* of these various formations within their language, and the styles that arise from them. We can review nouns by comparing how a passage of mostly abstract nouns differs from one containing mostly concrete nouns. We can compare the use of vague adjectives to vivid adjective choices, perhaps selecting passages from great works of literature. What is the effect of a passage written with the intentional use of many present participles? What happens when we attempt to eliminate any use of the verb *to be?* By the ninth and tenth grades students grow more conscious of qualities in writing that they merely felt before, and begin the attempt to imitate them.

By the final years of high school, one hopes that lessons in grammar can be applied in ways that the students can *achieve the effects* they want in their writing. This implies accuracy in details as well as in stylistic effect. They need to be in command of the placement of modifiers and punctuation just as much as they need to be able to formulate a sentence that expresses their intent. As wordsmiths, they need in their minds and at their fingertips the tools and skills to craft thought. Will complex sentences or compound sentences best serve this particular idea? Are there sufficient adjectives to allow the reader to create his or her own images while reading this piece? Have the details led effectively towards a general statement? Fine polish now must appear in the language work. After all, if our language has descended from the gods and been entrusted to us, does it not then deserve to be presented decently in our writing and speech? In this way, a curriculum of grammar study can guide students from correctness of expression through beauty of language to the culminating experience in high school of achieving the power of linguistic command.

Let's imagine some ways that such skill development in grammar can be accomplished. In the fifth grade, for example, one introduces active and passive voice. In addition, the children learn about plants; they focus on the plant as an entity living within the stream of time, and they learn how the plant world relates to the human world as they both evolve to greater complexity. Thus, the mushroom bears a parallel to the infant, and the parallel of the full flowering experience of a rose does not occur until one is about sixteen. By introducing the active and passive voice, a teacher might ask students to consider how life is for babies as compared to adults. The children readily offer something:

Babies	Adults
are fed	*feed others*
are held	*hold*
are carried	*walk and drive*

From these and countless other examples it becomes clear that children and youth fit somewhere between the emerging passive voice of infancy and active voice of full adulthood. Such considerations, relevant to real life, give pictures within grammar that can grow with the child.

When the subject of active and passive is considered again, perhaps in the sophomore year, students notice that they must assign accountability with the active voice. It has more dynamism. They might be asked to write about a campus incident involving student horseplay and damage to property—once in the active voice and once in the passive voice. Which is stronger? Which is more credible? "The door was accidentally broken!" or, "Josh broke the door when he pushed Devon into it." Write an explanation of why you want the time extended for the term paper—once in active and once in passive. "I was kept late for practice so my paper for biology wasn't finished on time," or "I planned poorly. I won't let it happen again." Read the sentences over and decide which you are more likely to submit. In this way, by seeing the effect of a particular grammatical point, and by learning to create within that awareness, students fully learn the style book adage: "Shun the passive!"

Imagine you want to work in the ninth grade with deepening awareness of the effect of concrete or abstract nouns. Ask the students to compare how they feel when reading a passage from the *Declaration of Independence*:

We hold these truths to be self-evident: that all men are created equal; that they are endowed by their Creator with certain unalienable Rights; that among these are Life, Liberty, and the pursuit of Happiness....

Compare that with a passage from *A Tale of Two Cities* that describes a wine cask broken in a street of Paris:

> ...the cask had tumbled out with a run, the hoops had burst, and it lay on the stones just outside the door of the wine-shop, shattered like a walnut shell.... men and women dipped in the puddles with little mugs of mutilated earthenware, or even with handkerchiefs from women's heads, which were squeezed dry into infants' mouths....

How do the students experience each of these passages? Does one seem more immediate than the other? Which draws them more into thought? Into their senses?

The next year, perhaps while building towards comparative essays, one might again use concrete and abstract nouns and look for metaphorical correspondences between them. First, a lesson in metonymy might lead the way.

> *Sceptre* and *crown*
> Must tumble down
> And in the dust be equal made
> With the poor crooked *scythe* and *spade*.

How do the concrete nouns reach beyond their usual domain? What is implying something beyond the sense experience? Thus one paves the way to work with metaphor, and one may ask the students to take a concrete noun and an abstract noun and quest for the relationship within. One such sophomore assignment, using pairs of words on cards drawn at random, produced this correspondence between *suspicion* and *a stone fence*:

All of us have suspicions. All people fear evil and wish to be protected from it. So, in order to be safe, we set up a barricade. Suspicion forms itself into a heavy, hard belief that we carry to the borders of our fear and lay down, one by one as we get older, and jaded by life's experiences. We hesitantly peep over this great stone wall and then run away from whatever is behind it, although we listen to the gossiping lizards who scurry through the rocks.—*Sophomore girl*

Through grammatical work such as this, we can see how a potentially dry skill can, in fact, lead to a quickening of wakefulness within the child's self. It enhances the path from unconscious to conscious living.

We need not fear the structure of language as a prison. Grammar, like anything else, can become harmful if misused. Rudolf Steiner urges teachers to know grammar, so that we can speak differently about it. We must acquire a feeling for the wisdom of the language. Through this feeling we can come to understand how the study of grammar, when approached with sufficient sensitivity and artistry, can lead to a greater appreciation for the cosmic origins of both language and ourselves. Rudolf Steiner said:

> Through the analyzing activity in grammar the children develop a greater wakefulness of soul and less inclination toward materialism. They attain a proper inwardness.

In an age when the unresolved conflicts surrounding students seem to be met increasingly with methods of "the sword," it is a truly worthy mission to resurrect the Word with the deepest possible understanding. Inasmuch as grammar plays an essential role in raising this understanding to a conscious level, it can help to lead us beyond dullness and doubt toward greater soul health. Whether or not we are aware of it, perhaps we are all being beckoned to take up the banner of the *Knights of the Word*. This mission seems to have been clearly perceived by Dag Hammarskjold,

Secretary General of the United Nations, who expressed his view contemporaneously with Max Herzberg, but who acknowledged the potency of the Word, at its source. Such a view may help us to find a way past a trivial stance toward grammar and to truer communication. In Hammarskjold's *Markings* we find:

> Respect for the word is the first commandment in the discipline by which a person can be educated to maturity— intellectual, emotional, and moral.

> Respect for the word—to employ it with scrupulous care and an incorruptible heartfelt love of truth—is essential if there is to be any growth in a society or in the human race.

> To misuse the word is to show contempt for humanity. It undermines the bridges and poisons the wells. It causes humanity to regress down the long path of evolution.

REFERENCES

Charles Dickens, *A Tale of Two Cities*
Declaration of Independence
T.S. Eliot, *Four Quartets*
Dag Hammarskjold, *Markings*
Jane Healy, *Endangered Minds*
Max Herzberg, Address, reprinted in *English Journal*, March 1994
René M. Querido, *The Golden Age of Chartres*
James Shirley, "The Glories of Our Blood and State"
Rudolf Steiner, *The Alphabet*
—— *Soul Economy and Waldorf Education*
—— *Conferences with Teachers*
—— *A Modern Art of Education*
—— *Basel Course*
—— *Practical Advice to Teachers*
E. A. Karl Stockmeyer, *Curriculum/Waldorf School*
Frank Lloyd Wright, *A Testament*

WE LOVE GRAMMAR

Dorit Winter

"I hate history!" or, "Arithmetic is horrible!" are sentiments no self-respecting teacher would entertain. Yet, "I hate grammar!" has been the desperate cry of more than one frustrated class teacher, as though grammar were beyond redemption. Not only is grammar redeemable, it is redemptive. Without it we might cackle and coo, rumble or roar, but as for speech—we would be in the true sense idiotic. Words might tumble at random through the universe, but sense—a sentence—would result only by chance.

When we try to learn a foreign language, we soon discover that grammar is not based on chance. Unless we *must* make ourselves aware of it, however, we simply accept the structure of the language we use. So by way of a small demonstration, try this: Formulate an answer to this question: "What will you accomplish tomorrow?" Before you answer, however, make sure you are fully conscious of *every* nuance of grammar—syntax, etymology, lexicology—which your sentence requires. Tedious, if not impossible, and likely to render you speechless, dumb.

Now, do this: Lift your right arm, but before you raise it, make certain you are fully conscious of *everything* that your muscles and bones, ligaments, tendons, joints, nerves must do to accomplish the deed. An impossible demand? Yes, and paralyzing.

Both movement through space (the physical manifestation of will impulses) and movement through language (the communicable manifestation of thoughts) happen more or less automatically. Yet, although we are perhaps not always entirely conscious of the controlling principles, the chaos which results from uncontrolled movement of speech is immediately apparent.

The body of language is structured by grammar; the physical body is structured by its skeleton. The joints which enable physical movement are the *articuli*. When we move through language with grace and precision we are *articulate*. Without grammar, language would remain inchoate; humanity would be dumb. Dumb means mute, but it also means stupid. We can judge the intelligence, the degree of awareness, of sensitivity, of consciousness, the refinement of a speaker's thoughts, by the degree to which he is articulate. Someone who is articulate can speak his thoughts clearly, can enlighten. Language illuminates. The intensity of the light cast upon a subject, or a discussion, or a description by a speaker, depends on his control of the *articuli*, the joints, the connections within the language. Flexibility of thought, light of reason, new light shed upon conventional ideas, these all depend on the mastery of the given structure of the language.

The Word was made flesh. The Word was the light that shone into the darkness. Historically, the Word was made flesh in Palestine. Individually, in each human being, the power of thought is made flesh by the word. Without the word, we cannot think. Without thought, we remain in darkness. Thought is a uniquely human activity. In relation to the *Logos* it is also the most divine human attribute. Without language, thought would be chaotic; without grammar, language becomes a chaos.

Without a skeleton, a child couldn't ever rise onto her two legs, or learn to grasp the world with her toes and fingers. Able to grasp the world physically, she can proceed to grasp the world through language. Language then enables her to think. First she holds onto the table, then she says, "table." Then, even when the table is not in sight, she can think: *table*. She is likely to be burned by the iron once before she learns "hot" so that she can understand the *danger*. And what about words like *love* or *thought* or *beautiful* or *good*?

The clearer one's grasp, the more articulate one's language, the more precise one's thought, the more enlightened one's understanding will be.

If we teach our children grammar so that instead of throwing bleached bones—isolated rules, definitions, labels—at them, we lead them with delight into the splendid intricacies of the skeleton/structure of language, then the spirit and soul as well as the body on which these are dependent will manifest themselves. If our children learn grammar joyfully, they will not be dumb.

Certainly there will be little joy for the students if the teacher is in pain. The teacher's relationship to language is decisive. Just as one's voice and gestures have a formative power, so do awareness and love of language leave their mark on the class. One may not love arithmetic, but in all likelihood one will find out about fractions because one must face them sooner or later. As long as one is not deaf and dumb or illiterate, however, one can "get by" without bothering about either the structure of English—its grammar, without which neither speech nor thought would be possible—or the art, the beauty, the nobility to which that delicate structure may aspire: literature.

"Getting by" is so much more possible with English because, after all, we use it all the time. Unlike the German or French teacher, the English teacher deals with children who already know the rudiments of the subject. Children who are old enough to come to school have already learned to use language. They can speak. They can understand. They have listened to their mothers, an older brother, a babysitter, television, and have absorbed a colossal amount from all of them. The English teacher does not start from scratch. Yet there is so much more to the mastery of language, to true literacy; so much to teach and so little guidance, that it is tempting to continue letting the children's environment instruct them, and to hope that in the end they will be fairly articulate, not make too many mistakes, and be able to read without fear.

Tempting it may be, but impossible. Consciously or not we teach English continually, with every word we speak or write, with our voices, our breath, with every story, instruction, explanation and greeting. Nor is it our vocabulary alone which instructs the child, nor even the correctness of our grammar and syntax (integral though these be) which the child emulates. It is, above all, the quality, the effort and deliberation behind our language, which impresses itself upon the children. Do we forge our meaning with our words? Are we precise? Are we logical? Does our language penetrate, or does it obscure?

When we speak, do we expect the children to listen? Do we repeat ourselves consciously or on purpose, or "show" because we haven't the patience to use language instead of our hands? Do we cater to the eye and neglect the ear? In short, are we conscious of the *how* of language, and not only of the *what?* Because, if we are, how can we do less than honor grammar?

The grammar of language determines the consciousness of nations. By teaching the native grammar, we provide a scaffold for the descent of individual consciousness. Knowledge of grammar is consciousness-raising. Deliberate use of language is impossible without control of form, of grammar. However, too much awareness of form brought too early to the children can also be debilitating; can destroy the naive joy in words which "every child may joy to hear." That is why we do not want to start too soon. Nevertheless, although the transition from the first three or four years (when we *do*—sing, recite, paint, act, etc.) to the upper elementary years (when we begin to *think*) is gradual, it is necessary.

Just as the block crayon of the early grades gives way to the pen of the later years, so the simplest sentence about the fox and the grapes copied from the board ought to result eventually in the original composition about Lorenzo de Medici or the French Revolution. The high school student will carry on with term papers, essays, poems, stories. As the children gradually become responsible for the design of a page, so they ought to become responsible for its language, the choice of words, the organization of ideas, the presentation of information. Out of the experience of color, sound, rhythm, rhyme, image and so on which their teachers have provided, the students work their way, with further guidance, into those loftier planes of abstract thought which language can achieve. Unconscious imitation gives way to the conscious struggle for articulate, correct expression. How can the students' struggles engender the joy that must come from ever greater prowess with language, and thus with the power of thought, if the teacher suffers the "I hate grammar" syndrome?

Reverence for language, based on deep understanding of its nature, is one of the gifts Rudolf Steiner offered teachers. Again and again he draws our attention to the cosmic essence in language. Again and again he connects those three momentous achievements of the little child: learning to walk, learning to talk, learning to think.

In the course of the six lectures given at Christiania, Norway, May 16-20, 1923, and published as *Man's Being, His Destiny and World Evolution*, Steiner reveals the magnitude of these first achievements, and provides a context for what is usually tossed off as "learning to talk."

. . .in this learning how to walk lies an element of utmost grandeur.

Simultaneously, the correct use of arms and hands is attained. And by placing himself, as a physical being, within the three spatial directions, the human being receives the foundation for all that is called *learning how to talk*....

Language develops out of walking, out of the grasping of objects, out of gestures flowing from the organs of movement.

Anyone viewing these things correctly will know that a child with the tendency to walk on his toes speaks differently from a child walking on his heels; employs different shadings of sound. The organism of speaking develops from the organism of walking and moving.... In the third stage, the child learns how to think.

... And all this has a deeply significant, practical side.... For many people, speech itself has assumed a materialistic character. It can be used only in connection with physical things. Undeniably, we live within a civilization making language, more and more, into an instrument of materialism....

The consequence will become apparent.... During the day, we talk with others. We make the air vibrate. The way in which the air vibrates transmits the soul content which we wish to convey. The soul impulses of our words, however, live in our inner being. Every word corresponds to a soul impulse, which is the more powerful, the more our words are imbued with idealism, the more we are conscious of the spiritual significance contained in our words.

"Yes, yes!" we shout ecstatically, "but what about subject-verb agreement, what about indefinite pronouns?" True, we must come to such details, to the specific grammatical laws, to the femur, the ulna, the metatarsals; to the bones which in*struct* us. When we do, let us keep in mind how it is the highest wisdom which in*forms* the bones, that it is in the very marrow of those bones that the life's blood is created. Let us become "conscious of the spiritual significance contained in our words." If reverence for language and an appreciation of the beauty, the dignity, and the mission of grammar support our knowledge and teaching of grammatical lore, then no matter how precise or rigorous our classroom task may be, our students will become articulate, not bored.

Now, filled though we may be with the potential magnificence of language, we dare not forget that the most glorious poetry, the wittiest prose, the most stirring eulogy, the most comprehensive book report, the grandest Achievement Test Essay all demand subject-verb agreement if they are to be understood. In the end, no matter how spiritually endowed our words, it is grammar, the organizing principle in language, which makes the sentence more than the sum of its parts.

How to discover a design which will lead our teaching from one part to the next, that is the challenge. What follows is meant to be suggestive, rather than prescriptive. Thus, the tempo and intensity with which these "lessons" are conveyed will be determined by the teacher and the class—a seventh grade, or perhaps a sixth, possibly even a fifth or an eighth, depending on the teacher's modifications. Of course the introduction to grammar in the third grade was quite different in nature, and the seventh graders will enjoy being reminded of their "Grammar Garden," or of their play about the verb-king and the subject-queen, or of how the red verbs stamped and hopped and slithered across the room while their orange adverbial companions accompanied and formed them. There, in the third grade, the process began gently, actively, simply. Throughout the elementary school years the children return again and again to the terrain of that Grammar Garden. They learn to discern and appreciate ever more intricate, often hidden, details of the landscape. The process is cumulative. The foundation of the children's knowledge is strengthened by each return to what should become familiar, secure. Like many subjects in our curriculum, grammar cannot be taught once and for all. After all, a true understanding of verb and subject presupposes a true understanding of time and space—a lifelong study.

Lightning cracks. Thunder roars. Branches sway. Leaves tumble down. The wind howls. Rain....

Now you turn to the class. You have said these words, and perhaps you have written them on the board. What does the rain do? It pours. It drips. It splatters against the window. There are other suggestions. You choose one and add it to the list. What else happens in a storm? What else do you hear? What else do you see, or smell or feel?

Birds struggle. Clouds tower. Puddles swell.

Before long your list covers the blackboard. All the time you avoid passive constructions or even direct objects as you try to keep the sentences as simple as possible. For homework, the children make their own lists.

Next time you might begin by asking the children whether they recall what the lightning does. It cracks. You write what it does on the board. Soon you have a list of verbs on the blackboard. All along you have kept the particular storm you are describing clearly in view. You know whether it is a storm at sea, a thunderstorm at night or a blizzard. Now you might read some fine descriptions of storms. Literature is full of them. George Eliot, Charles Dickens, Thomas Hardy provide beautiful examples. The children themselves might now write their own descriptions. They should be encouraged to make their compositions vivid. You want to know just what happened. Depending on the sophistication of the class's writing, you may allow a person or an animal to enter the setting; you may want to know how the storm began and ended. What you are after are verbs, even though you still have not mentioned the term in connection with these storms. Perhaps the children will underline all the words in their compositions which describe what *happened.* After you have read these assignments, you might find one which lends itself to a reading of just the verbs. You read only the verbs, and they tell the story of the storm. Now you are coming to the moment when you could say that there is a name for these words which tell you exactly what happens: verbs.

From the verb you now want to find a transition to the subject. The verbs by themselves almost tell the whole story of the storm, but not quite. The verb rules the sentence; it is the king, but every verb has a subject. What roars? The wind? Thunder? Thunder roars. Roars is the verb. Thunder is the subject. At this point you could reintroduce the color code that you built up in earlier years: the verbs are (underlined) active red and the subjects blue.

At this point you may want to mention the *nomen*, the name, the noun. In any event, you are now ready to say that when we have the verb/king and its subject, when you know what happened and what did it, then you have a sentence. It is called a sentence because together these two words make sense. Sense/sentence. Wind howled. Along the rugged cliffs, the strong wind howled. No matter how many other words surround the verb and the subject, a sentence needs at least a verb and a subject, otherwise it is not a sentence.

Out of this concept of the sentence as the unit, now follow the sentence fragment, the run-on sentence, the simple sentence, the compound sentence. You explain the prefix *co*. The *co*mpound sentence requires the *co*ordinating *co*njunction. You explain the simple verb (*simplex* = one in Latin), the simple subject, the compound verb, the compound subject.

Perhaps you are still using examples from the storm descriptions. (A word of caution: In his advice to foreign language teachers, Steiner warns that it is not the example, but the rule, which the children ought to retain.) More likely, enough time has now passed so that the children have written about other topics. If your examples relate to what the children have experienced commonly or to what they have written about, the entire process will benefit, because then the examples will not be superficial.

Before leaving the verb/subject, you may want to dwell on the different types of verbs and verb tenses. The verb *to be* is particularly crucial. It is the only verb in English to have much variety in its conjugation. It may be a helping verb or a linking verb. The continuous tenses—you *are* reading—merit special attention because they are peculiar to English (at least in comparison to French or German). Once you have brought in *to be* and the concept of conjugation, you have already touched on number—singular/plural, subject-verb agreement and pronouns. None of these concepts should be rushed. Neither, of course, should they be belabored. A lot depends on the teacher's temperament.

Having reached the pronouns, you are now in a position to introduce indefinite pronouns. *Does* everyone have *his* or *her* books? Indefinite pronouns are either singular or plural. *Everyone* is singular. Why are they called indefinite?

With pronouns, you may want now to introduce the direct object. The question always is, "How do you introduce the concept, the term?" A lot depends on the grade level. Even in the upper elementary grades the children will appreciate your attempts at ingenuity. One attempt could be this: You hold up an object. "Here is an object," you say to the class. Perhaps it is a piece of chalk. "Who will go outside while we hide the object?" You choose one of the eager volunteers. You hide the object. The volunteer returns. The class guides the pupil to the object by calling out "hot" or "cold." You choose different objects, different volunteers. Now you are ready to write on the blackboard: Anna found the object. Anna found the chalk. You may revert to your red and blue underlining. In any event the class can tell you that *found* is the verb and that *Anna* is the subject and now you can add that *chalk* is the object, the direct object. After you have spent some time with direct objects, and perhaps even indirect objects (though they are tricky and may come on the next circuit) and you have made up various exercises (or used any of the numerous books available for this purpose), you want to clarify the use of subject and object pronouns. You ask two children to circle the room. One walks behind the other. Now you ask them to change direction. Then you add a third child. One child follows two children. Then, two children follow the third. Can we find sentences to describe what took place? Timothy follows Michael. Michael follows Timothy. Michael and Timothy follow Stuart. Stuart follows Michael and Timothy. He follows him. He follows him. They follow him. He follows them. Why do I write *he* follows *him* regardless of whether Timothy or Michael is following? Why do I use *they* in that sentence and *them* in this one?

Having mastered subject and object pronouns, the class may be ready for relative pronouns. Who and whom are especially tricky.

Now that objects are clear, perhaps it is time for the preposition that is always accompanied by a prepositional phrase that contains an object of the preposition.

And so it goes. Adjectival phrases, adverbial phrases, one thing leads to another. One thing must lead to the next. You decide on the next step, but you make the connection clear. In this way, and by always working with complete sentences that are connected with the children's experience, you will convey to the children the recognition that the thing we call grammar is an organic, dynamic substructure, which makes expression possible.

Perhaps it is extreme to "love" grammar, but appreciation is always facilitated by sympathy. It may not be necessary to love thy neighbor's skeleton in order to love thy neighbor, and yet we know that a great deal of our being is revealed by our structure. Revulsion for thy neighbor's aspect will surely inhibit anything beyond a superficial relationship. So it is also with literature, language and grammar. If we can comprehend language to the depths of its structure, its being will be revealed; and with this revelation will come that power of articulation which profound sympathy always generates.

REFERENCES

Rudolf Steiner, *Man's Being, His Destiny and World Evolution*

BIOGRAPHICAL INFORMATION

. . . .

CHRISTY MACKAYE BARNES

was born and spent her summers in the hills of Cornish, New Hampshire. Her family moved frequently during the winters, following the career of her father, poet-dramatist Percy MacKaye. During high school she boarded at the Cambridge Haskell School in Cambridge, Massachusetts, where her remarkable English teacher became a lifelong friend. After two years at Smith College she traveled around Europe with her sister Arvia, and in Dornach, Switzerland, became a member of the Anthroposophical Society in time to attend the conference for the opening of the second Goetheanum. During the following years she waited tables at the Threefold Restaurant in New York City, attended Anthroposophical activities, and brought out a book of poems, *Wind-in-the-Grass,* with an introduction by Edwin Arlington Robinson, published by Harpers & Brothers.

Christy graduated from Rollins College in Winter Park, Florida, in 1933, and then taught for a year at the New York Rudolf Steiner School until she was invited by her former English teacher, Agnes Delano, to teach with her at Mount Vernon Seminary in Washington D.C. During summer visits to Dornach, she became interested in the art of speech formation; ultimately she decided to devote herself to this discipline full time and entered the Speech School at the Goetheanum.

While in Dornach, she married Henry Barnes in 1939. A year later, she received her diploma during a hurried visit to Marie Steiner in the Swiss Alps, just before returning to America due to war conditions. Later, Christy played the part of Maria in Rudolf Steiner's first mystery drama, *The Portal of Initiation,* under the direction of Hans Pusch.

Henry Barnes soon became Faculty Chairman of the New York Rudolf Steiner School where Christy periodically taught. When their daughter was ready to attend first grade, Christy taught a class, taking it through the sixth grade. Afterwards she taught literature in the high school until her retirement. She also edited *Journal for Anthroposophy* from 1972 to 1984, in the midst of her many other activities.

After their retirement, the Barnes' moved to Hillsdale, New York. Henry was active, together with Arvia and Karl Ege, in founding the Rudolf Steiner Educational and Farming Association in Harlemville, and was for a long time President of the Board. Christy directed the Christmas Plays and gradually took over management of the Adonis Press from its founder Arvia Ege. Adonis Press has published two books by Christy *A Wound Awoke Me* in 1994 and *Arvia MacKaye Ege: Pioneer for Anthroposophy* in 1995.

. . . .

ADAM BITTLESTON (d. 1989)

Priest of the Christian Community and adult educator at Emerson College in England; author of *Meditative Prayers for Today, Our Spiritual Companions*, and *Loneliness*, and editor of *The Golden Blade*.

. . . .

SUSAN DEMANETT

Waldorf class teacher in Hawaii and English teacher for Waldorf middle and high school grades in New Hampshire.

. . . .

L. FRANCIS EDMUNDS (d. 1989)

Lifelong Waldorf teacher and adult educator; founder and principal of Emerson College in England; author of *Rudolf Steiner Education, Renewing Education*, and *Anthroposophy as a Healing Force*.

. . . .

URSULA GRAHL (d. 1980)

Worker with handicapped children at Sunfield Children's Home in England; lecturer on the meaning of fairy tales; author of *The Exceptional Child*.

. . . .

A. C. HARWOOD (d. 1975)

Waldorf teacher and adult educator at Michael Hall School in England; for many years Chairman of the Anthroposophical Society in Great Britain; author of *The Recovery of Man in Childhood* (a seminal book on Waldorf education), *Shakespeare's Prophetic Mind*, and *The Way of a Child*.

. . . .

HUGH HETHERINGTON

Writer and high school teacher of literature at Michael Hall, a Waldorf school in Forest Row, Sussex, England.

. . . .

EILEEN HUTCHINS (d. 1987)

Pioneer of Waldorf education in Great Britain, co-founder of the Elmfield School in Stourbridge; author of *Introduction to the Mystery Plays of Rudolf Steiner* and *Parzival, An Introduction.*

. . . .

LINDA SAWERS

English and history teacher at various Waldorf high schools in the United States; Faculty Chairperson at the Washington Waldorf School.

. . . .

DORIT WINTER

Waldorf class and high school teacher; Director of the San Francisco Extension Program of Rudolf Steiner College's teacher education course.

. . . .

ISABEL WYATT (d. 1992)

Co-director of studies at Hawkwood College inGloucestershire, England; novelist and author of many children's books, among her titles on literary themes are *From Round Table to Grail Castle* and (in collaboration with Margaret Bennell) *Shakespeare's Flowering of the Spirit.*

A SPECIAL ACKNOWLEDGMENT TO

Journal for Rudolf Steiner Waldorf Education
(formerly *Child and Man*)

for permission to reprint L. Francis Edmund's "Literature in
the Upper School," which will form part of a forthcoming
collection of essays on English language and literature.
For details of this collection, write to:

The Secretary, Steiner Education,
The Sprig, Ashdown Road,
Forest Row, East Sussex
RH18 5BN UK